Intelligence Policy

Its Impact on College Admissions and Other Social Policies

ENVIRONMENT, DEVELOPMENT, AND PUBLIC POLICY

A series of volumes under the general editorship of
Lawrence Susskind, *Massachusetts Institute of Technology,*
Cambridge, Massachusetts

PUBLIC POLICY AND SOCIAL SERVICES

Series Editor: Gary Marx, *University of Colorado,*
Boulder, Colorado

Recent Volumes in this Series

AMERICANS ABROAD: A Comparative Study of
Emigrants from the United States
Arnold Dashefsky, Jan DeAmicis, Bernard Lazerwitz, and Ephraim Tabory

THE DIFFUSION OF MEDICAL INNOVATIONS: An Applied
Network Analysis
Mary L. Fennell and Richard B. Warnecke

DIVIDED OPPORTUNITIES: Minorities, Poverty, and Social Policy
Edited by Gary D. Sandefur and Marta Tienda

HISPANICS IN THE LABOR FORCE: Issues and Policies
Edited by Edwin Melendez, Clara Rodriguez, and Janis Barry Figueroa

INNOVATION UP CLOSE: How School Improvement Works
A. Michael Huberman and Matthew B. Miles

INTELLIGENCE POLICY: Its Impact on College Admissions
and Other Social Policies
Angela Browne-Miller

OSHA AND THE POLITICS OF HEALTH REGULATION
David P. McCaffrey

RACIAL AND CULTURAL MINORITIES: An Analysis of Prejudice
and Discrimination (Fifth Edition)
George E. Simpson and J. Milton Yinger

Other subseries:

ENVIRONMENTAL POLICY AND PLANNING

Series Editor: Lawrence Susskind, *Massachusetts Institute of Technology,*
Cambridge, Massachusetts

CITIES AND DEVELOPMENT

Series Editor: Lloyd Rodwin, *Massachusetts Institute of Technology,*
Cambridge, Massachusetts

Intelligence Policy

Its Impact on College Admissions and Other Social Policies

ANGELA BROWNE-MILLER

University of California, Berkeley
Berkeley, California

Plenum Press • New York and London

Library of Congress Cataloging-in-Publication Data

On file

The Cattell excerpt on p. vii is reprinted from Cattell, R. B. (1987). Intelligence and society. In *Intelligence: Its Structure, Growth and Action*, of Stelmach, G. E. and Vroon, P. A. (Eds.), *Advances in Psychology* (Vol. 35). New York: NHC, p. 619. The Eiseley excerpt is reprinted from Eiseley, L. (1957). *The Immense Journey*. New York: Random House, p. 55. Appendixes C.1–C.7 and C.12 are reprinted with permission of the University of California, Office of the President, Oakland, CA. *Introducing the University* is revised and published annually.

ISBN 0-306-44745-2

© 1995 Plenum Press, New York
A Division of Plenum Publishing Corporation
233 Spring Street, New York, N. Y. 10013

To my father, Lee Winston Browne, and
to my husband, Richard Louis Miller,
sages on the edge

If a trifling meteorite fifty miles in diameter hit the Pacific, it could cause such survival problems that, without a sufficiency of men of genius, we should all perish. Crawling on a planet's precariously stabilized skin, under which exist incredible pressures and temperatures, and gazing at the vast explosions in an as yet superficially understood outer universe, how can we doubt that understanding through intelligence is our only hope?

RAYMOND B. CATTELL
in *Intelligence: Its Structure, Growth and Action*

[E. D. Cope, the nineteenth-century paleontologist,] first enunciated what he called the "law of the unspecialized," the contention that it was not from the most highly organized and dominant forms of a given geological era that the master type of a succeeding period evolved, but that instead the dominant forms tended to arise from more lowly and generalized animals which were capable of making new adaptations, and which were not narrowly restricted to a given environment. . . [But] who is to say without foreknowledge of the future which animal is specialized and which is not?

LOREN EISELEY
in *The Immense Journey*

Foreword

When Angela Browne-Miller first came to my springtime-long field class in natural history, dressed in camouflage fatigues, the place began to buzz. Angela was, even then, back in 1975, as a senior undergraduate at the University of California, Santa Cruz, a predator of ideas for whom no old shibboleth was sacred. I can still hear her asking, "What do you mean by that? You've just told me. . . ." No old icon was safe, and no conventional wisdom was allowed to gloss over a shaky structure of faulty assumptions.

And she's still that way. In this marvelous book she's put all these rapier thrusts of hers in little boxes enclosed by black lines. You read along, following one of her clear arguments, and there will be a box, and in it will be a sentence that requires you to stop and back up. You must—she requires it of you—reconsider the very framework on which your emerging ideas are based. I've never met a book like it. But that's Angela for you.

What does she challenge in this book of hers? Well, if I were drawing the boxes, I'd say that in the first one would be a flat statement like this:

Our society constantly applies assessments of intelligence as decisions are made about admission, advancement, etc.

Angela would probably not allow me the "*etc.*" since she would want to know what I meant, and what I meant was that I gave up thinking about categories but that there are, I'm pretty sure, a lot of them. I can hear her focusing on the matter now, not letting me off the hook.

At any rate, in this book Angela probes and prods about this vital and combustible issue, clarifying the places where we have hidden things from ourselves. We humans are deathly afraid of being ranked or classed—and with good cause. The most luminous example of what can happen is the Holocaust, where people of all sorts—frail gentle old ladies, intellectuals, little children, and the rest—were labeled and killed for bearing the label. Who knows what that meant? Who applied the label? What shaped their decisions? In today's world, white journalists entering a black "homeland" in South Africa feel they are protected because of their empathy with the plight of the blacks, but then they have this shield stripped away when they see the visceral welling outrage of blacks they've never met. The confrontation sends them cowering for cover. In the wake of classification nothing remains but black and white. And that's what we fear, that is, that such classifications will polarize us and that labels will be misused.

And yet, beneath this fear we do rank each other. Constantly. Ponder the following unexceptional statement: "The University of California accepts the upper 12½% of California's students."

We must, in fact, perform such classification if our populace is to be trained and selected for the vastly diverse mental needs of our society. We must classify if we are to direct this or that young person into the places where he or she can succeed. But unless we know what we mean by intelligence, or what performance in a test signifies, we are surely engaged in a crudely defined process that will fail to do justice to many young people, and to our society more broadly. For many of them the anger may never leave.

Beneath this substrate of need are even more basic questions, and Angela teases them all out into the open. She spends many pages exploring questions like the following: If human minds are of multiple dimensions, can we be measured and ordered according to a simple scale? How can we approach the diversity of mind? If you rank minds according to a single scale and find that, for example, the races of the human species fall out in a regular order with so-and-so at the top and so-and-so at the bottom, does this really mean anything we can use to rank people by? Haven't we crammed a multivariate species into the peg holes that define a single curve? Don't those shavings that piled up on the floor when the pegs didn't fit represent the true richness of society, the stuff that matters most? What have we lost? How can we do better?

Angela explores another domain: How much is predetermined by the inherited mind, and how much can be shaped to fit the creations of our culture? Is the job of a grade school or university to mold minds, to shape and change intelligence? Or is it to take the diverse minds that stream through the admission process and allocate them, or let them allocate themselves, to the places in the smorgasbord of the educational establishment where they find they best fit and are most likely to succeed?

What Angela shows is that, after decades of trying, even the basic questions about ranking humans according to intelligence remain a morass of fuzzy thinking and that most ranking is done by a single generalized criterion that lumps us all together. The term *learning* is apt to be used coterminously with *intelligence*, and what intelligence might be remains as fuzzy as ever. Some neurobiologists insist we are of multiple minds, and yet the measures we use to gauge ourselves take little heed of this emerging fact.

All during my reading of this book I thought about my own mind and wondered what would be measured if I sat down to take a Spearman test or one of the other methods of measuring what I am like. There is no way the one-dimensional examinations would reflect me very well. At best they would come out with some sort of average assessment that took the best of my mind and mushed it up with the worst. The average test would steer me only in the most general way. The best thing somebody who assessed me might do would be to say, "Looks like there's something there. Turn him loose in academia and see what happens." The test would not tell the obvious places where I excel or those where I am woefully lacking. Now that I have retired and have a long career behind me, let me use my case to explain what I mean.

I am a naturalist-biologist (which means I like to work in nature), well known in a fairly narrow circle for my studies of thermal biology of desert animals and for similar work with fish and best known for discovering many aspects of the biology of dolphins, especially their echolocation and social behavior. My work, if you could call it work, has taken me all over the world, and I went as a scientist, which only superficially covered the fact that I am also an artist, captivated to the very deepest recesses of my being by the beauty and perfection I find in nature; in plants and animals; and in the physical world of wind and water, sun and rock. Most important of all, I see directly what is in front of me in nature, not stereotypes that I have filed in my mind. I can draw the animals and plants I see with elegant fidelity, if not artistic panache. My parents, one an artist and the other an outdoorsman-engineer, truly defined the limits and possibilities of my mind and what I have been able to do with it.

My own special stock-in-trade as a scientist has been a capacity to see in three dimensions and to perceive and think with patterns and with patterns within patterns—the gestalts of life, the surrounds within which all of us live, the ecologies, the sociobiologies, the cultures. This has been so strong in me that when faced with mathematics as a young student, I immediately applied my capacity for seeing relationships to it. In geometry everything was relationships, and they were visual. Piece of cake. Then came algebra. Forget it. I could see the quadratic equations okay, but when asked to deal with where it led, I was hopelessly mired. Algebra, I later learned from my mathematician daughter, just as I was about to retire, isn't like that. It's a chain of small logical steps, using tested rules, leading who knows where. How could I envision a thing like that? I couldn't, and most of mathematics for me became a sea of frustration as I tried over and over to apply the strength of my mind to it and failed. Algebra, and much else, had no obvious surround. So my part of science became the imaginative leap, and more and more I came to work with others who could do the one-step-at-a-time things, which included not only math but every instrument that imposed itself between me and nature as well.

Now, what would a Spearman test or any test of mental ability do with me? Certainly, the quality of my mind is difficult to measure. Certainly, measures of mathematical and verbal abilities are not good indications of how my mind performs best. Perception of gestalts isn't remembering or using words or numbers. In my view, it is preverbal. But analogies tests and spatial questions are also inadequate measures. Perhaps the quality of my memory is a better, but still incomplete, measure. There was a time when my long-term memory was stuffed with an amazing clutter. It's thinning out a little now. And this is good, I think.

My naturalist's ability to see in nature has always depended upon avoiding those stereotyped representations for trees, rocks, people, and animals that we file in our minds as a kind of shorthand and upon actually looking directly at these natural things. That capacity is apparently involved in crossovers between the various hemispheres and subsections of my brain. Such crossover has been very important to my intellectual activity, even central. What really tests that?

So, in my view, if a psychometrician wanted to test me successfully, most of the important things to know about me would be the interactive workings of the various nonverbal constructs of my mind. Only after gauging those things would one find any value in knowing about the trove of words I carry around or the large but idiosyncratic collection of ideas, concepts, and facts that I have never stopped gathering or constructing.

So I perk up when Angela lays out before the reader the simplicities of how we try to gauge what we warily call intelligence. She finds much basic theoretical confusion between the basic organizations of mind that predict performance and the results of working minds. She elegantly shows the dance that masks the ubiquity of intelligence assessment in our society, one that may well be based on false premises and mistakes in the basic constructs we use to explain intellectual performance.

Beyond these things, as I read this book, I wondered, "Is the university so much a creation of the dominant culture as to be inaccessible to others?" What does that statement, analyzed and pared into its pieces, mean? What does it have to do with mind, with this thing we call "intelligence"? We're back to that again.

Following Angela through this intellectual thicket is what the book is about. There's much more in it than I could tell here. If anyone is to lead us out of the mire of false premises and hidden agendas about how we gauge each other, it's likely to be Angela Browne-Miller.

KENNETH S. NORRIS

Professor Emeritus of Natural History
University of California at Santa Cruz
Santa Cruz, California

Preface

Intelligence Policy grew out of my long-term concern regarding the distribution of opportunity in a free society. I was taught by my parents, who immigrated to the United States before my birth, to cherish education as one of the greatest opportunities in life and to work hard for it. In fact, I remember that my mother, as she was dying during my senior year in high school, made it clear that one of her greatest regrets in dying young was not being able to see her three children through college. Many other parents experience similar regrets, not because of their untimely deaths but because their children experience limited access to the opportunity to complete a higher education and a baccalaureate degree at a university of their choice.

The failure to realize one's potential is increasingly viewed as being related to the lack of opportunity to construct and then to realize one's educational dreams. This failure is felt to be a kind of death. It seems to me that the bell tolls for all of us each time a human mind is wasted. The challenge, then, is to understand the obstacles to the utilization of all the actual and potential mental ability within a society, and, for that matter, around the globe. The challenge is also to integrate, into a democratic society, the difficult and often unproductive debate regarding the sources of human intelligence, a debate rearing its dangerous faces again on the wave of *The Bell Curve*, a book released in 1994 by Richard Herrnstein and Charles Murray.

I have written this book in response to these challenges. My goal is to contribute to the development of an ethical and conceptually eclectic analytic tool that can be used to examine the impact of social policies that utilize or fail to utilize mental ability. We must never stop scrutinizing our decisions in this arena. To stop asking is to block the flow of truth within and among belief systems and to allow further empowerment of the dangerous cesspool of prevailing paradigm.

ANGELA BROWNE-MILLER

Tiburon, California

xiii

Acknowledgments

So many interactions, fleeting and longterm, enter into the writing of a book. Even a book-length summary of these would be barely adequate acknowledgment of all who have in some way contributed to this project. I will, therefore, take this opportunity to mention but a few key players in the inspiration and encouragement of this work.

Bernard Gifford, Professor in the School of Education at the University of California at Berkeley, inspired me to complete and refine my analysis of this topic during the years when he was chair of my doctoral committee as well as Vice President of Education at Apple, Inc., and Chair of the National Commission on Testing and Public Policy. The sheer dedication and talent of this man are evidenced in his assuming such a combination of posts. Yet his specialness cannot be captured in job titles. To watch this man think on his feet before an audience of one or many is to sit in awe of both the mind and the presentation. To come to know his ability to shift with skill among several fields of theory and endeavor is to learn what it means to be a modern Renaissance person of the intellect. But what I admire most about him is his ability to apply his intelligence to real-world problems. I thank you for the modeling, the direction, and the inspiration, Dr. Gifford.

And I must somehow, in mere words, express my gratitude to Aaron Wildavsky, my dear colleague and special mentor, professor in the Department of Political Science at the University of California at Berkeley and founder of the School of Public Policy at the same university, who cannot be on the planet for the publication of this book. Aaron's untimely death in the fall of 1993 marks the departure of one of the most prolific and greatest thinkers of our time. To attempt to describe in words the caliber and brilliance of Aaron's mind is to reduce his intelligence to a feeble representation of his awesome intellectual power. I had the privilege of working with Aaron as his doctoral student and as coauthor of the new chapters in the third edition of *Implementation,* an experience that changed my life. That collaboration was fantastic training and will influence all my writing for the rest of my life. Aaron, I cannot find a way to say an adequate good-bye, except to acknowledge your immortality as you live on in my work and in the work of many others. Thank you for believing in me.

I have a few other very dear people who must also be named here. Lynne Byrne has been the most valuable editorial, research, and administrative assistant I could ever hope for. Every author should be as fortunate as I have been to find the intelligent dedication to a project of which Lynne is capable. And my family—Richard, Sarana, and Evacheska—are always respectful of my almost continuous desire to write, even though I have been known to burn dinners, spend entire vacations typing, and commit other seemingly antisocial acts while writing books.

And there is my father, Lee Browne, who wanted to live to see the completion of this book but did not. Lee taught me to cogitate and to avoid sloppy thinking, and started doing so the day I was born. Thanks, Dad.

Contents

Foreword *by Kenneth S. Norris* ix

Introduction *by Raymond B. Cattell* 1

1. The Bell Tolls 5

    Specific Objectives 6
    Definitions and Structure 10

I. THE DEMAND FOR AND ASSESSMENT OF MENTAL ABILITY

2. The Supply of and Demand for Intelligence 15

    Demand 16
    Meritocracy Emerges 19
    Populist versus Classicist Views of Access 21
    Questioning the Connection between Education and Democracy .. 22

3. The Juxtaposition of Individual and Institutional Assessment ... 25

    Tilting at Windmills 28
    Anatomy of the Cover-Up 40
    Consequences 50

II. MAPPING SOCIAL POLICY AGAINST A THEORETICAL BACKDROP

4. Mapping Admissions and Other Social Policy against a
   Philosophical Backdrop 59

    On the Learnability of Intelligence 60
    A Model of Societal Investment in Intelligence 62

5. Academic Merit versus Fair Representation: A Case Study of
   the Undergraduate Admissions Policy at the University of
   California at Berkeley   65

   Access to Opportunity   66
   The Evolution of a Modern Admissions Policy   69
   Basic Components of U.C. Admissions Policy   73
   Explicit Shifts in the Balance of Admissions Policy   78
   Admissions Policy as Opportunity Allocation   79

6. Intelligence versus Higher Education as a Determinant of
   Worldly Success: The Sociopolitical Perspective   81

   Pressure for Homogenization of Intellectual Standards   82
   School as an Agent of Social Stasis   83
   Belief Systems in Conflict   88
   Conflict between Belief Systems Regarding Intelligence   90
   The Power of Prevailing Belief Systems   92
   The Systematic Transfer of Cognitive Abilities and Intelligence ...   94
   The Flow of Theory   99
   Testing for Intelligence   102
   Constructing Society around Inequalities   103

7. Academic Aptitude versus Achievement: Scientific
   Interpretations of Intelligence   105

   Testing   106
   Intelligence   109
   Giftedness   113
   Sociological Aspects of Intelligence   116
   The Platform of Cognitive Science: A Conceptual Bridge?   118

8. Rationalist versus Empiricist Views: The Philosophical
   Backdrop on the Learnability of Intelligence   125

   The Legacy of Rationalism   127
   The Surge of Empiricism   131

9. The Illusory Faces of Implicit Intelligence Policy   137

   Seeking Truth in Policy   138
   The Environmentalism Face   139

The Definitional Face 140
The Economic Face 141
The Selection-Testing Face 141
The Ability-Shift Model in Selection Policy 143

III. THE IMPACT OF IMPLICIT INTELLIGENCE POLICY
ON EXPLICIT POLICY

10. The Potential Value of Impact Analysis on Intelligence Policy   149

Policy Analysis 149
Ecological Rationality 151
Impact Analysis 152

11. The Impact of Implicit Intelligence Policy on Explicit
University Admissions Policy   153

The University of Tomorrow 154
The Difficult Issue of Matching 158
An Undercurrent of Tension 159
The Implicit Undergrid 161
Tension 1: Academic Merit versus Fair Representation 163
Tension 2: Intelligence versus Higher Education as a Determinant
of Worldly Success...................................... 166
Tension 3: Aptitude versus Achievement 168
Tension 4: Rationalist Views versus Empiricist Views 170
Impacts 172

12. Recommendations and Conclusions: Toward a Coherent and
Explicit Intelligence Policy   179

Basic Questions to Ask of Admissions Policy 180
The Potential Role of Impact Analysis 181
Specific Proposals for Admissions Policies That Specify Their
Relationship to Intelligence Policy 182

13. From Here to a Coherent and Explicit Intelligence Policy   185

Mapping Intelligence Policy to Make It Explicit 185

Speaking Truth to Power 187
Diminishing Demand for Intelligence Diminishes Its Supply 189
For Whom the Bell Tolls 190

APPENDIXES

A. Relevant Models of Impact Analysis 193
B. Adaptation of Impact Analysis to Intelligence Policy Analysis 205
C. Relevant Documents 209

Notes 223

Index 245

About the Author 255

Introduction

By Raymond B. Cattell

Distinguished Research Professor Emeritus of Psychology
University of Illinois

So important and comprehensive a work as this book by Angela Browne-Miller, which deals with the social and policy aspects of intelligence, needs a very firm understanding of intelligence itself. In a feat of conceptual synthesis Dr. Browne-Miller pulls together a vast and interdisciplinary array of theory regarding mental ability in support of her policy-analytic approach to the matter.

We see how much of our utilization of human intelligence is, for better or worse, test based. This is an area in which I have been deeply involved. I have seen that the history of intelligence testing falls into two very distinct streams. First is the theoretical-scientific approach, which organizes human intelligence into primary and secondary components. This approach began in 1904 with Charles Spearman's article "Intelligence Objectively Determined and Measured," in which he, using the statistical method he invented—factor analysis—identified a general factor, "g," common among intelligence tests. The second stream evident in the history of intelligence testing is the more pragmatic commonsense approach that has as its end the identification, use, and training of human intelligence rather than merely listing its characteristics. This approach began with Alfred Binet and Theodore Simon's construction of a successful field test, also conducted in 1904.

The latter approach drew far more attention and was carried forward for the next 80 years by an army of inventive psychologists. The former approach, Spearman's invention of factor analysis, drew all kinds of ingenious objections, primarily because most psychologists were short on mathematics. A few years later, Louis Thurstone cleared up most of these objections while seemingly substituting his theory of multiple primary abilities (such as verbal, mechanical, numerical, and the like) for Spearman's concept of the single general factor, "g." The matter of Thurstone's primary abilities supplanting Spearman's "g" was soon resolved, however, by the discovery that a single common factor lay behind all of Thurstone's primaries (which, in statistical terms, were positively correlated).

In 1940 I made the rather startling discovery that the supposedly single intelligence or "g" behind Thurstone's primary abilities was actually *two* intelligences, two so-called general factors: "fluid intelligence," which is largely biologically determined, and "crystallized intelligence," which is much more susceptible to environmental stimulation. Later, A. R. Hakstian found as many as 21 mental abilities and showed that when these abilities are analyzed for common factors,* they yield some five or six very broad factors in the cognitive ability field. These include the two intelligence factors I identified as well as speed, memory, and perceptual ability factors.

This line of research has led to the development of a rather scientific arm of psychology. The two intelligences I discovered by factor analysis have been further elaborated and substantiated by several different kinds of experiments. For example, we know that the life curve of what I call "fluid intelligence" (or "g_f") reaches a maximum at the age of 20 and declines slowly but steadily thereafter whereas "crystallized intelligence" (or "g_c") remains steady for most of one's life.† We find what we call the "heritability" (or inheritance) of fluid intelligence to be largely‡ explained by genetic inheritance. On the other hand, the heritability of crystallized intelligence is much less** explained by genetic inheritance. Crystallized and fluid intelligences have proven distinctly different in character. We even find that, as Donald Hebb suggested, the effect of brain injury on intelligence is a relatively local one for crystallized intelligence—limited to the scientific abilities most concentrated in the particular part of the brain that has been injured—but is proportional to the degree of the injury for fluid intelligence. It happens also that the visual shapes used in testing for spatial intelligence have been found to most closely represent fluid intelligence.†† Test questions involving these spatial-shape issues generally are culture fair, meaning they do not result in artificially contrived racial or cultural variations in test scores owing to the degree of exposure to the information being used in the test questions. By contrast, more verbal "g" tests (such as the Wechsler Adult Intelligence Scale), even with the modern fairness-inspired translations, are not culture fair and tend to measure crystallized intelligence.

The two streams of endeavor named at the outset of this introduction end very differently. The pragmatic Binet–Simon approach to intelligence ends in a marshland of misleading conglomerates of subtests in which the definition of intelligence is reduced to an impoverished "intelligence is what intelligence tests

---

*As statisticians would say, "factored," in this case, to the "third order."
†Note that we find that the standard deviation of IQ is about 15 to 16 for "g_c" whereas that for "g_f" is 24.
‡80%.
**Only 40%.
††Statistically speaking, to "most highly load on g_f."

measure." On the other hand, and perhaps more realistically, the approach that began with Spearman's discovery of a basic and common intelligence factor defines and measures intelligence as "the capacity to perceive relations." Today, the purest measures of intelligence available are "culture-fair tests." From these, the surest predictions regarding mental ability and performance-based mental ability can be made, involving all that we now know about the psychological and physiological nature of the intelligences.

With this foundation, it is possible to look around at the political, social, and educational aspects of intelligence and to consider the policy implications of our various assumptions and theories regarding intelligence. This book does just that. One of my first concerns in such an endeavor (although, as you will find, it is not one of the concerns expressed in the book) is, unfortunately, almost totally neglected by the press and by politicians: the genetic deterioration or "dysgenic decay" of intelligence in industrialized countries. This concern has been not only controversial but dangerous for a scientist to express in that it engenders fears of racial bias and visions of officially conducted genetic selection. Related research has, unfortunately, been overlooked for its implications regarding overarching trends in the distribution of intelligence. Consider the following findings: It was shown in Britain as early as 1937 that children of IQ 85 have an average family size of between three and four siblings whereas the family size for children of IQ 130 was one and a fraction siblings. In 1938 an article appeared that calculated a decline in the average IQ of the general population in industrialized countries of one point per generation and predicted that in 50 years there would be a decline in school standards (such as SAT scores), an increase in delinquency, and an unabsorbable increase in unemployment at the semiskilled level. More recently, in 1991, the population statistician Daniel Vining repeated a similar survey about declining population IQ in the United States and came out with the same figure. Meanwhile, the changes predicted by the earlier studies are now here for us to lament. It is most unfortunate for the human species that the causes of these changes are considered either too complex or not of great enough concern for journalists and politicians to address.

It has been the standard for quite some time to base estimates of scholastic performance on intelligence tests. This practice has been considered sound because the correlation between school or college performance and measured intelligence has been typically found to be statistically significant. Of course, observant people have long realized that character, motivation, and environmental circumstances must also be taken into consideration in the evaluation of scholastic performance and of intelligence. However apparent this may have been to many observers, it was years after the factor analysis of mental ability was achieved that the factor analysis of personality structure was able to reach some firm conclusions. Before then, there was no way to perform the feat of conceptual and analytic design that would scientifically verify these observations.

Between 1940 and 1980 much solid progress was made in the development of temperamental scales, such as the High School Personality Scale and the School Motivation Analysis Test. These have been checked numerous times as to the correctness of the 14 or more traits covered. In 1968 my colleague, John Butcher, and I made a thorough study of what could be predicted from such instruments. In the end, we found that in the objective measure of various school performances, there was a strong relationship between intelligence level and school performance, and that this relationship appeared to raise to an even stronger point of prediction than other measures by emphasizing fluid intelligence.

Among those resisting the measurement of intelligence and the utilization of such measurement are some who say "character is more important than measured intelligence." Although many research findings now support the truth of this statement, it is nevertheless a dangerous and all too widespread error to underestimate the importance of intelligence in life. Intelligence correlates with everything from walking through a door to understanding Einstein. It correlates positively with earnings, social status, stature, freedom from disease, success at cards and chess, intelligence of the marriage partner, and reduced frequency of car accidents. The correlations may be small, but they are significant. Given that the effect of intelligence on a single life can be considerable, the effect of intelligence on the life of society and of the human species must be profound. This is, indeed, a pressing matter for social policy.

1

The Bell Tolls

No man is an *Iland*, intire of it selfe; every man is a peece of the *Continent*, a part of the *maine*, . . . any mans *death* diminishes *me*, because I am involved in *Mankinde*, And therefore never send to know for whom the *bell* tolls; it tolls for *thee*.

JOHN DONNE [1]

Many allocations of opportunity made within educational, corporate, and other social policy arenas reflect unstated and inconsistent views regarding the definition, treatment, and utilization of human intelligence and mental ability. [2] These views are often silent but, nevertheless, powerfully operative, and they have profound societal impacts. Whether or not such views are made explicit, debates about social policy reflect conflicting views regarding the degree to which apparent differences in school, job, and life "performance" are linked to individual differences in measured intelligence, the degree to which intelligence is learnable, the degree to which intelligence can be realistically measured, and the degree to which these differences are socioeconomically determined and can be socioeconomically remedied.

Although the importance and definition of intelligence is unclear, unspecified assumptions and tensions regarding intelligence are allowed to exert significant, albeit oftentimes subtle, influence on educational and other policies in both the private and public sectors.

Instead of naming a "Minister for the Development of Intelligence" or similar official (the likes of which has been done in some countries [3]), we make the assumption that existing legislative processes and offices and departments of education adequately address the matter of intelligence. We make such an assumption for the following reasons:

- There is no consensus regarding the definition of intelligence [4].
- Intelligence is not only scientifically and professionally debated but politically controversial [5].

- There is no clear commitment as a nation to protect, develop, and utilize the vast and varied intelligence resources, whatever they may be.
- There is, therefore, an unarticulated implicit intelligence policy.
- The public is rarely cognizant, let alone respectful, of the societal impact of implicit intelligence policies.

Controversial, conflicting, biased, costly, sporadic, ineffective, and frequently detrimental mandates, laws, programs, budgets, and policies related to the development and utilization of intelligence reflect a lack of explicit intention and theory. They suggest the persistence of general, confused, and conflicting prejudices regarding the characteristics of mental ability. *They also suggest the existence of societal inhibitions regarding the explicit treatment of intelligence and the clarification of values that drive intelligence and mental-ability-related policies.*

At the same time, competition on the international front is calling the nation to enhance the development of human resources, especially in occupational areas requiring technical competence and ingenuity. [6] The health of the economy is seen by business, academic, and government leaders to "depend on the ability of American enterprises to compete successfully with foreign companies. And successful American enterprises rely primarily on the skills of an educated workforce." [7] It is time to examine and to clarify the various elements and societal impacts of heretofore implicit intelligence policies. This will permit more effective budgeting and organization for the fair treatment of human intelligences in a culturally diverse society, a society that is facing profound pressure from within and economic competition from around the globe.

Questions must be asked. What biases lurk behind even seemingly unbiased social and corporate policies? Some of these are biases regarding human intelligence. Whether or not the issue of human intelligence is addressed directly, it is a powerful force behind policy. To the degree that this force remains unrecognized, implicit, its effects are unpredictable and uncontrollable. Policy that is based on ambiguous and unspecified assumptions has ambiguous and potentially damaging consequences. Ignorance is dangerous. The goal of this book is to help lift the shroud of ignorance regarding intelligence—a must in our turbulent times.

SPECIFIC OBJECTIVES

The specific objectives of this book are, therefore, threefold. Part I considers the emergence of what can be called "unarticulated and implicit intelligence policy" in modern higher education, in light of economic and other implicit influences. Part II maps higher education admissions policy against an omnipresent and multifaceted theoretical backdrop. Part III postulates and then demonstrates an evaluation of the effects of implicit intelligence policy on explicit policy and the outcome of explicit policy. As a demonstration, the notion of impact analysis is applied to the troubled case of higher education admissions policy, a social policy that incorporates many assumptions regarding intelligence and mental ability. Given the tensions extracted from the analysis in Chapter 3 and in the chapters of Part II, admissions policies, specifically those at the University of California at Berkeley—a university grappling with pressures soon to be faced, if not already being faced, by most universities—are examined in terms of the assumptions and tensions among the assumptions that may drive them. Assumptions regarding measured and actual mental ability and intelligence are identified in order to estimate their impacts on admissions policy and its outcome. This study does not pretend to represent a survey of philosophies of mind held by current admissions officers and other players in the admissions policy process; instead, it infers these assumptions from the policies as publicly presented and relates them to the bodies of theory and tensions within those bodies that are examined in Part II.

The shift in admissions standards has become a national issue that requires careful analysis. The admissions policy at the University of California at Berkeley (U.C. Berkeley) is waiting for just such an analysis. This campus is one of the foremost universities in the world and has been at the forefront of political controversy across several decades. The issue of admissions standards has become a locus of that political controversy. Because of its size, visibility, world renown, public status, and multiracial mix, the experiences of U.C. Berkeley hold lessons for colleges and universities around the world.

Among the many pressures faced by U.C. Berkeley and the university system of which it is but one campus are intense economic pressures. Few, if any, institutions of higher education will proceed through the next decades without such pressures. In this sense U.C. Berkeley again offers an excellent lesson for colleges and universities seeking to maintain academic standards *and* respond to the demands of diversity while confronted with economic limitations. As David Gardner, past president of the University of California system, stated in 1991, "It will require from all of us continued and vigorous effort to sustain this institution and to preserve it for succeeding generations." [8] Gardner also explained that if state funding and increases in student fees prove unable to fully fund the university's essential needs, "then we . . . have only one alternative left, and that is reducing enrollment to match available resources." [9]

Such a trade-off marks the turning point of an era of expansion in higher education. Now enrollment must be *reduced*. Now there are limited slots for students, and there is an increased demand for these slots. Given concurrent pressures to accommodate the requirements of increasing racial diversity, a new brand of competition results. The increasingly central question is, How can social policy fairly distribute such a precious opportunity for an education at an excellent institution while preserving its outstanding reputation?

With respect to the gravity of this and related dilemmas and in an effort to contribute to the calibration of these issues of fairness, Part II of this book organizes theories of and assumptions regarding intelligence that influence higher education admissions and other policies into four areas of tension (see Tables 1.1 and 1.2):

- *Academic merit versus fair representation*, a tension inherent within the design of admissions, hiring, promotion, and other areas of policy, one that pits academic achievement against identification with particular socioeconomic groups
- *Intelligence versus education as a determinant of worldly success*, a sociopolitical tension between the belief in inherent and unchanging ability levels and the faith in education and training to affect the level of ability
- *Aptitude versus achievement*, a tension running deep within science and related research, which weighs measured intellectual potential against actual school, job, and life performance
- *Rationalist views versus empiricist views*, the basic philosophical tension driving each of the aforementioned tensions, an age-old dilemma which implicitly serves to polarize all views regarding ways of thinking, knowing, learning, and problem solving

As explained earlier, admissions policy, specifically, the undergraduate admissions policy of U.C. Berkeley, is presented herein as the example of the way impact analysis can be applied to intelligence policy. Admissions policy is especially intriguing in that it has undergone considerable scrutiny and debate in recent times, and it is a field of policy in which the heavy shroud of denial, which usually hides implicit intelligence policy, has worn quite thin.

Universities either apply a purely "merit-based" method of admissions or

Table 1.1.   Implicit Intelligence Policy
Impacts Higher Education Admissions Policy

Intelligence Policy Arises (see Part I of this book).
Tensions Mold Implicit Intelligence Policy (see Part II of this book).
   Philosophical tensions affect
   Scientific–theoretical tensions that affect
   Sociopolitical tensions that affect
   Policy tensions.
   Societal investment in education thus reflects implicit intelligence policy.
Implicit Intelligence Policy Impacts Admissions and Other Social Policy (see Part III of this book).
EXAMPLE: Higher Education Admissions Policy
   This is an opportunity allocation.
   There is a tension in the formulation of policies that distribute this opportunity.
   This tension must be recognized as impacting policy and policy outcome.

Table 1.2. Tensions Involved in Implicit Intelligence Policy*

THE RANGE OF ADMISSIONS POLICY OPTIONS

Merit-based admissions policies ⟶ 50–50 approach ⟵ Complimental admissions policies
                                      (Chapter 5)

⟵——⟶

IMPLICIT INTELLIGENCE POLICY CONSISTS OF THESE TENSIONS

TENSION 1: Regarding the level of societal investment in the development of intelligence and mental
   ability

Academic merit (to uphold ⟶   Tension   ⟵ Fair representation (to diversify
   academic performance)   *(Chapter 5)*   student body)

TENSION 2: Regarding the perceived potential influence of educational intervention upon individuals
   and society

Intelligence determines worldly ⟶   Tension   ⟵ (Higher) education not intelligence
   success   *(Chapter 6)*   determines worldly success

TENSION 3: Regarding the perceived learnability of intelligence and mental ability

Aptitude ⟶   Tension   ⟵   Achievement
                                      (Chapter 7)

TENSION 4: Regarding the philosophical view of the mind

Rationalist views of knowledge ⟶   Tension   ⟵ Empiricist views of knowledge
   acquisition   *(Chapter 8)*   acquisition

*These tensions impact, to varying degrees, policies of educational opportunity, such as higher education admissions
   policy.

find other strategies for reducing or at least balancing enrollment to match it with
available resources. Behind these critical decisions lurks the implicit favoring of
selected assumptions about intelligence and mental ability. In this manner, policy
decisions assume positions along the aforementioned four continua of tension
diagrammed in Table 1.2.

The book concludes by recommending several major amendments in admissions policy and in the matriculation of students through the higher education
system. It also recommends that impact analysis be applied in the analysis of
social policies whether they be admissions, curriculum, "learnfare," "workfare,"
hiring policies, or other methods of opportunity allocation (especially those
requiring work, training, or learning in exchange for money). All such policies
affect (either directly or indirectly) and/or utilize human intelligence and mental
ability. The results of this book are relevant as a philosophical/conceptual meter
and as an analytical meter in educational planning, policy development, training,

and in the ongoing development of education science. Honest scrutiny of implicit intelligence policy can move us toward a rational calibration of fairness.

The sources of human intelligence have been long debated. No resolution to this debate is in sight. Yet while theory may be debated forever, the impacts of belief in these theories must be measured in the present. Lloyd Humphreys, a professor emeritus of psychology at the University of Illinois, who has a long history of major contributions to the fields of psychology and psychological testing, wrote in his 1980 article "Race and Intelligence Reexamined" that "it is possible to devise social policies that can, in good conscience, be supported by both hereditarians and environmentalists while avoiding policies that are supported by one position but are contraindicated by the other." [10] If Humphreys was correct about this possibility, the adaptation of the *intelligence policy impact analysis* proposed herein may help to devise the most effective policies with the broadest social value and support.

DEFINITIONS AND STRUCTURE

Basic to this discussion is an understanding of *implicit policy*, a subtle and relatively intractable network of attitudes and tensions, and actions based on these attitudes and tensions. Compounding the abstract quality of the discussion of the role of implicit policy in the formulation of explicit policy, such as that of higher education admissions, is the issue of intelligence. So controversial and so elusive that its mention is frequently avoided and its relevance fervently denied, *intelligence* is a difficult to describe human attribute that has some relationship to academic performance, occupational attainment, worldly success, and other human behaviors. Whether intelligence is viewed primarily as a product of the individual and societal environment, as a product of genetic inheritance, or as the result of an interaction of these, it is a determinant of, and often a synonym for, *mental ability*. It is the numerous, and often conflicting, assumptions and theories regarding mental ability and intelligence that form the basis of *implicit intelligence policy*.

A significant portion of this book (Parts I and II) is, therefore, dedicated to the unearthing and mapping of implicit intelligence policy. Chapter 2 in Part I begins with a brief consideration of the modern history of implicit intelligence policy in higher education and concludes with a look at psychologist Raymond Cattell's graphic representation of the supply of and demand for intelligence in changing economic times. Such a shift in demand, although economically driven, suggests a shift in perception. It indicates that *societal perceptions of intelligence*, its utility, its distribution, and even its definition, fluctuate in response to cultural factors such as economics, political pressure, and theoretical fashion. The opening chapter of Part II (Chapter 4) maps societal investment in intelligence based on the perceived malleability of that intelligence. This map is developed against the age-old philosophical backdrop of the rationalism-versus-empiricism argument, which is integrated into the heuristic map drawn in Chapter 4. Although other dilemmas in the discussion of intelligence and mental ability may or may not be viewed as being parallel or related to this basic philosophical tension, Chapter 8 contends that this basic tension foreshadows and permeates all other levels and angles of the discussion (see Table 1.2). The impact analysis demonstrated in Part III supports this contention. Let us proceed then to interrogate intelligence policy for the truth.

I

The Demand for and Assessment of Mental Ability

2

The Supply of
and Demand for Intelligence

In the age of information, knowledge is capital, and the ability to get and use
knowledge is the key to productivity.

ROGER J. PETERS [1]

As stated in Chapter 1, this book examines the relationship between implicit
intelligence policy and explicit social policy, focusing on college admissions at
highly selective universities as the primary example. Because implicit policies are
unarticulated and, therefore, elusive, this relationship must be viewed in terms
of the various underlying pressures at work on the overlay of explicit policy. Many
of these pressures grow out of influential bodies of theory. As a prelude to the
examination of theoretical pressures in Part II, Part I looks at the general issues of
access to the university and assessment of academic performance once access to
the university is attained. This first chapter of Part I considers the problem of
access—of opportunity allocation—from two important historical standpoints:
university biases (regarding those other than the "white male elite") and the
emergence of conflicting merit and populist standards (in response to elitist
admissions policies).

Building on this overview of the evolution of access, the economic pressures
of supply and demand are linked to the demand for and definition of mental ability.
Simply stated, when there is an abundance of opportunity for higher education, a
broader segment of society is admitted to the university; when there is a scarcity or
shortage of opportunity, selection pressure mounts and definitions of mental
fitness for higher education narrow. In this manner, implicit intelligence policy,
whether it leans toward an elitist or a populist direction, is influenced by economic
pressure. Elitist solutions are a common response to scarcity of opportunity.

The ebb and flow of access to higher education responds to the sociopolitical
and economic tenor of the times. To explain this, an economic model of the

15

demand for intelligence can be applied. But first, a word regarding differing demands for mental ability among differing occupations is necessary.

DEMAND

It has been argued that occupations differ in their demands for general intelligence and that persons scoring low on traditional intelligence tests have a low probability of succeeding in occupations with a high demand for intelligence. [2] Educational psychologist Arthur Jensen contends that this is due, at least in part, to the differing levels of what he labels "g-demanding" (to be called "intelligence-demanding" for now) educational requirements of various occupations and, also in part, to the differing intelligence demands of the various occupations. [3]

The notion that occupational level is, at least generally, positively related to educational level is a concept that is less controversial than the contention that intelligence is the key determinant of educational level attained. Some argue that one's level of general intelligence acts as a "probabilistic threshold" for worldly success [4], which is dependent on educational and occupational level. Others argue that the sociopolitical environment is the key determinant not only of worldly success but of the very measured intelligence that is said to predict that success. [5]

Support for the opposing sides of this argument waxes and wanes over time. Assumptions regarding the origin and utility of differing levels of measured intelligence mirror political and economic expansions and constrictions. Economic interpretations themselves have political ramifications. Cattell brilliantly depicted this shifting demand for what is measured as intelligence. According to his model, this demand shift corresponds to the shift from times of economic affluence to times of economic hardship (see Figures 2.1 through 2.4). According to Cattell, the perceived utility of various levels of intelligence expands under affluent conditions in a technocratic society. Hence, there is more demand for the utilization of average and lower levels of mental ability. In times of economic constraint, the demand for utilization of mental ability moves up the spectrum. The apparently more mentally able are in greater demand and the apparently less able are in less demand. [6] This shift as it relates to the demand for complex ability is powerfully illustrated by Cattell in Figure 2.1 (note that the "g" levels in Figure 2.1 refer to a "general" or core intelligence). As the complexity of a job increases, the price of the work will increase, as shown by Cattell in Figure 2.2 (first curve). The reward curve in Figure 2.2 (second curve) illustrates the waning percent of the population in high-earning complex occupations. In this model the combination of high IQ and high educational level correlates with high-priced work (see Figure 2.3). Cattell's "ability-shift theory" is clearly illustrated in

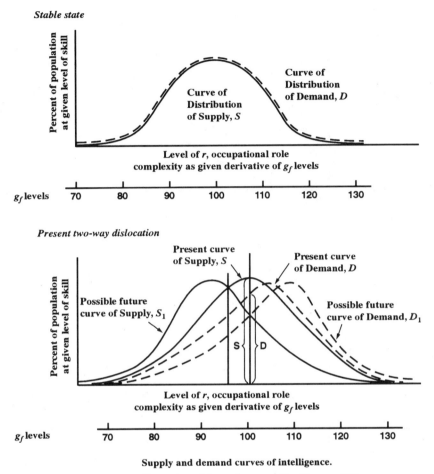

Supply and demand curves of intelligence.

Figure 2.1. Cattell's supply and demand curves of intelligence. [25]

Figure 2.4, where he depicts the average IQ employed in times of prosperity as being lower than the population mean and the average I.Q. employed in times of recession as being higher than the population mean. Such access to occupational opportunity is limited by perceptions of the mental ability of job applicants. Implicit assumptions such as the ones fueling this relationship affect the distribution of opportunity.

The ability-shift theory of Cattell suggests that economic perceptions help to define the value society places on mental ability. While the demand for and actual utilization of intelligence may be driven by the economic constraints described by

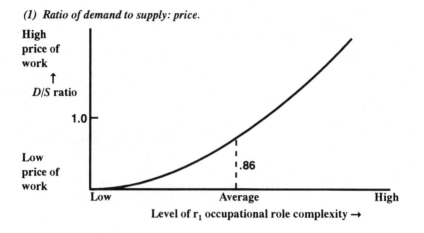

(1) Ratio of demand to supply: price.

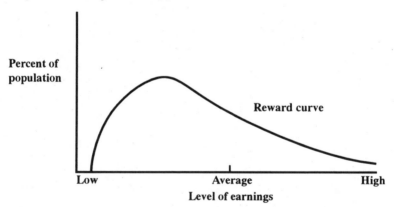

*(2) Distribution of earnings to be expected
from natural adjustment to (1):*

Figure 2.2. Cattell's ratio of demand to supply: price and earnings effects. [26] Note that these curves are illustrative and are not based on any exact data.

Cattell, the understanding of intelligence is powered by deep-seated and often implicit assumptions. As Part II maps implicit intelligence policy, the aforementioned fundamental economic pressures are retained as the overarching dollars-and-cents reality.

In order to see the substance of the admissions process with respect to intelligence and mental ability, it is necessary to look beyond economic pressures on admission standards. Candidates for university enrollment must be seen as

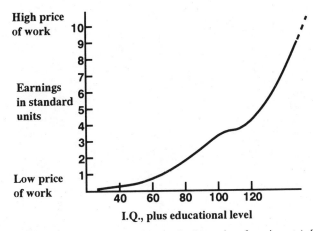

Figure 2.3. Cattell's ratio of demand to supply (i.e., price of earning rate). [27]

products of a social order that has both explicitly and implicitly sought to form them and that has brought their intelligences as far along as possible (or necessary). A multitude of contemporary factors feeds this social order. Before proceeding to an extensive examination of these factors, consider briefly the historical context for the emergence of meritocracy.

MERITOCRACY EMERGES

· Harvard University was traditionally regarded by many students as out of their social, cultural, and intellectual league. This image began to change as a consequence of events related to World War II. A distinct break in tradition occurred when wartime female Radcliffe students were taught jointly with men owing to various constraints presented by the war. The female students actually raised the grade average and placed the Harvard males under new scholastic pressure.

The GI Bill of Rights brought to universities around the nation a new breed of student: veterans of the war who were more mature, more serious about schooling, less interested in the social aspects of university life, and impatient with issues of social status. A boom in higher education began, which opened the range of recruitment to a larger population of students. Students who would never have been told that universities, including Harvard, might be open to them began to hear this news in their high schools. [7]

The privileged few who were once guaranteed attendance at Harvard and similar universities saw a change on campus. Derogatory terms emerged. "Exces-

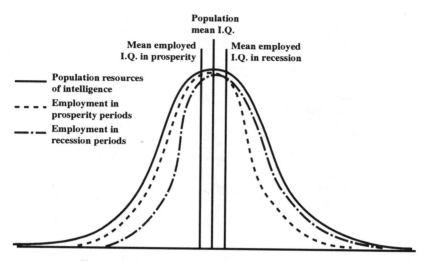

Figure 2.4. Cattell's ability-shift theory of business cycles. [28]

sively studious" students (hard-working students admitted on the basis of their academic merits), admitted under the new "democratized meritocracy," were called "wonks" by the "cavalierly bright" students (of presumably "higher" social status). Later, the term "jock" came along, derisively describing athletes who were presumably admitted for their athletic ability rather than their social status or their academic merit. [8]

While merit-based admissions were first viewed as a development that would broaden opportunities for access to higher education, basing admissions on merit rather than social status was interpreted quite differently by the 1960s. As Professor David Riesman, a member of the Carnegie Commission on Higher Education in the 1960s and an eminent social scientist, explained:

> Meritocratic selectivity, earlier of course seen as the path of equity, became in the eyes of many another form of racial discrimination, once it was evident that equality of opportunity produced anything but equality of results. . . . there was a loss of humane solidarity consequent upon competitiveness in a society where equality of opportunity results in the losers condemning themselves for nonachievement, the winners for manipulativeness. [9]

Riesman did not find meritocracy to be the absolute panacea for social inequities. He found the impact of meritocracy on the occupational hierarchy and occupational opportunity to be minimal. [10] Rather than let this be an indictment of meritocracy, consider it an indication that meritocracy alone cannot change the organization of the encompassing society.

POPULIST VERSUS CLASSICIST VIEWS OF ACCESS

Amidst the plethora of lofty assumptions and disputed theories of intelligence, education policy attempts to address the needs of real people and real institutions. Such policy is so very enmeshed in this web of implicit assumptions and tensions that it cannot but represent and be an extension of the web. Implicit intelligence policy manifests itself in explicit policy. Witness, as an example, the evolution of populism and classicism in higher education.

Higher education has long been viewed as the gateway to economic and social opportunity. However, the question of opportunity for whom has had a variety of answers in different eras and has been debated at several points in modern history. The question, pivoting around changing perceptions of various social groups, is this: Who is believed to have the ability to take advantage of higher education, to fully harvest the knowledge, and to best return the educational investment to society? Access to higher education has expanded greatly in recent decades, but it was not so long ago that participation in higher education was almost entirely limited to the white elite, often of particular religious inclination and usually of the male gender. [11]

Historically, access to higher education has not only been limited for women but limited for anyone other than the most affluent members of the dominant culture. Definitions of the role of the university in society have clustered around two opposing views. The "classicist" view maintains that the university has three basic obligations: to transmit high culture to a select group, to create new knowledge through pure scholarship, and to train and certify numbers of learned and elite professionals. [12]

Thomas Jefferson, considered the foremost educational statesman of the Revolutionary generation, saw the positive relationship between a system of broadly accessible free public education and a society that would improve the condition of mankind. Hence, Jefferson proposed his "Bill for the More General Diffusion of Knowledge" to the Virginia legislature in 1779. In Jefferson's vision, the state university was the "crown" of the public education system. (Note that University of California President David Gardner once described his university system as California's "crowning jewel." [13]) In fact, the state university system described by Jefferson flourished in the southeastern United States in the 1700s and early 1800s because it did not have to compete with earlier colonial colleges such as those in New England and because the regional organized religions were not powerful enough to strongly oppose public education. [14] (Of course, the public college system of Virginia served a predominantly male student body.)

By contrast, the "populist" viewpoint sees three very different obligations as being basic to the university: to provide educational opportunity to all citizens, to provide ordinary citizens the opportunity to enter elite occupations, and to generate "fluidity in the class structure." [15]

In short, the populist view contends that higher education is a right rather than a privilege. Defenders of the classicist view argue that the primary mission of higher education is intellectual and that it is dangerous for institutions of higher education and for society to subordinate this mission to social goals. [16]

Access to high school became universal at an earlier stage of educational history, and now access to higher education has expanded to appear, at first glance, almost universal. Yet access to 4-year colleges and universities is an obstacle course littered with bureaucratic and sociopolitical hurdles. Applications involve hours of filling out forms and writing essays under deadline pressure and usually with an accompanying application fee requirement. For those families who can afford it, proprietary college application services are available, costing as much as $1,000 per student in the San Francisco Bay area in the early 1990s. [17] Admissions testing brings its own set of hurdles, ranging from test biases to test fees. And admissions themselves occur in an environment of scarcity. Not everyone can be admitted to and can afford to attend the college of his or her choice. Some students are not admitted to their first, second, or third choice; others dare not apply to their first, second, or third choice, knowing that their chances of admission are slim or nonexistent. In this way, *self-selection* emerges in times of diminishing opportunity. Self-selection reinforces perceived and actual admissions policies and, in so doing, represents a special form of implicit intelligence policy, one implemented not by admissions committees or politicians but by young people across the nation.

QUESTIONING THE CONNECTION BETWEEN EDUCATION AND DEMOCRACY

In times of economic affluence it is somewhat easier for a society to move in the direction of sharing at least some of the wealth. If educational opportunity is a form of wealth—a wealth of knowledge and a wealth of resources and time involved in educating students—then it is easier to share educational opportunity in times of economic affluence. The decade of the 1990s has witnessed the shrinking of the affordability of and opportunity for high-quality higher education in proportion to the demand for it. As opportunity for high-quality university education shrinks and/or becomes more costly, perceptions of students' fitness for such an education shift. This shift in perceived qualifications of students is often subtle but must not be ignored. A good candidate for admission in one era may be a poor candidate for admission in another, even if he or she has the same qualifications and academic ranking.

Consider the trend in California at the beginning of 1992: University of California (U.C.) regents voted to raise student fees 22%, which was the third time fees were raised in 3 years. These raises were aimed at reducing the statewide budget gap. Fees were also raised at the second-tier feeder system level of higher education, the California State University (C.S.U.) system, not part of the U.C. system. C.S.U. raised its fees 40% in early 1992, following a 20% increase the year before. [18] California Assemblyman Tom Hayden, chair of the Assembly Higher Education Committee, spoke to this matter: "California's historic guarantee of higher education for every qualified resident is coming to an end." And Hayden did not feel that the effects would be positive: "Closing the doors of higher education will have calamitous consequences." [19] Hayden consequently proposed that student fees be charged on the basis of income, rather than have the state continue to pay $11,000 of the cost of education for each U.C. student. He claimed that the sliding fee scale he proposed would save the state $50 million. To save another $10 million, Hayden also proposed that higher fees be charged for students in professional programs, such as law, that "are not in undersupply and thus less appropriate for public subsidy." [20]

Removal of public subsidy of the education of well-to-do students may do more than save the state dollars. It can promote a new level of competition for students who can pay their own tuition among universities. It can also alter the nature of the competition for admission among applicants; self-selection, driven by economic status, can increase. And, winners of the competition for admission may be viewed as being more intellectually suited for university education than losers, whether or not they are.

As public universities become as costly as their private counterparts, *selection of universities by applicants on the basis of tuition costs* may be replaced by *selection of universities by applicants on the basis of other reputational characteristics*, such as status and alumni achievements. Theory suggests that this should increase competition among universities, should generate greater competition in the educational marketplace. Yet this shift in *selection style* will occur most fully among those well-to-do students whose public university tuition increases. These are the students who will pay close to the same tuition either way, whether they choose a public or a private school or an in-state or out-of-state one. They may be even more likely to select the universities with the best reputation. Those students who cannot afford private universities, who will not pay the same tuition either way, and who will not have the same degree of choice will at least have guaranteed access to local public universities. Thus, the competition among universities resulting from a sliding fee scale in the public system may be a lopsided one. Knowing that enrollment by those less affluent is not as lucrative, universities may compete for the most affluent students, implicitly defining their particular academic characteristics as the most qualified. True fairness and fully equal opportunity are then further jeopardized. Such a catch-22, the perceived trade-off between democracy and economic efficiency, is typical of what has been termed the "neo-liberal political economy." [21]

Other theorists have argued that free-market competition among schools could remove education from this trade-off between democracy and economic efficiency but that an increase in educational efficiencies and standards may not follow from this "marketization" of education. [22] Again, this is because the market is politically and culturally constructed in such a way that it affects the behavior of the education consumer but not necessarily of the education supplier. [23] Market-led education may not be structured to deliver the minimum necessary requirements for democratic citizenship and to distribute the skills and understandings necessary for life in an economically sophisticated, increasingly technological democratic society. [24] Market-led education allows the market to influence definitions of fitness for university education. Although this book in no way intends to indict the market, it does seek to alert policy makers to the many implicit influences on admissions policy. An explicit part of admissions and all social policy making should include ongoing consideration (the beginnings of which can be found in Cattell's supply-and-demand diagrams included earlier in this chapter) of how the market interacts with, and even feeds, policy. Allow this consideration to linger throughout the following discussion.

3

The Juxtaposition of Individual and Institutional Assessment

> As a nation, we're caught on a hook of defining intelligence in certain ways and then letting our colleges and universities be defined in the same narrow ways.
>
> WILLIAM HISS [1]

The social order, which explicitly and implicitly seeks to form candidates for university enrollment, is fueled by powerful philosophical, scientific, and sociopolitical factors. These factors contribute to the ongoing formation of the college candidate from birth, through youth, and into adulthood. These factors not only affect the development of the college applicant prior to admission (or rejection) but also affect the academic performance of that student once (or if) he or she is admitted to college.

The quality of the admissions process, and of the institution doing the admitting, is implied by the academic performance of the students it admits. Simply stated, students who "do well" make the university look good. The purpose of this chapter is, therefore, to consider the presence of implicit and confused assumptions regarding intelligence in the assessment of the appropriateness, success, and quality of higher education.

In examining assumptions behind various interpretations of academic outcome, assumptions behind admissions policies designed to corral and even to guarantee certain academic outcomes are clarified. An individual-versus-environment dilemma surfaces: if an institution of higher education receives a positive assessment, is this reflective of the "quality" of the institution or the "quality" of its students? Will highly selective admissions policies lead to outstanding institutional assessments? The assumptions behind the answers to these and related questions are "implicit": although they may be articulated within the contexts of both scientific investigation and casual conversation, they are not out on the table for all to see during the drafting and implementation of either admission or assessment policy. The harm in these implicit assumptions lies in the fact that they are ambiguous and that, as a result, policies are driven by these ambiguous forces. In this way, largely unspoken assumptions about the nature of intelligence are powerful modulators of all education policies, including those pertaining to admissions and assessments in higher education.

A note about assessment: it is not the author's intention to cast assessment in a negative light. Assessment is a valuable endeavor that, when conducted carefully, can help improve the quality and the accountability of education. The concern is that as the assessment movement is growing, it is burying even more deeply the assumptions about intelligence, obscuring the effects of these assumptions on both admissions and assessment, and adding a superficial layer of data to the camouflage. In order to delve deeply into the world of assessment in higher education, portions of this chapter journey into narrow and precise aspects of assessment, since implicit assumptions are often buried beneath details.

What has remained implicit will serve better if it is made explicit. Otherwise, there remains an inadvertent cover-up of unspoken assumptions and subsequent manipulation by them. Therefore, in the first section of this chapter the presence of an implicit undergrid of thought and theory in the assessment of academic outcome is discussed. (Academic outcome may also be viewed as *admissions outcome*; refer to Figures 3.1 and 3.2.) The problematic definitions and assumptions that perpetuate the undergrid are reviewed. It is this undergrid that is inadvertently covered up. There are also definitions of assessment and assessment policy, as well as commentary on intelligence policy. In the second section of this chapter the anatomy of the cover-up is investigated. Also considered are the effects of increasing pressure on higher education to assess its performance, the generation of great expectations by lofty educational missions, the euphemism of the value-added approach to assessment, the muddle of generic academic outcomes, the ambiguities of measurement, and confusion about what students actually contribute to their own educations. In the third section the consequences of the cover-up are discussed, as are concerns regarding the undermining of assessment and admissions by implicit assumptions about intelligence. As long as things remain unspoken, no one has to talk about what it means to hear them. However, it is simply not true that "what we don't know won't hurt us."

Throughout the following discussion of or brainstorming regarding assessment, assumptions behind the various aspects of assessment are inferred and then identified. These are listed in boxes throughout the text. The chapter concludes by organizing the assumptions inferred from this examination of assessment policy into three of the four basic areas of tension (depicted in Table 1.2).

Intelligence is a murky and controversial concept. Therefore, the author refrains from favoring a single, specific, and highly elaborated definition of intelligence. It is best to admit to a running overture of consensual and conceptual

CONSEQUENCES
Damage from implicit assumptions
Danger in reliance on test results
Threatened homogenization of outcome
Undermining of assessment by implicit assumptions
Such consequences are the result of the cover-up.

ANATOMY OF THE COVER-UP
Pressure to assess
Generation of great expectations
Euphemism of value-added approach
Muddle of generic academic outcomes
Ambiguities of measurement
Confusion regarding student contribution
This anatomy is built on an undergrid.

IMPLICIT UNDERGRID
Implicit undergrid of thought and theory about intelligence
Murky definitions and airy assumptions
Hidden intelligence policy
The above results in a denial of implicit assumptions.

Implicit undergrid —> Cover-up —> Consequences

Figure 3.1. The impact of the implicit undergrid (thematic diagram of Chapter 3).

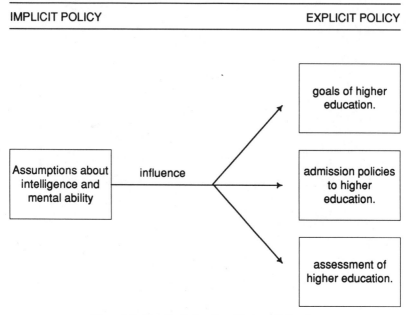

IMPLICIT POLICY   EXPLICIT POLICY

Figure 3.2. How implicit policy affects explicit policy.

haziness and tension with regard to the relationships between intelligence, ability, and learning. If any readers are uncomfortable with this degree of ambiguity, this is a request to take advantage of this discomfort. Readers are encouraged to inquire of themselves and of their colleagues exactly what assumptions—clear or vague— they hold about intelligence and how these assumptions influence their own work. Readers should also ask themselves how they differentiate between, and fuse, the notions of intelligence and ability. Ability is usually viewed as less restrictive and more expansive than intelligence. No matter how much debate surrounds the learnability of intelligence, ability is something that sounds as if it *can* be learned. There is ambiguity about the acquisition of intelligence but less so about ability.

TILTING AT WINDMILLS

In assessing academic outcome it is student performance or institutional performance, or both, that is being evaluated. When an institution performs poorly, it can hold itself responsible or it can place the burden of responsibility on the student. When the student performs poorly, the student can blame the university or can accept responsibility for the poor performance. Sometimes the university and the student willingly share responsibility for the academic outcome. Regardless of where the responsibility falls officially, the admissions policy that brought the student to the institution in the first place deserves scrutiny (and possibly more than that) when academic outcome is poor.

The Implicit Undergrid

Academic assessments cannot help but imply something about admissions policies. Why? Because assessment evaluates the performance of those who are admitted. The following discussion examines the implicit undergrid connecting admissions and assessment (see Figure 3.2).

Relationships between unarticulated vague notions of intelligence and articulated specific assessment program designs are elusive. It is perhaps easier to specify some connection between unarticulated notions of intelligence and articulated *goals* of higher education. When assessments are conducted to evaluate performances of colleges and universities against their stated goals, these assessments are influenced by implicit assumptions about intelligence that underlie these goals. If nothing else, the simple implicit assumption that the majority of people exposed to higher education can learn from it is persuasive enough to expose and, therefore, *admit* this majority to higher education.

Assumption: The majority of students exposed to higher education can learn from it.

Stated goals of higher education are particularly illuminating. Most colleges and universities share basic goals. Higher education seeks to serve democratic or "purportedly democratic" [2] purposes. It seeks to cultivate the following:

- Its citizens
- Talent among its citizens [3]
- Participants in the economy
- Persons who will contribute to society and culture [4]

Higher education seeks to train students to be competent in various fields of human endeavor and to prepare them for adulthood, for life. It seeks to promote the general welfare by increasing "the supply of educated intelligence." [5] In so doing, it aims to raise the level of the collective intelligence. Supporting these goals is the belief that they can be achieved by higher education and that the raw materials, students' minds, are amenable to the desired effects of higher education.

> *Assumption:* The goals of higher education can be achieved by higher education.
>
> *Assumption:* Students' minds can be molded to acquire the desired effects of higher education.

The distribution of higher education among an increasing number of citizens is viewed as being instrumental in increasing the viability of the society. Institutions of higher learning are the distributors of the instrument for major social change: advanced education. In order for these institutions to distribute the benefits of higher education among their own student bodies, several things must happen. The education they offer has to be designed to actually produce the effects society desires. Students must be willing to achieve that which society desires. Moreover, students must be *able* to do so. In order for the desired effects of higher education to be fairly distributed, or at least for them to be distributed to a critical mass of students via an equal distribution of educational energy, students must be relatively equal in their willingness to receive (or acquire) these effects. They must also be relatively equal in their *abilities* to receive (or acquire) these effects, in their abilities to learn. Without the ability to learn what higher education intends to teach, students do not accrue the desired effects of higher education.

> *Assumption:* The distribution of higher education to an increasing number of citizens increases the viability of society.
>
> *Assumption:* The education offered by institutions of higher education has to be designed to produce the effects desired by society.
>
> *Assumption:* Students are willing to receive these effects.
>
> *Assumption:* Students are able to receive these effects.
>
> *Assumption:* Students are relatively equal in their willingness to receive these effects.
>
> *Assumption:* Students are relatively equal in their abilities to receive these effects.

The focus shifts briefly to this *ability* to learn. Is there a link between learning ability and intelligence? Some would say so. Psychologist Arthur Jensen posits that the ability to learn is, in reality, indistinguishable from intelligence:

> Although learning and intelligence can be conceptually distinguished in terms of formal definitions and measurements, a review of evidence on the relationship between individual differences in measures of learning and of intel-

ligence suggests that no clear distinction can be made between the cognitive processes that contribute to individual differences in these two definitionally different realms. [6]

According to Jensen, the view that learning and intelligence overlap is widespread.

> It has been observed that some people acquire knowledge and skills 10 or 20 times faster than others. . . . Certain people can acquire particular knowledge and skills that some others cannot acquire at all with any amount of training. Such conspicuous individual differences in learning are most commonly thought of as differences in intelligence. Indeed, ability to learn is part of many psychologists' definitions of intelligence, and most educators and the laity hardly make a distinction between learning and intelligence. [7]

Assumption: The ability to learn is indistinguishable from intelligence.

It is not surprising, then, that the general goals of higher education implicitly bank on the learning ability, and also the intelligence, of students. The large societal investment in higher education speaks of a societal faith in students' abilities to receive its intended effects. Somewhere embedded in this faith is the belief either that students' intelligence, as it corresponds to learning ability, is of a level that can receive the effects of higher education or that higher education raises students' level of intelligence and learning ability to make it possible for them to receive these effects.

Assumption: Students *do* arrive in higher education with the necessary learning ability and intelligence.

---

versus

Assumption: Students *do not* arrive in higher education with the necessary learning ability and intelligence; however, higher education can raise the levels of learning ability and intelligence as needed.

These supposedly opposing assumptions about intelligence affect higher education policy. In the former assumption, the college student's intelligence is a given and is static. In the latter, intelligence is malleable. Unfortunately, these assumptions are not openly discussed; they are hidden amidst the red tape of program and policy. The public, unclear about its own assumptions regarding intelligence, simply assumes that educators and educational policy makers can use tax dollars to turn theories about educating into actions of educating. Assessment of higher education is then expected to measure the success of this transformation. And yet the transformation desired is vague and built on the two foregoing assumptions.

Assumption: Educators and policy makers can use tax dollars to turn theories into actions.

Assumption: Assessment can measure the success of this transformation.

The flaw in all public and private policy is the presumption that the direct translation of theory into action is generally possible. [8] Theory and action are not expressed in equivalent languages. Moreover, to think that theory can be directly and flawlessly translated even further—that is, through actions into results—is even more naive [9]. But when theories are not clearly specified and underlying assumptions are potentially conflicting, it is even less likely that ideas will be taken through to actions and on to intended results. This means that assessment, no matter how scientifically conducted and goal driven, is evaluating an ambiguous and undefined process. *Assessment of an ambiguous process is ambiguous.* This also means that the admission of students, who will later be assessed for college performance, is one of the first steps in this long and ambiguous process.

Assumption: Theory can be directly and flawlessly translated into actions and desired results.

Murky Definitions and Airy Assumptions

In education as in many other fields, the details on the map of the journey from theory into action and on to results are difficult to specify. Can one really get there from here? Exact material links in the chain of causality remain unknown [10] while only representations of them are studied in the artificially contrived forms of research variables and analytic factors.

Intelligence has been described as a "cultural invention." [11] It can be suggested that ambiguity about intelligence is also a cultural invention, with science being but one of its inventors. There is no complete consensus regarding relationships between learning, mental ability, and intelligence, even for elements of these theoretical concepts that proponents of standardized tests claim to measure. Which of these is dependent on the others? Which is a prerequisite for the others? Are these items at all related? Are they, in essence, the same?

Where it is agreed that a person may be more intelligent than others, it is not commonly agreed that that person may have *acquired* more intelligence than others. For all the argumentation in support of the notion that environmental influence is a powerful determinant of intelligence, there is an absence of references to particular examples of acquired intelligence. Instead, it is the *abilities that have been learned* that are discussed. At least in casual conversation, ability is now mentioned more frequently than intelligence as an explanation for academic outcome. [12] Educators go so far as to "dismiss intelligence as an outmoded and harmful notion." [13] Many scientists have done the same. Just mentioning intelligence can upset many a social gathering. Is intelligence really passé or is it actually too disturbing to talk about? As Sandra Wood Scarr, Commonwealth Professor of Psychology at the University of Virginia, points out,

> In times of optimism, human nature is presumed to be perfectible, and individual differences attributable to easily remedied differences in experience. In pessimistic times, human nature is seen as difficult to change or even immutable. From such general cultural views flow ideas about intelligence. [14]

Times may be pessimistic or optimistic. Educators and assessment professionals may never speak the word "intelligence." Yet these very same people operate with a curious set of assumptions about it.

Assumption: Ability is learnable; intelligence is not.

Assumption: Intelligence is a harmful and outmoded notion.

Assumption: There is no such thing as intelligence.

Folk Assumptions about Intelligence

A diverse array of assumptions about intelligence exists among the lay population. These have filtered into the general pool of knowledge from scientific, political, and philosophical sources. Conflicting "folk concepts" [15] include ideas concerning the flexible mental capacity of the individual and the unalterable nature of this capacity. Stemming from the latter assumption, that this mental capacity called intelligence is unalterable, are beliefs that intelligence is inherited, fixed at birth, and fixed from generation to generation. [16]

Assumption: Intelligence is fixed at birth.

Assumption: Intelligence is unalterable.

---

versus

> *Assumption*: Intelligence is somewhat alterable.
>
> *Assumption*: Intelligence is entirely environmentally determined and entirely alterable.

For every one of these definitions of a fixed and static intelligence, there is a broad definition of the opposite or nearly opposite viewpoint. Thus, intelligence is variously seen as somewhat alterable, entirely alterable, only partially inherited, not at all heritable, entirely environmentally determined. And to further complicate the discussion, intelligence is also said to take the form of any number of talents and capacities.

Scientific Assumptions about Intelligence

Whether folk assumptions inspire the development of the scientific assumptions or vice versa, folk and scientific assumptions about intelligence generally mirror each other. And it is most likely that ancient philosophical debates inspire both folk and scientific debate about intelligence.

Yale psychology and education professor Robert Sternberg organizes the scientific theories regarding intelligence into three basic groups, which he calls "loci" of intelligence. These are the loci of the individual, the environment, and the individual–environment interaction. [17] This Sternberg framework indicates (as well as organizes) the profound diversity of scientific theories of intelligence and of the differing views regarding the sources or causes of intelligence.

> *Assumption*: Intelligence exists at various loci.

Scientific rationalizations of intelligence range from the biological to the environmental. On one extreme is the view that intelligence is a specific mental capacity in which one basic process, that of efficient neural transmission, underlies all intellectual ability [18] and in which several specific intellectual components are always present in the same proportion to each other. Together these components represent a single factor, Spearman's "g" [19], a factor formulated by Charles Spearman, the inventor of factor analysis, a statistical method that is one of the cornerstones of psychometrics.

> *Assumption*: Intelligence is a specific capacity: neural transmission.
>
> *Assumption*: Intelligence is a single factor: Spearman's "g."

Another approach to intelligence is to speak of types of intelligence. It has been argued that the tasks most common in school settings and on IQ tests are measures of so-called "academic intelligence." [20] This academic intelligence is especially relevant to this discussion, since it brings its own set of characteristics to the field of assessment and draws attention to what actually might be sought after in the admissions process. Tasks that are designed to measure academic intelligence are characteristically viewed as being:

- Of little or no intrinsic interest to the student [21]
- Removed from the student's ordinary experience outside of school [22]
- Usually narrow but well-defined [23]
- Associated with only one correct answer or solution [24]
- Usually associated with only one correct method of solution [25]

Emory University Professor Ulrich Neisser contrasts academic intelligence against what he describes as "practical intelligence." This practical intelligence determines students' responsiveness to situations in ways that help them realize their goals, or at least not to work against these goals. [26] Higher education appears to address both academic (classroom) and practical (more worldly) intelligence. When intelligence is defined this way, there is an implication that it is malleable, at least from the practical standpoint, and therefore at least partly environmentally determined. Inasmuch as practical intelligence determines the application of academic intelligence within and outside the classroom, academic intelligence is also malleable, even if and when it is argued that it is based on a static, unchangeable core such as Spearman's "g."

Assumption: There are various types of intelligence rather than a single type.

Assumption: Academic intelligence is one type of intelligence.

Assumption: Academic intelligence is malleable.

Assumption: Practical intelligence is another type of intelligence.

Assumption: Practical intelligence is malleable.

There is, of course, a tension between definitions of intelligence such as Spearman's "g" and Neisser's academic-versus-practical differentiation. It is doubtful that Spearman's "g" can be affected by higher education as its curriculum is presently designed. As addressed later, the measured IQ of graduating college seniors rarely changes during the course of 4 years of college.

Concerned that disagreement over the definition of intelligence is detrimental, Jensen warns, "We should not let the *word* 'intelligence' block the path toward understanding an important phenomenon." [27] However, he then clarifies this statement, restricting intelligence to a narrow range:

> If we want to talk about this phenomenon in a scientifically productive way, it is a mistake to implicitly assume a larger universe of phenomena than we actually want to discuss, or, in fact, than can be properly dealt with in a scientific manner. [28]

Assumption: Disagreement over the meaning of intelligence is detrimental.

Jensen suggests omitting the larger universe of phenomena from the discussion of intelligence. This universe may include everything that appears to be malleable by higher education.

Assumption: It is best to omit the larger universe of phenomena from the discussion of intelligence.

Others who believe that genetic determination plays an important role in intelligence have argued that there are serious social consequences in denying that individual differences in intelligence exist. In his book *Storm over Biology*, Bernard Davis warns that "if we refuse to recognize the importance of genes for human behavioral diversity, and if we reject the use of science to help us to understand and to build on that diversity, our society will lose more than it will gain." [29]

Assumption: Society will suffer if the genetic role in determining variation in intelligence is not recognized.

The confounded goals and consequent assessments of higher education exist amidst an undercurrent of disagreement regarding the degree of malleability, the best definition, and the true nature of intelligence. How can a policy controlling admissions into an institution supporting and supported by such a theoretical morass be straightforward?

Implicit Assumptions about Intelligence

So what are some of the standard implicit assumptions that emerge from the plethora of definitions of intelligence and the social tensions surrounding them? Some of these may be organized as follows:

- Intelligence does not exist.
- Intelligence does exist.
  - Intelligence can be clearly defined.
  - Intelligence is some kind of ability, but there is no distinct boundary to it.
  - Intelligence tests measure intelligence.
  - Intelligence tests do not measure intelligence.
- Intelligence is unchangeable, fixed at birth.
- Intelligence is either partially or entirely environmentally determined.
  - Intelligence is learnable.
  - Education is a powerful part of the environment that determines intelligence.
  - Higher education is a powerful part of a student's environment and experience and therefore influences intelligence.
  - Higher education is more than merely classroom experience. Therefore, if intelligence can be influenced by higher education, it is influenced by a variety of social and academic factors in higher education.
  - Higher education may be more than classroom experience but only classroom experience influences intelligence.
- Intelligence is something that is the same as, or overlaps with, learning ability.
- Intelligence is purely cognitive.
- Intelligence can take any of a number of forms. Some people are intelligent in the area of mathematics, others in music, others in athletics, other in leadership, etc.
  - Higher education can address these various intelligences. It can even enhance them. In fact, it can teach them.

Each of these lofty assumptions in some way addresses human ability; each in some way addresses the educability of ability. Educational assessment that intends to measure educational outcomes or gains must unearth the assumptions that are operative in its design. If it does not do so, assessment does not enjoy the support of an identifiable theoretical structure. Admissions policy that intends to result in any form of programmatic or social change must likewise unearth the assumptions that are operative in its design. If it does not, there is no control over the educational outcome or the assessment of this outcome or the changes made based on the findings of this assessment.

The concept of intelligence has become implicit because intelligence is viewed as being confusing and controversial. The concept of intelligence has actually been suppressed because a fear exists that policy that addresses intelligence can be dangerous in the wrong hands. And yet, educational institutions and those who design assessments of them are drawing conclusions and making critical decisions (such as admissions quotas, curriculum content, and funding) based on implicit and suppressed assumptions about intelligence.

Assumption: Intelligence is a confusing concept.

Assumption: Intelligence is a controversial concept.

Assumption: Policy that addresses intelligence is dangerous if it falls into the wrong hands.

The Role of Assessment

The definition of assessment is, presumably, less murky than that of intelligence. However, just as the assessment of higher education is an evolving process, so too is the definition of assessment. Presently, there exists a "conceptual muddle" in assessment. [30] Broadly speaking, assessment of higher education is any and all evaluative activity aimed at (but not necessarily guaranteeing) the improvement of learning and knowledge that accrues from student attendance at colleges and universities. [31] Assessment has been described as a catchall term that refers to a range of efforts aimed at improving the quality of education. [32] This is because assessment supposedly exceeds mere evaluation by providing specific feedback regarding educational effectiveness and outcome.

Testing is, naturally, one of the most common methods of assessment. It is so common that most laypersons assume that *testing* is synonymous with *assessing*. Utilization of testing is based on its historical roots in education, blind faith in its relative validity, its convenience, the aspects able to be quantified and standardized, and the limited number of available alternatives. Testing is used in admissions, in achievement evaluation, at graduation, and in application to graduate school. [33]

Whether it be by testing or other methods, most assessment is designed to produce outcome data, data that measure the effects of higher education. "Student outcomes assessments" are those that measure student performance after exposure to a particular educational intervention (an activity, course, or curriculum). [34] "Value-added" and "talent development" approaches to assessment involve baseline and then post- and continuous measurement of, and testing for, the addition of valuable knowledge or the development of talent as a result of learning from education. [35]

There is no direct reference to measurement of intelligence in definitions of assessment in higher education. Perhaps this is because intelligence is assumed to be, deep down at the roots of the theoretical web, ultimately unchangeable at the college level. There is a great deal of disagreement over the key terms and methods used in assessment. [36] Whatever type of assessment is conducted, its contemporary goal is, in the main, to provide evidence (usually to the public) regarding the quality of higher education.

During the 1980s the primary focus of assessment shifted from the individual student to the program or institution. The original purpose of assessment was to measure student learning and then to improve student performance. This purpose then shifted to, or at least added the aim of, improving the program and, eventually, improving institutional effectiveness. [37] This shift resulted in assessment having as its focus multiple levels of analysis, including the student, the department, and the institution. [38] This shift in purpose is underscored by questions of worth such as the following: Is the academy conducting activities that are truly worth the investment of societal resources? (By itself this question is too general to produce a satisfactory answer.) What exactly are these activities? How do these activities work? Do they raise the general intelligence of society? Can they raise collective student performance by raising collective intelligence in lieu of raising individual learning ability and intelligence? (Although the most recent trends in assessment seem to be back toward the individual and the improvement of individual learning, the institutional pressure that suggests these questions continues.)

Hidden Intelligence Policy

When official plans are made for the assessment of colleges and universities, an assessment policy is formed. This is a policy to assess particular academic processes and/or outcomes at prescribed intervals, at certain levels of institutional activity, and with certain methods of assessment. Above all, it is an overall policy to assess. Policies to assess are being adopted at an increasing number of institutions. [39] As assessment expands, the underlying ambiguity regarding the role of intelligence in the goals and gains of higher education also expands. While assessment is directed toward (some sort of) improvement of the level of some sort of mental ability, it is not actually claimed anywhere that assessment, in itself, can enter the process and directly cause such an improvement.

Assessment has become increasingly important as the educational system has fallen under growing scrutiny. With most countries having official education policies and departments of education pressing the development of their educational systems, the United States is experiencing pressure to compete. Some countries have gone so far as to make explicit their drives to raise the intelligence level of their citizens. [40] Perhaps the willingness to be explicit about the policy of developing the collective intelligence of one's society is an advantage. At least the assumption that intelligence can be developed has been made explicit. Such explicitness might allow assessment policy to approach gains in intelligence more directly. Otherwise, the efforts of assessment in support of intelligence policy remain implicit and intelligence policy itself remains implicit.

> *Assumption*: It is possible for public policy to raise the intelligence level of its citizens.

ANATOMY OF THE COVER-UP

In the absence of explicitly stated societal intelligence policy, other labels for the type of improvement desired in higher education are sought. One label being used is "prosperity." Assessment is thus alleged by some policy makers to demonstrate that the education provided has enhanced societal prosperity.

Increasing Public Interest in Assessment

Public policy makers are increasingly vocal about the importance of assessment. As stated by the advisory committee to the legislatively commissioned New Jersey College Outcomes Evaluation Program,

> The evidence is growing that a state (or country) cannot prosper, cannot successfully compete in markets, without a sufficient number of people with the level of education our colleges and universities can and have provided.
>
> We believe that the American system of higher education, combining quality with access and diversity, is as good as any system anywhere in the world. We also believe it can improve.
>
> . . . Assessment can play an important role in achieving excellence. Assessment is a technique for demonstrating that our efforts have been worthwhile, that we are making progress, that we can accomplish our goals. [41]

Is there any link between the prosperity of a state and higher education? And with the assessment of higher education? The statement just quoted suggests that there is. Is the prosperity of the state linked in any way to the level of societal intelligence (the sum total or average of all citizens' intelligences)? If institutional quality in education is built on the quality of changes in an institution's students and if there is a link between institutional excellence and the learning ability of students, then to raise institutional excellence may involve raising learning ability. Policies that seek to bring about institutional (university) excellence in order to bring about societal excellence must explain these causal links.

> *Assumption*: There is a link between the prosperity of the state and higher education.

Growing Concern over Educational Quality

Another label for the desired outcome of higher education is "excellence." As is indicated by the foregoing quote, assessment is emerging as the perceived guarantor, or at least one of the perceived guarantors, of excellence in higher education. The call for assessment of higher education stems from increasing public awareness that serious problems have been identified in the undergraduate curriculum. [42] Many college students appear to need remediation. [43] College test performances are declining. [44] Faculty members find today's students are less interested in learning than were those of the past. [45] Taxpayers, the media, business, and industry all seek to hold higher education responsible for its actions. [46]

Assumption: Assessment is a guarantor of excellence in higher education.

Since the latter half of the 1980s, there has been an increase in external involvement in assessment; government agencies (especially those at the state level) have become more concerned about, and involved in, the assessment of higher education. [47] Politicians have seized the opportunity to make a mark and are now attempting to appease taxpayers by appearing to lead the crusade against what seems to be sloppy and unaccountable education. [48] There has, consequently, been pressure for assessment to move from the limited focus of instructional improvement to a more profound view of institutional accountability. [49] But again questions surface. What is it, exactly, that institutions should be held accountable for? If they are to be held accountable for achieving presumed or stated goals, then the assumptions regarding learning ability and intelligence that drive these goals must be unearthed for all to examine.

The Generation of Great but Naive Expectations

Explicitly stated and rather lofty missions of colleges and universities not only avoid the goal of raising societal intelligence but generate great expectations among their constituents. Consider, for example, the following excerpts of the mission statement for the California State University system:

> To advance and extend knowledge, learning and culture. . . .
> To provide opportunities to develop intellectually, personally, and professionally. . . .
> To prepare significant numbers of educated, responsible people to contribute to California's schools, economy, culture and future. . . .

To encourage and provide access to an excellent education to all who wish to participate in collegiate study. [50]

What is not made explicit are the assumptions behind these statements. A mission statement such as this one, which aims to accomplish the stated goals, implies that education can actually have the effects described—extending knowledge, providing opportunities, and so on (see Table 3.1).

Assumptions behind Great Expectations

A brief examination of the verbs used in the foregoing excerpts suggests that higher education can "advance," "extend," "provide," "prepare," and "encourage" a range of desirables, including knowledge, learning, and intellectual development. These operations are, for the most part, intended to be performed directly on individual students. It is thus assumed that higher education has the power to mold the minds of its students, that learning and intellectual development are indeed malleable. Is it also assumed that the core of intelligence is malleable? Is it also assumed that intelligence is clearly distinguishable from learning and intellectual development? It is possible that (implicit) assumptions are being made, namely, that as an increasing percentage of the population receives higher education, the culture becomes more intelligent, composed of more intelligent citizens. It is possible that contemporary admissions policies reveal these assumptions.

Assumption: Higher education advances, extends, provides, prepares, and encourages a range of desirables, including learning and intellectual development.

Assumption: As increasing numbers of citizens receive higher education, the culture becomes more intelligent.

Table 3.1.   Elements of Commonly Stated Explicit Assumptions

A INTERVENTION		B OPERATION		C GAIN OR OUTCOME
Higher education	→	advances and extends	→	knowledge, learning, and culture.
Higher education	→	provides	→	opportunities to develop intellectually, personally, and professionally.
Higher education	→	prepares	→	people to contribute to schools, economy, culture, and the future.
Higher education	→	encourages and provides	→	access to an excellent education.

Value-Added as a Euphemism, but for What?

Somehow, assessment must provide information as to whether or not the great (or even average) expectations, vague as they may be, that society has for higher education are being met. The controversial value-added approach to assessment has thus emerged. It is based on the premise that it is the measurement of gains in academic quality and excellence, rather than average student body graduation scores and institutional reputation and resources, that should indicate the educational effectiveness of an institution. Focusing on this critical development in assessment will aid in understanding how even what is considered by some to be the truest form of assessment, "value-added," is engaged in a cover-up of assumptions.

Value-added and related types of assessment seek to measure (but not to compare among students) the gains made by individual students as a result of higher education. In value-added terms, students can begin college at different ability levels. A student at a lower academic level may make greater gains and, thus, actually achieve more than a student who begins at a higher academic level. The student adding more "value" to his or her education thus "achieves" more. Value-added assessments are made for the semester, the academic year, and the duration of college (from the time of admission to the time of graduation). Other, more traditional, assessments of excellence do not measure the respective gains experienced by individual students. They do not address the varying degrees of academic progress—change—made by individual students.

Unfortunately, the meaning of value-added assessment is not entirely clear. [51] In practice, value-added assessment varies greatly. It ranges from specific blueprints for using specific tests at different points in students' educations and for subsequent comparison of baseline and posttest scores to more general definitions such as "the institution's ability to affect its students favorably, to make a difference in their intellectual and personal development." [52]

The advantages of a value-added approach to assessment are many. [53] This approach allows "room at the top" for more than just the richest and most famous institutions, at least on a new continuum of educational quality. This is because filling the top notches on the scales of institutional reputation and measurement of total worth of resources does not guarantee student gains. [54] The value-added approach is more honest than other approaches because it takes pre-, post-, and ongoing measurements rather than single outcome measures. Value-added assessment offers the possibility of measuring change rather than a static outcome state at the end of 4 years. [55] Value-added assessment creates the possibility of defining the greatest academic success as the greatest gain, gain that can be achieved by an academically average or even a less than academically average student. Value-added assessment provides ongoing feedback by considering gains made *during* the process of education rather than only those made by the end of the process of education. Value-added assessment is also used to measure changing levels of student involvement in learning, that is, changing amounts of time and energy spent by students on learning.

> *Assumption*: Value-added assessment measures the value of a higher education.

According to its advocates, value-added assessment causes students at all academic levels to become more motivated and to spend more time on learning. Their performance, test scores, and academic gains improve. Faculty interest in the level of students' performance increases. Much of its success can be attributed to the fact that value-added assessment helps to clarify educational goals for students, professors, and entire academic communities. Yet value-added assessment is a euphemism for ambiguity. Even when research designs are scientifically structured, value-added assessment assumes that something of value is being added and that this is what is being measured. Value-added assessment does not necessarily address the deeper and more complex intellectual changes that may be involved in producing the measurable value of education. Again the malleability of intelligence is an issue implied but avoided. This results at least in part from the tension regarding the definition of intelligence.

Unfortunately, value-added assessment, even with its advantages over mere outcome measurement, has potential liabilities. It threatens to erode emphasis on any clearly set standards regarding the competency that higher education must produce. Instead of measuring students' level of actual competency at graduation, value-added assessment measures students' gains over time. Gains scored on Graduate Record Examinations or other achievement tests may be high for students who have far from satisfactory levels of competency. The problem of defining gain is inherent in value-added assessment. It may not be realistic to just say that change should be measured. [56] On a deeper level, the assumptions driving the measurement of change must be questioned. It seems that there is an obvious assumption, namely, that change is possible. However, what brings about change, and what type of change is it? [57]

> *Assumption*: Change as a result of higher education is possible.

Value-added assessment may change the mission of higher education. Rather than encouraging students to reach particular levels of competence, it may merely encourage students to improve as much as they can. This may say that improvement is all that can or should be expected by a broad range of students. Is this because they cannot be expected to achieve more or because there is a question about how to teach them to learn more? Learning ability cannot be guaranteed, and therefore learning outcome cannot be guaranteed. This line of thought suggests that learning ability is fixed. What an irony!

Assumption: Value is added simply if students improve, not only if they reach a particular level of competence or knowledge.

Moreover, value-added assessment incorrectly assumes that true and specific educational change can be accurately measured. [58] It is very difficult to know how much real gain in student learning results from the education being measured. The challenge is to use or develop measures specific enough to be sensitive to students' educational gains but general enough to rise above the trivial. This challenge has not yet been met.

Assumption: Specific and important educational change can be measured.

As in most testing processes, the value-added assessment technology is still emerging, and much of what is used, despite its occasional claims to the contrary, is simple pre- and posttest comparison. These are especially fallacious. Measurements being used are not always reliable for both baseline and follow-up scores.

Furthermore, how can it be said with any certainty that a gain of 20 points on a low test score is equivalent to a gain of 20 points on a high test score on the same test? Or any test score on another scale or test? [59] A remedial math student may have to work very hard to increase his or her test score 20 points while an average math student may find that learning a few formulas and practicing them for a month makes the 20-point gain relatively easy. Evaluating these gains in the same manner is unrealistic. Construct validity and consistency must be longitudinal in value-added assessment. Unfortunately, this is difficult, if not impossible, to achieve. A test does not always measure what it claims, and if it does so at one point in time, it does not necessarily do so at another. It is difficult to attribute student gains to academic progress. Error variance and maturation are two of many factors that confound scores. Moreover, no two students learn at the same speed and in the same way, let alone the same things. And what of learning ability and intelligence? These may be more malleable in some students than in others. Can this difference be detected and controlled in assessment research?

Dilemmas result. Will students who begin at high academic performance baselines gain less academically than those who begin at low baselines? Which is preferable? What should be the institutional response to the various situations?

How does an institution appear to the public as it tries to make these decisions? [60] Teachers may begin to teach for the tests. Students may begin to learn only for the tests. The public focuses increasingly on tests, as if they were measures of institutional quality. The assumption is that the higher-order cognitive learning that higher education is trying to stimulate can actually be tested. However, testing is better at reporting the additive types of learning that occur much earlier in life. Higher-order learning is difficult to assess, regardless of the method used. When it is being assessed, the propensity to learn and the level of intelligence involved in learning are also implicitly being assessed.

Assumption: Tests can measure learning.

Assumption: Higher-order learning can be tested.

The Muddle of Generic Academic Outcomes

The assessment of the product of higher education avoids defining and measuring intelligence, but it muddles its other findings in with intelligence. The Educational Testing Service (ETS) often uses the phrase "general learned abilities" to describe the variables measured by its tests. These variables are usually divided into two groups: "verbal ability" and "quantitative ability." [61] These abilities are presumed to underlie academic work across the curricula and are most often measured at two main transition points in education: application to college and application to graduate school (or graduation from college, which occurs about the time many students apply to graduate school). Learned abilities are measured by the Scholastic Aptitude Test (SAT) at application to college and by the Graduate Record Examination (GRE) or a more specialized admission test upon application to graduate school. [62]

Although general learned abilities are described as being "learned," the ETS has at times described these abilities as being almost static, permanent, and unchangeable. [63] For example, the quantitative problems in the GRE require nothing beyond high-school-level algebra and geometry. The learned abilities being tested for are thus presumed to be stable enough to be unaffected by the intervention of higher education (by participation in its educational programs). General learned abilities are considered too stable to be indicators of college learning. These abilities were learned somewhere, however. Children are not born with these abilities. They do not arrive at elementary school ready to pass the SAT. The high school experience must cement these abilities. Yet if the same high school experience would provide all entering college students with the same level of general learned abilities, then all students would be able to enter college at the same level and then, perhaps, they could leave at the same level as well.

A muddle is created. Academic outcomes are not easily delineated by or attributed to specific academic activities. Education professor Leonard Baird distinguishes among three "interrelated types of variables: basic skills, general learned abilities, and generic academic outcomes." [64] Although these can be described as separate effects of education, in reality they are conceptually linked and even overlapping. Perhaps they are even indistinguishable outside of the context of scientific analysis.

Consider the nature of these three variables. Basic skills are more specific and more basic than what are termed general learned abilities. Basic skills are tested in order to determine readiness for college-level work as well as the need for remedial work in order to bring about this readiness. [65]

At the other extreme are generic academic outcomes, which are founded on basic skills and are somewhat dependent on learned abilities. [66] These generics are the specific outcomes expected to result from college-level academic work. These outcomes are difficult to identify. They focus on critical thinking, problem solving, and reasoning capabilities. These are complex cognitive processes that are generally derived indirectly from the academic curriculum. Courses in heuristics, or what are often called problem-solving methods, that are not domain specific are rare. Even when courses such as these are taught within domains, they are camouflaged. Students are seldom taught that these heuristics are important or that some of them are transferable. These competencies are rarely called components of intelligence; however, intelligence tests tend to look for such competence. Perhaps the implicit assumption is that these forms of mental competence can be taught, and even picked up "along the way." Researchers in this area of metacognition may agree in principle, although they disagree among themselves, regarding the value of teaching heuristics and the transferability of these heuristics. [67]

By definition, general learned ability falls somewhere in between basic skills and generic outcomes. Yet all three outcome variables are apparently learned abilities. They simply occur at different levels or in different arenas of academic experience. The slippery term *learned ability* is a convenient way of avoiding a discussion of the following assumptions:

- Some learning is enabled by intelligence.
- Accumulation of learning might possibly result in an accumulation of some type of intelligence.
- Intelligence can be taught.

Is Intelligence Dynamic?

The innocuous phrase *learned ability* allows us to suggest that a specific ability can be learned by anyone who undergoes a specific learning experience. Generic academic outcomes are built on academic (and other) experiences and accumulated academic (and other) abilities. In the societal explanation of this process there is uncertainty not only about the nature of intelligence but about whether intelligence stays constant while these other things change, whether intelligence changes as well, and whether intelligence is a relevant entity (see Figure 3.3).

Postulating in absolute terms, if intelligence stays entirely static but educational outcomes can be dramatically varied based entirely on input, then intelligence is irrelevant in education. Or, on the other hand, if intelligence can change from static to dynamic under enough pressure from academic input, then intelligence is not only relevant but a potentially hidden yet desirable outcome. Isn't it a common desire to have an increasingly intelligent society? Or if intelligence is always dynamic, then it is, quite possibly, an important product of college outcome. Thus far, standardized intelligence tests are unable to prove anything other than that intelligence stays the same during a college career [68] and that students with higher levels of measured intelligence perform at a higher level in college.

The Ambiguities of Measurement

Assessment is a difficult undertaking. It is based on the assumption that intelligence is static when measured over time whereas achievement is dynamic when measured over that same time frame. Yet achievement itself is difficult to measure. [69] This is evidenced on several levels of measurement. Although tests vary in measuring the upper limits of ability, students who score lower at admission tend to show greater gains on achievement tests after 4 years of college whereas students who enter with higher scores on achievement tests tend to show less change in their scores after 4 years of college. [70] The high scorers who appear to change less over time are frequently subject to the "ceiling effect," which limits the amount of growth that can be shown. [71] However, differences in total gains are inconsistent not only across high and low entering score groups; students in different majors advance differently on achievement tests. [72]

Selection of the changes to be assessed is a delicate process. [73] It is important to ask what is being measured by the tests used in assessment and to

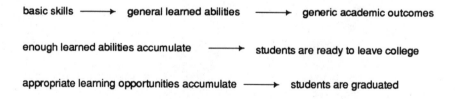

(Does intelligence stay static through all this?)

Figure 3.3. Do all forms of intelligence stay static during these processes?

determine whether test results intended to measure achievement actually discriminate between achievement and intelligence—or whether they actually measure intelligence along with achieved "gains." General cognitive tests, for example, border in nature and content on intelligence tests. [74] Tests of language skills often overlap with tests of general mental ability. [75] They frequently have a high correlation with intelligence tests. [76] Clearly, one of the difficulties in using tests is the potential (or actual) lack of discriminant validity from the measurement of "g" on standard IQ tests. [77]

Even without the confusion between achievement and intelligence, there are statistical dilemmas in assessment testing. There is frequently too much error and variance to know what is being measured even if it can be separated from intelligence. [78] There are problems with matching pre- and posttest instruments. For example, the SAT is sometimes used as the pretest and the ACT-COMP as the posttest, but the tests have different average residuals and a comparison of these in order to measure gain may not be reliable. [79] In other words, the two tests are not identical and the student has matured in the meantime. Whatever the method of assessment, the intellectual heuristics that affect what is being measured are present not as a result of anything learned in a particular course but as a result of the whole experience of life and college. Complex aspects of learning are difficult to measure when they result from a combination of higher education and life experiences. [80]

Yet another dilemma: if the focus of an assessment measure is too general, there is confusion. Cognitive tests that are highly general overlap in variation with intelligence tests. [81] On the other hand, if an assessment measure is too specific, it may gauge some things more efficiently [82] but miss the learning, which is better tested with more holistic measures. The choices are difficult. On the one hand, the choice can be to measure virtually nothing. On the other hand, the effort can be made to measure a great deal, including changes in mental ability and some aspects of intelligence. But then, there must be an admission that intelligence, in all of its conceptual haziness, will always muddle an assessment.

Student Is Not a Passive Agent

This discussion has centered on the effects of higher education *on* students. This suggests that students are passive agents; that they merely "receive" the effects of higher education; that they might be bringing not only static intelligence but also unalterable degrees of motivation, self-esteem, and so on; that education happens *to* them; and that there is no separate, independent student evolution. However, this is known to be untrue.

That the student is not a passive agent again presents a dilemma. The value-added approach to assessment is actually derived from the economic concept of "human capital," with student learning as the product. [83] In this vein, value-added assessment measures differences in the product of higher education. Can value-added or any form of assessment actually separate the effects of higher edu-

cation from independent student evolution? (Even if mental ability and intelligence are malleable, where does the molding originate—in the student or the university?)

The impact of student learning may not be purely value-added. Although there is frequent reference to the effect of college on students, the student is not a passive agent. The way the student "uses college resources" makes a major difference in the gains he or she makes. [84] Is the ability to use resources an innate or an acquired ability? Can it be taught to students? Does any particular type of intelligence have anything to do with this ability? Assessment and admissions policies must explain, in their policy wordings, their relationships to presumed answers to such questions.

Students bring a number of abilities and tendencies to their college experiences: motivation; desire to succeed; previous success; levels of self-esteem; and, of course, the prior knowledge they have gained, at least in part, from their high school education. They may or may not bring an immutable intelligence of a particular sort with them. If they are measured in terms of the Spearman's "g" type of intelligence they bring, they are not likely to show a change in this measure over the years of college [85], regardless of the changes their psychological, social, and economic characteristics undergo. This leads again to the ever unresolved problems of delineating types of intelligence, discovering which of these are malleable, detecting which of these interact with other characteristics, and finding out which of these intelligences students can actually be motivated to develop and apply. An admissions policy that takes no explicit stand regarding these various areas of intelligence is weak and founded on ambiguity.

CONSEQUENCES

This chapter has journeyed into the assessment world in order to place admissions policy in the context of academic outcome and to show that there are institutional pressures on admissions policy makers to create (admit) a student body that will assess well. Where admissions policy does not do so, assessment may adapt its methodology to meet the institutional need to look good, because assessment findings often serve as feedback on admissions policies.

Damage from Implicit Assumptions

Implicit and muddled assumptions about intelligence drive assessments of higher education as well as the admissions process. Curricula and assessments of them are frequently influenced by fiercely biased assumptions such as the following:

- All students can learn up to at least a certain level of knowledge.
- Some students can only learn with remediation.

- Students who cannot learn cannot be taught to learn.
- Intelligence is fixed.

Danger in Reliance on Test Results

Whatever tests and measures are used in assessment, the findings will therefore be confused with intelligence or with various intelligences. There is a tendency to ignore and deny the claim that intelligence cannot be identified because it cannot be satisfactorily defined. This denial places dangerous importance on theoretically unclear test results and assessment designs and leads to policy decisions based on these misunderstood results and designs. Again, ignorance is dangerous.

Threatened Homogenization of Outcome

Encroachment of the advancing assessment movement on the academy may have serious consequences. Because the tendency of movements is to standardize their ideals, the assessment movement, as it becomes centralized and national, threatens to narrow and to homogenize instruction. Such a trend will encourage increasing standardization of methods, including assessment testing and testing requirements. Because there is considerable racial and ethnic variability in students' outcome test scores, assessment could have a far-reaching and discriminatory impact on access to education and tracking in education. [86] Policies, curricula, and budgets addressing this variability may severely limit the pre- and postadmission opportunities of those with low test scores or low gain scores (not necessarily the same subpopulation). The growing diversity of educational subcultures, and of admissions and curricula that address this diversity of abilities and desires, is then threatened. Is this threat to diversity something that should be consciously allowed, something that assessment policy and then admissions policy should enable?

Without unearthing the assumptions society harbors about intelligence, an explicit plan to protect higher education from a reactive drive toward homogenization cannot be created. Quality of education and its outcome may become viewed as only one state of affairs. Assessment is confronted with the truth about quality in education; academic quality, whether it be institutional or individual, is very difficult to define. Steps to tangible results are vague. [87]

Even the purportedly egalitarian value-added form of assessment poses moral problems. Every gain in student scores may be falsely interpreted as a gain in student learning and even in mental ability, whether it is or not. This is a risky undertaking, based on weak assumptions; changes in test scores over time are actually attributable to many variables. Changes in test scores may be entirely unrelated to the quality of education. On the other hand, the quality of education may be entirely related to the future of human intelligence: it may determine its character, its homogeneity or diversity, its place in the curriculum, its fate.

Implicit Assumptions Undermine Assessment

Until assumptions regarding intelligence and their exact impacts on policy are made very explicit, they will influence assessment and admissions driven by assessment results without being recognized as doing so. Either higher education influences societal and, thus, individual intelligence or it does not. Either higher education does something ambiguous with regard to what is already ambiguous—intelligence—or it does something clear. Admissions policy makers would do well to explicitly state the assumptions about intelligence that drive it and to clearly explain how these assumptions relate to institutional goals. This would create pressure to clarify the design of the assessment of academic outcome (or of what is actually admissions outcome) in terms of the assumptions about mental ability that drive it.

Sets of Assumptions Active in the Assessment of Higher Education

There are far more assumptions that affect the assessment of the quality of higher education, from both the student and the institutional standpoint, than those unearthed in this chapter. However, the assumptions that have been highlighted are representative of the assumptions that are continually at work. Listed here for review are the assumptions that appeared in boxes throughout this chapter. Many of these readily organize into the first three of the four thematic divisions of the basic tensions that affect admissions policy. As will be shown later, all of these reflect the underlying rationalist versus empiricist tension.

Tension 1: Assumptions Regarding the Level of Societal Investment in Intelligence and Mental Ability

> Disagreement over the meaning of intelligence is detrimental.
> Intelligence is a confusing concept.
> Intelligence is a controversial concept.
> Policy that addresses intelligence is dangerous if it falls into the wrong hands.

and

> Society will suffer if the genetic role in determining variation in intelligence is not recognized.

Tension 2: Assumptions Regarding the Influence of Educational Intervention on Individuals and Society

> Educators and policy makers can use tax dollars to turn theories into actions.
>
> Theory can be directly and flawlessly translated into actions and desired results.

and

> As increasing numbers of citizens receive higher education, the culture becomes more intelligent.
>
> There is a link between the prosperity of the state and higher education.
>
> The distribution of higher education to an increasing number of citizens increases the viability of society.
>
> The education offered by institutions of higher education has to be designed to produce the effects desired by society.
>
> Students are willing to receive these effects.
>
> Students are able to receive these effects.
>
> Students are relatively equal in their willingness to receive these effects.
>
> Students are relatively equal in their abilities to receive these effects.

and

> The majority of students exposed to higher education can learn from it.
>
> The goals of higher education can be achieved by higher education.
>
> Students' minds can be molded to acquire the desired effects of higher education.
>
> Higher education advances, extends, provides, prepares, and encourages a range of desirables, including learning and intellectual development.
>
> Change as a result of higher education is possible.

and

Students arrive at institutions of higher education with the necessary learning ability and intelligence.

versus

Students do not always arrive at institutions of higher education with the necessary learning ability and intelligence; however, higher education can raise the levels of learning ability and intelligence as needed.

Tension 3: Assumptions Regarding the Learnability of Intelligence and Mental Ability

The ability to learn is indistinguishable from intelligence.
Academic intelligence is one type of intelligence.
Academic intelligence is malleable.
Practical intelligence is another type of intelligence.
Practical intelligence is malleable.

versus

Ability is learnable, intelligence is not.

or

Intelligence is a specific capacity: neural transmission.
Intelligence is a single factor: Spearman's "g."

and

Intelligence is somewhat alterable.

or

Intelligence is entirely environmentally determined and entirely alterable.

versus

Intelligence is unalterable.
Intelligence is fixed at birth.

and

Intelligence is a harmful and outmoded notion.
There is no such thing as intelligence.
Intelligence exists at various loci of social and biological organization.
There are various types of intelligence rather than a single type.

Assumptions Regarding the Assessment of Higher Education in Light of the Foregoing Assumptions

Assessment can measure the success of the transformation of tax dollars
into actions.
Assessment is a guarantor of excellence in higher education.
Value-added assessment measures the value of a higher education.
Value is added simply if students improve, not only if they reach a
particular level of competence or knowledge.
Specific educational change can be measured.
Tests can measure learning.
Higher-order learning can be tested.

II

Mapping Social Policy against a Theoretical Backdrop

4

Mapping Admissions and Other Social Policy against a Philosophical Backdrop

> The unspoken assumption is that [minority students] are anti-scientific, or, at best, ascientific. . . . We're wasting enormous amounts of brain power.
> BERNARD ORTIZ DE MONTELLANO [1]

In the chapters of Part II the many factors that constitute implicit intelligence policy are organized around four areas of tension. Recall that these areas of tension result from the following dichotomies:

- Academic merit versus fair representation
- Intelligence versus education as a determinant of worldly success
- Aptitude versus achievement
- Rationalism versus empiricism

It seems that all of the tensions inherent in intelligence policy tend to polarize (albeit very implicitly) around the fourth dichotomy, or what has become of this dichotomy in modern times. This polarization is so extreme in its implicitness that many academicians, philosophers, and policy makers actually overlook and even deny its reality. This viewpoint is understandable given the intricate, multilayered, and obscure relationship between the ancient philosophical dilemma represented in Tension 4 and current social, psychological, and political theory.

The following chapters therefore build up to rather than begin with a discussion of this fourth and ultimate dichotomy, a process that culminates in Chapter 8. Chapter 7 discusses some of the newest aspects of the policy conundrum, aspects generated by the primarily unintentional but nevertheless definite overlay of recent cognitive science onto ancient philosophy. Although new developments in cognitive science may serve as a conceptual bridge across the relevant philosophical and other dilemmas, they do not necessarily ease and most certainly do not clarify the tensions among them. Chapter 6 looks at environmental influences on intelligence that may be too subtle to fully substantiate in a laboratory or classroom setting, namely, the sociopolitical influences on actual, measured, and manifested intelligence and mental ability that may be too powerful to measure, as it is so difficult to see the forest through the trees. Chapter 5 investigates the tension inherent in debates regarding educational admissions policies, policies that reflect, in a subtle but forceful manner, conflicting perspectives regarding the acquisition and social value of knowledge as well as the mental ability necessary to acquire that knowledge. Note that one can examine implicit policy by beginning with an explicit policy (as is done in Chapter 5), by then turning to and attempting to relate to each other the various bodies of theory behind that policy (as is done in Chapters 6 and 7), and by then digging deeper to detect the deepest philosophical roots of that policy and of the tensions within and surrounding that policy (as in Chapter 8).

In preparation for the detailed examination of the forces forming intelligence policy contained in this section, this opening chapter of Part II draws a theoretical map of societal investments in the development of mental ability against the ubiquitous but frequently obscure philosophical backdrop of Tension 4: rationalism versus empiricism. This map, explained in the following pages, is presented in Figure 4.1.

Public university admission is now one of the primary, if not the most significant, meters of societal investment in the development of its citizens' minds. In Part II this issue is addressed from a theoretical standpoint that is built on but reaches beyond Cattell's economic model (found in Figures 2.1, 2.2, 2.3, and 2.4). This discussion seeks to demonstrate that it is not only the demand for "g," as depicted by Cattell, that is highly pliable in the face of economic shifts, but the assumptions and theories about intelligence that guide the demand and lack of demand for "g" (these assumptions and theories being expressed by public and private policy). The tensions and assumptions about intelligence that are fueled by supply and demand can be and must be identified. Certainly, societal investment in education will increase in times of economic abundance; there is more money available to fund programs. However, this is not the whole story. Other political, theoretical, and cultural factors shift in the swing from scarcity to abundance and back. What this says is that the prevailing "facts" on which public and private sector policies are built are transient and subject to economic influence so large and so all encompassing that this influence is difficult to detect.

ON THE LEARNABILITY OF INTELLIGENCE

Admission to high-quality public higher education is an opportunity that is awarded to those young citizens most likely to reward society for its investment in

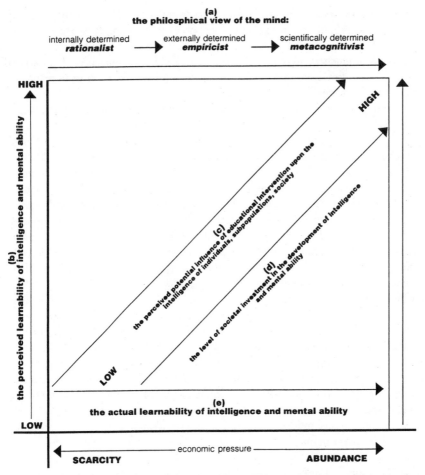

Figure 4.1. Heuristic map of hypothetical relationships. (This map is not a representation of an independent against a dependent variable. It is, instead, a depiction of interrelationships among several factors.)

their education. This determination hinges on unspoken assumptions regarding the malleability of college-age students' mental abilities: if their mental abilities are malleable, then admission need not be restricted to those already demonstrating high ability. If it is not malleable, admission is driven in a more selective direction. Although many other factors influence admissions policy, this philosophical and theoretical undercurrent is ever present.

Perceptions regarding the learnability of intelligence change alongside evolving theories of knowledge production and assimilation. But how much can the human mind actually learn? What proportion of mental ability is static, innate, immutable, and unaltered by education? Educators cannot help but wonder how deeply the influence of external reality can enter into the core of individual thought. Each time a concept or process is taught, there is an effort to reach into that core and to develop the intelligence therein.

At this stage in the evolution of education science, it is quite clear that at least some educators view some forms of what they call intelligence as learnable. It is not clear which forms of intelligence are not or cannot become learnable. Professor Andrea diSessa, a specialist in mathematics, science, and technology education at U.C. Berkeley, contends that in physics and in other domains education confronts, disassembles, and reshapes "inappropriate" or "naive" knowledge structures. In young children such educational intervention can take place before the "wrong" knowledge structures become deeply embedded. As students mature and reach high school and college age, these "wrong" structures do become more deeply embedded; in that case, the work of educators who attempt to reshape what diSessa describes as naive and inappropriate knowledge structures becomes more difficult and more profound. Education directs students to build functional, correct, appropriate, and "officially approved" knowledge structures. Unfortunately, education tends to classify students as "failing" when they do not follow the directive. These students may be failing to think competently under the appropriate heuristic paradigm, but they may have elaborated clever and even complex knowledge structures that are merely deemed inappropriate. The mental ability and intelligence of a student is not necessarily indicated by the appropriateness of his or her basic knowledge structure. He or she may bring an elaborate knowledge structure from a subculture that is misunderstood in the mainstream classroom. Nevertheless, it is considered to be in society's best interests to invest in mainstream education, a process that attempts to ensure that what are considered the most appropriate knowledge structures are shared by the greatest number of citizens.

A MODEL OF SOCIETAL INVESTMENT IN INTELLIGENCE

It was noted in Chapter 1 that although some countries have formulated education policies that include the development of intelligence, this is not a typical component of education policy. In the United States there are no funds explicitly earmarked for this purpose. Still (as documented in the following chapters of Part II), the belief that mental ability and even intelligence are malleable with respect to environment and education is prevalent. Much of education is implicitly viewed as a potential, if not an actual, influence on mental ability and intelligence. How different education would look if the opposite view of the mind prevailed in the classroom! How different the amalgam of education policies would look if students' mental abilities were viewed as being *entirely* unalterable and their intelligences *entirely* predetermined.

To the degree that intelligence is viewed as being learnable, educational intervention can be viewed as having the potential to affect the intelligence of individuals, subpopulations, and all of society. Figure 4.1 maps the relationship between philosophical views regarding the mind (continuum a), the perceived learnability of intelligence (continuum b), and the potential influence of educational intervention (continuum c). A fourth and fifth continuum have been added to this figure. Continuum d, the level of societal investment, suggests that as the potential for educational intervention to influence intelligence increases, societal investment in intelligence may also increase. This increase may actually be determining of as well as contingent upon the actual learnability of intelligence. This shifting learnability is depicted as movement along continuum e, which was added to this graphic in response to the possibility that humans can create their own reality. Perhaps intelligence can become increasingly learnable as its mechanism and structures are probed more deeply. The economic pressure described in Chapter 2 has also been depicted in this diagram. Economic pressures can lead to the redesigning and shifting of policies in order to respond to scarcities and surpluses. In times of abundance, labor, specifically in the forms of labor-intensive educational methods of careful tutoring that might reshape students' mental abilities, is more affordable. In times of scarcity, cutbacks shift everything to the left and downward on the continua in Figure 4.1. The actual learnability of intelligence may respond to the shifting level of societal investment in educating intelligence. In times of abundance, intelligence may be more learnable; in scarcity, it may be less so simply because it may be too costly to treat intelligence as learnable. These implicit relationships influence admissions, hiring, and many other social policies, as discussed later.

As the theoretical backdrop of implicit intelligence policy is examined, it is important to see intelligence as a moving target. What was once called and recognized as the "mind" may actually evolve, under its own pressure, into a new form of mind. The possibilities for molding intelligence may change with the evolving mind. Given that the mind can reach into its own intelligence to define, and maybe even to amend and extend, its own intelligence, educators who seek to train human minds may be unprepared for the vastness and ultimate power of malleability with which the mind is endowed. Admission to higher education must grapple with this reality: intelligence and related academic performance may be highly malleable. How then can students be admitted fairly to higher education? Can admissions analysts predict which students' minds will be most responsive to university exposure?

Those formulating admissions and other educational and social policies would do well to analyze their policies' relationships to notions about intelligence.

This analysis is especially important with regard to those notions that perceive intelligence as becoming increasingly:

- Defined that way
- Educated that way
- Viewed as being that way (malleable)
- Viewed as being malleable even at the previously obscure microbiological levels
- Evolving in its ability to manipulate itself

The discussion will now proceed to an examination of the four basic tensions that form the implicit intelligence policy behind explicit admissions policy, an examination beginning close to the surface, with college admissions policy itself.

5

Academic Merit versus Fair Representation

A Case Study of the Undergraduate Admissions Policy at the University of California at Berkeley

> Amidst the minutiae of debates about particular admissions policies, however, Berkeley must remain guided by a larger vision of its mission. In the 1990s, this mission must include taking a leadership role in the construction of a genuinely pluralistic environment in which the best students from all segments of California's diverse population can meet and debate in an atmosphere of enlightenment and commitment. This is a vision that is well worth pursuing, and it is a particularly appropriate one for an institution which has long prided itself on maintaining the highest academic standards, while continuing its tradition of service to the public that has so generously supported it.
>
> Committee on Admissions and Enrollment
> University of California at Berkeley [1]

For a university to set as its goals the maintaining of "highest academic standards" and the continuing of a "tradition of service to the public" is highly laudable. It is also quite ambitious in an era in which these goals emerge in apparent opposition. For example, in California, as in some other parts of the country, the cultural diversity of the general public is increasing more rapidly than is the cultural diversity of the pool of what are, by traditional standards, high academic achievers (Figure 5.1). Confronted with different rates in the progress of these trends, authors of higher education admissions policy enter a territory where trade-offs, compromises, and redefined priorities are increasingly deemed essential. That admissions policies of the 1990s and beyond to the new millennium are serving and will

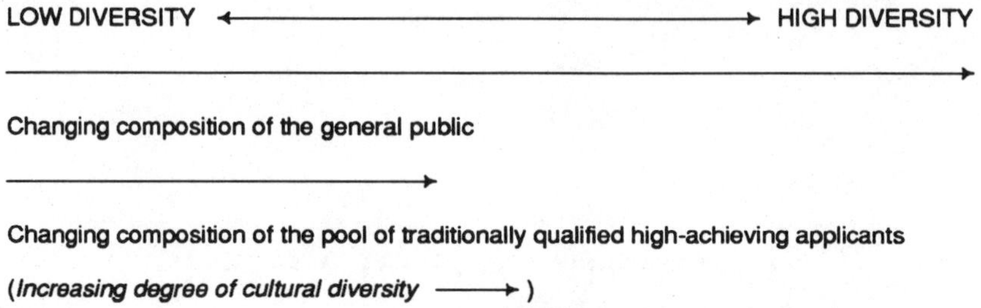

LOW DIVERSITY ◄──────────────────────────────────► HIGH DIVERSITY

──►

Changing composition of the general public

────────────────────────────────►

Changing composition of the pool of traditionally qualified high-achieving applicants

(*Increasing degree of cultural diversity* ──────►)

Figure 5.1. Contrasts in progress toward cultural diversity between the general public and qualified applicants.

continue to serve a public of growing diversity means that, more than ever, they answer to competing constituencies. There is no unified public from which to select. Especially for public colleges and universities, "public service" becomes service to a heterogeneous mix of cultural subpublics. "Public service" may therefore have to call for the loosening rather than the maintaining of those "highest academic standards," traditionally defined by the dominant culture along a rather narrow continuum of grades and test scores. This will be interpreted as a public service, at least for those socioeconomic groups (or subpublics) who may not be served by the maintenance of these traditional academic standards. These standards are viewed as barriers by those who are denied educational opportunities at the most selective universities. Consistent with this view is the argument that says that barriers to higher educational opportunities result in later barriers to higher occupational opportunities, which in turn result in barriers to socio-economic parity among the many subcultures housed within society. Admissions policy can thus be the most critical barrier.

This chapter describes the first of the four basic tensions present within explicit admissions policy. It is also the most explicit. Tension 1, the contrast between academic merit and fair representation, is actually spelled out in written policy statements. However, as explicit as this tension may be, it is rooted in deeper, less visible assumptions. It is just the tip of the iceberg. Subsequent chapters will unearth the deeper assumptions that support this tension.

ACCESS TO OPPORTUNITY

Those who view mental ability as being the product of the sociopolitical environment, that is, as being the result of opportunities for, stimulation toward, and access to knowledge and mental development within the environment, see the problem of access to opportunity as one that self-perpetuates in the absence of profound intervention on the level of social policy. Higher education admissions policy is one example, a very potent example, of the role that policy can play in redressing disparities of opportunity. Education is the currency of empowerment for individuals and social subgroups. The old adage that "knowledge is power" continues to be respected as an integral part of sociopolitical reality. Education, by virtue of being an intervention on the part of a citizen's environment, is a powerful form of nurturing, one that relies on the ability of the mind to absorb information and to structure itself in response to the environment.

Those who take an alternate stand note that although there have been significant advances in access to education at all levels experienced by minority groups, these have not resulted in equivalent changes in measured levels of intelligence. Professor Linda Gottfredson contends that although differences between African-Americans and whites in educational levels have been on a steady decline, the differences in "g" (as defined by Spearman), or general intelligence, between these groups "is not only very real but also very stubborn." [2] As this type of research finding has emerged, the emphasis on the value of intelligence has shifted. Intelligence was once viewed as important because it enabled students to earn educational credentials that would open the door to occupational opportunity. Now it is argued that educational practices must be changed in order to break the links between measured intelligence and achievement in school, and between measured intelligence and educational level attained. [3] Disagreeing with this argument, Gottfredson contends that "misconception about the value of schooling versus intelligence has been particularly mischievous in public life, because it turns well-intentioned but failing educational remedies for difficult social problems into additional sources of rancor, with educators and employers often receiving much of the blame for these failures," a conclusion similar to that of Murray and Herrnstein in *The Bell Curve*. [4] In this line of thought, what is borne out of the effort to use education as the solution to social problems may be a complication of these problems. Environmental interventions may not be as powerful as expected, and therefore the efforts of educators and employers may appear to fall short of expectations.

The picture is not a simple one, however. Research supporting the view that educational intervention has overextended itself to remediate inequities of opportunity concludes, rather ironically, that racial differences in IQ appear to correspond *negatively* with years of education and even with admission to college. For example, some studies claim that more African-Americans who enter college obtain more years of education than do whites with the same levels of measured intelligence. [5] Many researchers have measured African-Americans as having lower mean IQs than whites of the same educational levels. Differences between African-Americans and whites in SAT scores are consistent with these patterns. [6] What this suggests is that specific correlations between IQ and educational achievement are not consistent across races.

The discussion of racial differences in measured intelligence, academic performance, and educational opportunity expands beyond the realm of differences between African-Americans and whites. For example, by the end of the 1980s differential treatment of Asian-Americans and non-Asian-Americans in the admissions selection process at U.C. Berkeley became the focus of public controversy. Between 1981 and 1987 whites gained admission at a consistently higher rate than did Asian-Americans despite the fact that Asian-Americans had higher overall academic scores [7], and in the early 1990s African-American and Hispanic applicants were "(2000 per cent) more likely to be accepted for admissions than Asian-American applicants who [had] the same qualifications." [8]

In 1987 an Asian-American applicant for admission was turned down despite his straight-A average, his SATs in the 98th percentile, and his long list of prestigious academic honors. Shortly thereafter, he and his family discovered that they knew of several students with lower grade averages, lower SAT scores, and fewer academic qualifications who had been accepted. It became apparent to them, and to the Asian-American community, that U.C. Berkeley did not impose the same admissions criteria on applicants of different races. Berkeley applied merit criteria *within* rather than across groups. [9]

This effort to selectively apply merit criteria was made in the interest of fairness, with the unit under consideration being the racial group as opposed to the group defined by level of academic performance. In his controversial book *Illiberal Education*, Dinesh D'Souza, a former White House domestic policy analyst, reported that during the latter part of the 1970s and during the 1980s the affirmative action program at U.C. Berkeley "went from one of recruiting Black and Hispanic applicants to lowering admissions standards in order to raise their representation in each freshman class." [10] He added, "Since Berkeley's faculty could be expected to protest the dilution of the intellectual quality of the student body, the then Chancellor Ira Michael Heyman called for rapid implementation of preferential treatment so that, by the time the faculty committees took up the issue, he would have achieved proportional representation or something close to it." [11]

Chancellor Heyman was successful enough that by 1988 white students were actually underrepresented and in 1989 white admissions dropped to one-third of the freshman class. Asian-Americans and whites began experiencing what appeared to be policies of exclusion. [12] Although the emphasis on "exclusion" was implicit, appearing more as a by-product than as a basic tenet of policy, the emphasis on "inclusion"—of fairly representing underrepresented minority groups such as African-Americans and Hispanics—was explicit.

What does this suggest about the implicit assumptions that drive such an admissions policy? A policy of inclusion is likely to be based on the assumption that inclusion will have a positive effect on the individuals or on the public or subpublic it serves. Inclusion into educational opportunity assumes that those included can benefit from and utilize that opportunity to gain occupational and cultural opportunity. Policies of exclusion, even if relatively implicit, do not directly affect recipients in a positive manner but do seek to achieve some form of broader social good. The exclusion of some leaves room for the inclusion of others. The inclusion of others is a public service to specific subpublics and, by the laws of externality, to society at large. Proponents of exclusion assume that a trade-off between academic merit and fair representation is acceptable and that society can afford to exclude some of its higher academic achievers in order to create a satisfied and fairly represented public. The consequent assumption is that the public will gain as much or greater satisfaction from fairness than from academic excellence if these two functions are at odds.

It is quite probable that these and other basic assumptions have a powerful impact on admissions policy development, implementation, and outcome. However, the elements of admissions policy and therefore the impacts of admissions policy are somewhat more complex than this. This book examines the elements of U.C. Berkeley admissions policy as a primary example of the workings of implicit intelligence policy and as an excellent example of what colleges and universities are, or will be, facing as they adapt their admissions policies to a changing world.

THE EVOLUTION OF A MODERN ADMISSIONS POLICY

The University of California at Berkeley (U.C. Berkeley) is the oldest campus in the world-renowned University of California system (see Appendix C.1). U.C. Berkeley is one of nine campuses in the public U.C. system, administratively linked under the jurisdiction of the state of California. The particularities of and challenges to the admissions policy of U.C. Berkeley are an important case to be studied in the examination of the impact of implicit intelligence policy. (See Appendix C.2 for a general statement of U.C. admissions policy and Appendix C.3 for more specifics.) As noted at the opening of this chapter, the U.C. Berkeley Committee on Admissions and Enrollment states that its mission "must include taking a leadership role in the construction of a genuinely pluralistic environment." The construction of this environment is largely dependent on the selection of students to be admitted into that environment. Admissions policy can thus be a powerful tool in the construction of a truly pluralistic and egalitarian society.

Inherent in admissions policies is a mass of assumptions regarding the nature, educability, and utilization of mental ability. Because these assumptions are implicit and, thus, difficult to unearth, swings in or the general evolution of admissions policy must be observed for indications that intelligence policy is at work. The *1960 Master Plan for Higher Education Policy in California*, adopted by the California legislature in 1964, set the stage for the evolution of modern admissions policy throughout the University of California system, when it officially sought to "raise materially standards for admission to the lower division."

[13] Especially in public colleges and universities, the shifting of admissions standards over time are a response to changing societal views and pressures regarding the education and utilization of mental ability. (The general admissions policy statement for the entire U.C. system is shown in Appendix C.)

Raising Academic Standards

In order to *raise* academic standards, the Master Plan changed eligibility for all U.C. campuses from the top 15% of California public high school graduates to the top 12½% of these graduates. [14] This "top 12½% policy" was renewed by the California Commission for Review of the Master Plan for Higher Education in 1987, and remains in place as of this writing. [15] However, because competition for admission to the U.C. system has been, and continues to be, most intense at U.C. Berkeley, the "top 12½%" no longer have guaranteed admission there. [16]

Academic Standards versus Fair Representation

The background for the U.C. Berkeley situation is the increasing number of applicants as well as the increasing number of turn-aways. Over the years a decreasing proportion of all applicants, whether in the top eighth of their high school class or not, were admitted to U.C. Berkeley. In 1975, 3,896 of the 5,035 applicants were admitted; in 1980, 4,885 of the 9,115 applicants were admitted; in 1985, 6,329 of the 11,913 applicants were admitted; and in 1988, 17,731 of the 22,439 applicants were admitted. [17] The marked increase in applications during the 1980s continues into the 1990s, fueling an already challenging policy problem; how can U.C. Berkeley maintain an admissions policy that is equally fair to each of California's ethnic groups, that allows U.C. Berkeley to maintain its high academic standards and prestigious reputation, and that garners the support of its constituents, namely, California taxpayers? The *Karabel Report* on admissions policy at U.C. Berkeley, released by the Berkeley Academic Senate in 1989, explained that "the growing number of qualified applicants should make it possible for the campus to maintain and, indeed, to raise its academic standards at the same time that it broadens and deepens the process of diversification of its student body." [18] Although the report claimed, "This will not be an easy process, and it is sure to arouse controversy along the way," it expressed optimism that the policy could achieve these goals despite the officially recognized "tension" between them. [19]

The tension between academic standards and fair representation is perhaps the greatest and most explicit dilemma faced by modern admissions policy makers. It is within this tension that the tip of the iceberg surfaces and the hint in the wind materializes; it is here that implicit intelligence policy becomes apparent. By delving into this tension, the machinations of implicit intelligence policy can be explored and otherwise invisible, unspoken, and denied connections between implicit and explicit policies can be retrieved.

*(The following discussion of selected elements of pre- and post-*Karabel Report *admissions policy is based primarily on the* Karabel Report. *For a fuller understanding of the report and the elements of admissions policy described in this chapter, readers can refer to the* Karabel Report. *Any and all suggestions that elements of admissions policy reflect what is herein called "implicit intelligence policy" are the author's and in no way reflect, nor seek to contradict, statements made in the* Karabel Report. *Wherever this book discusses or interprets quoted statements or cited facts, it is going beyond official* Karabel Report *findings and recommendations to further the examination of the implicit intelligence policy driving the explicit admissions policy.)*

Diversification

From 1964 to 1974 U.C. Berkeley sought to diversify its predominantly white student body, a student body which, as of the early 1960s, was 90% white, middle- and upper-class. The Educational Opportunity Program (EOP) was started in 1964 to assist students from economically disadvantaged backgrounds, students who would otherwise have been unable to afford to attend. The U.C. regents maintained the 1960 Master Plan requirement that 2% of all admissions be offered to those students who did not meet the top 12½% standard. In 1968 the regents increased the size of this special group from 2% to 4% of all admissions. This Special Action category allowed the university to admit minority students and to bring in athletes who might not otherwise qualify. [20]

By 1971 the California Council of Chancellors had established a "50–50 criterion" for U.C. admissions policy. [21] This policy reserved half of the admission slots for applicants selected on an entirely academic basis and half for those selected for other reasons. This 50–50 split between the two admissions formats can be interpreted as an attempt to balance academic standards and fair representation efforts, to strike a balance not only between political pressures but also between opposing views regarding mental fitness for university education. The academic merit stand calls for rigorous maintenance of the university's reputation for upholding top academic performance standards and therefore for a rigorous admissions process. The fair representation stand maintains that students overlooked by rigorous admission standards can also perform well at the university and after graduation. The former view implies an expectation of a relatively static mental ability before and after admission. The latter view implies that the university can affect the mental ability of its students.

The official 50–50 balance of 1971 did not remain static. After 1986 this criterion was shifted to 40–60, decreasing the percentage of students who qualified solely on the basis of academic scores, and in 1991 it was set again at 50–50 on the basis of Karabel Report recommendations. [22] (Appendix C.4 does not reflect this most recent reversion to the 50–50 policy.) Swings in this balance reflect shifting demands for and changing perceptions of mental ability.

These efforts at mixing admissions criteria did not make a significant difference in minority enrollment. Eight years after the criterion was initiated, only 3.9% of the 1979 freshman class was African-American and only 4% of it was Hispanic. [23] The official goal to diversify the student body, even with EOP and Special Action efforts, was not realized at the end of the 1970s. Over the years the slowness with which the U.C. system student population was moved toward matching the makeup of the state's population of graduating high school seniors prompted the state legislature to become, in the words of the *Karabel Report*, "increasingly explicit about what it [considered] to be the public service responsibility of the University of California, emphasizing the need for it to serve *all* of the state's citizens." [24] However, as public policy became increasingly explicit in this area, it did not become increasingly explicit about the assumptions regarding mental ability that drove the increasingly explicit elements of admissions policy.

Principle of Broad Representativeness

In rendering admissions policy "increasingly explicit," the principle of "broad representativeness" emerged. This principle was ratified by the California State Assembly in 1974 and again in 1983 and 1988, as indicated in Table 5.1. This principle established that "each segment of California public higher education

Table 5.1.   Policy on Undergraduate Admissions Adopted
by the Regents of the University of California in May 1988 [51]

The undergraduate admission policy of the University of California is guided by the University's commitment to serve the people of California and the needs of the state, within the framework of the California Master Plan for Higher Education.

The entrance requirements established by the University follow the guidelines set forth in the Master Plan, which requires that the top one-eighth of the state's high school graduates, as well as those transfer students who have successfully completed specified college work, be eligible for admission to the University of California. These requirements are designed to ensure that all eligible students are adequately prepared for University-level work.

Mindful of its mission as a public institution, the University of California has an historic commitment to provide places within the University for all eligible applicants who are residents of California. The University seeks to enroll, on each of its campuses, a student body that, beyond meeting the University's eligibility requirements, demonstrates high academic achievement or exceptional personal talent, and that encompasses the broad diversity of cultural, racial, geographic, and socioeconomic backgrounds characteristic of California.

Because applicant pools differ among the campuses of the University, each campus shall establish procedures for the selection of applicants to be admitted from its pool of eligible candidates. Such procedures shall be consistent with the principles stated above and with other applicable University policies.

shall strive to approximate by the year 2000 the general ethnic, gender, economic and regional composition of recent high school graduates, both in first-year classes and subsequent college and university graduating classes." [25] The statement quoted here is the 1988 version. The 1973 version called for broad representativeness to be in place by the year 1980, which clearly did not occur. Broad representativeness thus became as fundamental to admissions policy as the basic "top 12½%" requirement, but not necessarily as readily achieved. While competition for admission led to exceeding the "top 12½%" standard at U.C. Berkeley, it has not resulted in a rapid realization of the goal of representation.

BASIC COMPONENTS OF U.C. ADMISSIONS POLICY

Admissions is a complex process. The discussion herein covers particular characteristics of admissions policy that are, or may be, relevant to the discussion of implicit intelligence policy. The use of measures of learning and indicators of intellectual qualities in the admissions process demonstrates a strong emphasis on the intellect. This is not surprising in that much of higher education is an intellectual process. The following discussion seeks to unearth the juxtaposition of intellectual or academic merit criteria with nonacademic criteria applied in the admissions process by using the U.C. Berkeley admissions policy as the prime example. (Appendix C.5 is an official summary of the U.C. Berkeley admissions process.)

Academic Index Score

The Academic Index Score or "AIS" is the most important criterion applied in freshman admission. This score combines the applicant's high school grade point average with the results of five standardized tests: the verbal sections of the Scholastic Aptitude Test (SAT), the mathematics sections of the SAT, and three College Entrance Board Achievement Tests (CEBs). Each of these five tests has a maximum possible score of 800 points. Therefore the maximum test score total is 4,000. The high school grade point average (GPA) is multiplied by 1,000 points (since the basic upper limit on the GPA is 4.0, the maximum GPA score is 4,000). The test score total and the GPA total are thus equally weighted. Together, these totals render a maximum AIS of 8,000. [26]

Admission by Academic Criteria

U.C. Berkeley, in its own official words of policy, "believes it has a responsibility to dedicate a major proportion of its available freshman places to those young people particularly throughout California who have worked hard to prepare themselves for university studies, and have demonstrated a commitment to further accomplishment through their academic attainments." [27] U.C. Berkeley "therefore assigns a high percentage of its freshman admissions to those applicants who have obtained the highest high school grades and test scores." [28]

Blind Process of Academically Eligible Admissions

Selection of freshman who have obtained the highest test scores and high school grade averages is accomplished by means of what is called a "blind" process, in which a computer rank-orders all applicants by Academic Index Score. (The computer automatically grants enrollment to the top-ranked applicants up to a number equal to half of the open admission slots. This designated percentage— 50%—can be changed—and has been changed, as noted earlier—by admissions policy makers.) (See Appendix C.6 and C.7 for breakdowns of student admissions by GPA and test scores.)

The Pre-Karabel Tier System

A policy admitting students based only on grades and test scores would yield a freshman class at U.C. Berkeley derived from the top 3% or 4% (along this AIS gradient) of California's graduating high school seniors, a class "overwhelmingly White and Asian." [29] Given its commitment to cultural diversity, U.C. Berkeley has "consciously rejected a policy of admitting students purely on the basis of grades and test scores." [30] Instead, only a portion, about half of its freshman slots, are filled this way. These are described as "Tier 1 admits." [31] Refer to Appendix C.8 for a sample breakdown of applicants by admissions tier.

The remainder of the admits are based on other criteria. Prior to the implementation of the *Karabel Report*, this remainder was, by policy prescription, broken into the following groups:

- "Tier 2 admits" were students whose Academic Index Scores were not quite high enough to meet Tier 1 criteria. These admits were reviewed on the basis of their AIS plus "supplementary criteria," the list of which was continuously controversial. This list of supplementary criteria included the following: California residency, economic background, an essay, and high school course work. [32] Points were awarded on the basis of both the supplementary criteria and the academic index ratings. Students in this group with the highest point totals became the Tier 2 admits. The percentage of total Tier 2 admits has fluctuated from year to year (18% of the total admits were Tier 2 in 1986, 21% in 1987, and 16% in 1988 [33]) because it has been dependent on the numbers of "Tier 3 admits" (see Appendix C.8).

- "Tier 3 admits" were from what was officially described as the "complemental admissions category." This "complementality," delineating a politically important category, included students who had overcome physical or social disadvantages or who showed unusual excellence in a nonacademic area such as athletics, music, or drama. Tier 3 added diversity to the student population. [34] Tier 3 admits were all U.C. eligible but did not have academic scores meeting the level of Tier 1 or Tier 2 admits. Without the policy of complemental admissions, Tier 3 admits would not have won admission in the face of Tier 1 and Tier 2 competition. The contribution of Tier 3 to the total admits varied over time. In 1986 it was 28.1%, and it was 38.9% in 1988. [35] Note that Tier 2 admit contributions to the total were smaller and were determined on the basis of the size of the Tier 3 contribution. This suggests that complementality had higher priority than the nearly top-notch academic standards achieved by Tier 2 applicants.
- "Special Action" students were those who were not officially "U.C. eligible" (well over 90% of the total U.C. admits, regardless of their Tier qualification, were U.C. eligible) but who appeared to have a reasonable chance of graduating. The Special Action group was composed primarily of students whose racial or economic backgrounds placed them at a disadvantage or who had special (usually athletic) talents. [36] (See Appendix entries C.9 and C.10.)

Post-*Karabel* Amendments to the Tier System

The *Karabel Report Recommendations* were implemented in 1991. Under the auspices of Tier 2, the *Karabel Report* formalized and added several new secondary review categories, combining them with the list of old Tier 3 complemental categories. Although the old Tier 2 was formally eliminated, many of its elements remained essentially in place, namely, consideration of student essays, extracurricular activities, and extra course work as supplements to the AIS. The new Tier 2 or secondary review categories proposed in *Karabel* aimed to broaden the student body and are as follows:

- One new category was established to socioeconomically diversify the entering class. The report noted that although significant progress had been made in the area of racial and ethnic diversification, less than one-fifth of the entering class was coming from families with an annual income below the national median and that students with highly educated parents continued to be overrepresented. [37] (Refer to Appendix C.11 for a breakdown of freshmen parental income by race and also Appendix C.12 on fees and expenses.)

- A second new category provided a secondary review to mature or "reentry" students. The report noted that although many of these students had "extensive work experience and [were] highly motivated," adding to the "intellectual and cultural richness of campus life," [38] the majority of them were women who found it difficult to qualify for admission to U.C. Berkeley. The report attributed this difficulty to two basic sources: "gaps in their now-distant high school records" and "relatively low standardized test scores," which, the report explained, are "often the product of having been out of school for some years." [39] Here, an official and explicit explanation for low SAT scores was made, and explicit policy was built around it.
- A third new *Karabel* secondary review category included students "whose academic index scores narrowly missed gaining them admission in Tier 1." These students were described as "virtually indistinguishable from one another academically." Nonacademic criteria were therefore explicitly made the primary selection criteria *within* this group. [40]

The *Karabel Report Recommendations* avoided major departures from what were Tier 3 complemental admission policies prior to 1991. However, specific Tier 3 targets (or "quotas" as some called them [41]) were changed to *flexible targets*, or acceptable *ranges* of admissions, from among various applicant subpopulations. The only amendments of complemental groupings were an expansion of the rural high school category to increase scanty admissions in this area; the combining of the former special talent and administrative review categories in order to promote the admission of a larger number of students with special talents; and the reduction of the "Filipino target" in response to an increase in the number of Filipino students qualifying for Tier 1. [42]

The *Karabel Report* also recommended that the Special Action admission category be reduced in size. The new limitation stated that no more than 1 place in 20 in the fall freshman class be Special Action admits but that at least two-thirds of these students be from socially or racially disadvantaged backgrounds. With this stipulation came the additional stipulation that all Special Action admit students be given "adequate support services," noting that only one-third of the Special Action students who entered U.C. Berkeley between 1978 and 1982 graduated in 5 years, a significantly smaller proportion than the percentage of regular admits (more than 60%) who graduated in that same time span. [43]

Concept: Admissions Policy Must Be "Balanced"

The basic stance of the *Karabel Report* is that a "fair and equitable admissions policy is not . . . a *neutral* one." [44] Instead, it is a policy that establishes "a reasonable equilibrium among legitimately competing goals, values, and interests." [45] In this way the report chooses to accept, incorporate, make highly explicit, and, in effect, build on the merit-versus-representation tension.

Concept: Admissions Policy Must Have an Educational Foundation

The *Karabel Report* defines an acceptable policy as having an "*educational foundation.*" [46] In so doing, the report maintains strong support for academic criteria.

Concept: Admissions Policy Must Monitor Itself

The *Karabel Report* also requires that those who alter admissions policy continually monitor the "*social* consequences" of that policy and alterations of it. [47]

Ten Policy Principles of Karabel

Within the spirit of balance, the *Karabel Report* derived 10 principles of admissions policy [48]:

1. As an institution of international renown and as one of the nation's leading research universities, Berkeley has an obligation to admit students with exceptionally distinguished academic records.
2. As a taxpayer-supported public university, Berkeley must strive to serve all of California's people.
3. Berkeley should actively seek diversity—socioeconomic, cultural, ethnic, racial, and geographic—in its student body.
4. Berkeley will absolutely not tolerate quotas or ceilings on the admissions or enrollment of any racial, ethnic, religious, or gender groups.
5. In its admissions criteria, Berkeley will recognize outstanding accomplishment in a variety of spheres, including (but not limited to) art, athletics, debating, drama, music.
6. While continuing to grant preference to California residents, Berkeley will continue to admit (highly qualified) out-of-state students.
7. Berkeley should accept only those students who have a reasonable chance of persisting to graduation.
8. The admissions process should include a human element and must not be based on grades and test scores alone.
9. In constructing and altering Berkeley's admissions practices, the faculty should insist upon at least a co-equal role with the administration.
10. The admission criteria and practices of the College of Letters and Science as well as those of the Professional Schools should continue to be described in detail and to be made fully available to the public.

EXPLICIT SHIFTS IN THE BALANCE OF ADMISSIONS POLICY

The balance sought by the *Karabel Report Recommendations* required subtle but definite shifts in several facets of policy. Policy principles described as "preferential treatment," "parity," and "total protection" were retired (at least temporarily) in favor of flexible and increased emphasis on academic merit. The implicit message behind this shift in favor of intellectual criteria is that increased emphasis on mental ability is deemed valuable.

Parity Recedes

The implementation of the *Karabel Report* represented a general departure from the previous stance taken by admissions policy. The explicit drive to "reach" explicit "parity" began to recede. Recall the earlier discussion of broad representativeness, which, as quoted there, calls for higher education to "strive to approximate . . . the general ethnic, gender, economic and regional composition of recent high school graduates." From the standpoint of this approach, parity sounds more exacting. In this context, to reach parity means to achieve an enrollment rate on a U.C. campus that is the same as the high school graduation rate for any given group. Because the old pre-Karabel Tier 3 targets were specific and aimed at achieving this explicit parity, the critics of this tier of the admissions system argued that the university actually had a quota system. [49]

Targets Become Flexible

Specific targets were replaced by "flexible" targets, ranges based on the availability of qualified students as well as on the desired balance of the student population. The *Karabel* recommendation in this area aimed to protect the campus's ability to meet its mission to serve the full spectrum of the California population and at the same time to avoid having its process legally jeopardized, as a quota system might have been. The old Tier 3 process was replaced by a more holistic review in which a would-be Tier 3-type applicant was evaluated in a multidimensional grid-like manner rather than on the basis of but a few variables that were subordinate to the dominance of specific targeting. New targets for secondary review were defined as having "rough" upper and lower bounds, with enough flexibility that even lower bounds of targets were not to be met if the number of qualified applicants was insufficient and upper bounds were to be exceeded if there was an unusually strong pool of target applicants in the secondary review category. In fact, during each admissions cycle, targets were to be adjusted based on the relative strengths of applicant pools. Sheer eligibility (or "total protection" policy) no longer would guarantee any particular applicant group admission; "total protection," therefore, ended. [50]

Return to the 50–50 Balance

Recall that *Karabel* recommended a return to the 50–50 criterion. This departure from the old 40–60 balance again placed selection by academic merit on an "equal" footing (50–50) with selection via a broader range of criteria. Of course, both halves of the 50–50 plan must be "U.C. eligible." This means that all applicants *must* meet the "top 12½%" criteria to be considered and are therefore all selected on the basis of some degree of academic merit, with the exception of Special Action admits. It is important to note that even the fair representation admission route has an academic base. Maintaining this base implies some degree of emphasis on previously demonstrated learning and mental ability to learn. For example, students in the top 12½% are eligible for admission, but students in the bottom 10% are not expected to succeed at the university. Why is this? Most likely this is because they have not demonstrated the mental ability or academic intelligence that is deemed necessary to perform.

ADMISSIONS POLICY AS OPPORTUNITY ALLOCATION

In this chapter the fundamentals of admissions policy at U.C. Berkeley have been examined for their most explicit characteristics. The 50–50 balance between academic merit and complemental criteria is one way of explicitly incorporating the tension between two contrasting approaches to admissions into one policy. The second approach, incorporated into the complemental tier, seeks to fairly represent a multitude of subpublics (i.e., older females, rural students, the economically disadvantaged) and is in itself an incorporation of several different approaches to admission into one bundle.

As the Committee on Admissions and Enrollment reemphasized, one of the primary goals of admissions policy at U.C. Berkeley is "service to the public that has so generously supported it." Yet, in an era of increasing cultural diversity, "the public" is more difficult to identify in the form of a single unified body. "Service to the public" becomes service to an array of often competing subpublics with different needs and characteristics. Now more than ever, admissions policy at U.C. Berkeley allocates a highly prized opportunity to competing constituencies.

Bernard Gifford, Chancellor's Professor of Education at U.C. Berkeley, who has also served as head of the National Commission on Testing and Public Policy, spoke of testing as an "allocative mechanism." [51] Indeed, it powerfully serves as such in the merit-based half of U.C. Berkeley admissions policy. It is also most definitely at work in the other tier of admissions. Again it must be noted that the entire concept of "U.C. eligible" has been built on academic criteria, emphasizing test scores for identifying the "top 12½%" of California's high school seniors. [51] Admissions policy is permeated with test score criteria. And where admissions policy considers test scores less significant than other criteria, as it does in the new Tier 2 (and old Tier 3) admissions policy, test and grades-based admissions criteria are nevertheless still functioning as an "allocative mechanism," allotting the precious and coveted opportunity for education at U.C. Berkeley. Even fair representation is merit based.

What really drives the allocation of higher education opportunity in a democracy? What fuels decisions as to who is most likely to return to society, and in the most beneficial manner, the investment made in his or her education? In answering these questions, the observation can be made that the allocation of educational opportunity cannot occur in the absence of implicit assumptions regarding intelligence and mental ability.

The next chapter looks behind the merit versus representation tension to the powerful sociopolitical forces that fuel beliefs about the effectiveness of education and about students' mental abilities. The next three chapters delve deeply into several different theoretical areas that are rarely, if ever, related explicitly to admissions policy. This analysis is designed to unearth the implicit intelligence policy that drives admissions policy and to crystallize the implicit tensions that Tension 1 reiterates and makes explicit in policy form.

6

Intelligence versus Higher Education as a Determinant of Worldly Success
The Sociopolitical Perspective

Knowledge is power.
Old adage

According to the document that has become known as the *Karabel Report*, written by the University of California Committee on Admissions and Enrollment, the U.C. Berkeley campus faces the "obdurate reality of large-scale differences in patterns of academic performance among California's racial and ethnic groups—differences that are reflected in a high-school drop-out rate among African-Americans and Hispanics at least 50 percent higher than whites." [1] The report adds that "racial and ethnic differences in rates of eligibility for the University of California reveal an even more dramatic pattern," with 5% of African-American high school graduates meeting U.C.'s requirements and 4.5% of Hispanic, 15.8% of white, and 32.8% of Asian-American high school graduates doing so. [2] The *Karabel Report* states that these differences are "deeply rooted in larger patterns of racial and ethnic inequity" and that these differences "constitute a formidable problem . . . in trying to construct an admissions policy that is responsive to all of the major social groups that comprise California's population." The *Report* adds, "How well Berkeley can respond to these challenges will be a crucial measure of its success as California struggles to adjust to the reality of multi-culturalism." [3]

Admissions policy thus wrestles with the "formidable problem" of "larger patterns of racial and ethnic inequity." The impact of these inequities, and of their sources, on the selection of criteria for admission is extensive. This chapter examines some of these sources of inequity and their involvement in implicit intelligence policy and in the creation of Tension 2: intelligence versus higher education as a determinant of worldly success. Within the parameters of this tension can be found the support for Tension 1, academic merit versus fair representation in admissions. If admissions are aimed, at least in part, at raising the level of worldly success of admittees, either these individuals must arrive in college with the mental ability to achieve this success or this mental ability must be acquired there. The following pages consider the means by and extent to which the sociopolitical environment determines the expression of intelligence, and perhaps intelligence itself, on an individual as well as on a societal level. (Because the development of the college-age young adult begins in childhood, comments herein include effects on childhood development.) Worldly success, inasmuch as it is related to academic success, is linked to the same socioeconomic factors that determine the expression of intelligence.

PRESSURE FOR HOMOGENIZATION
OF INTELLECTUAL STANDARDS

The discussion begins with the sociopolitical determination of intelligence and its implications. This chapter presents information favoring the position that the *expression* of intelligence can be taught and encouraged—and it can be neglected and obliterated. This is because the development, the measurement, and even the definition of intelligence reflect the environment or context in which these activities take place. The institution of education at the primary, secondary, and higher levels prepares the mind to fit into the encompassing social system, to find a place along a predefined continuum. The risk inherent in an institutionalized process of mental training, such as the established system of education, is that it encourages the stratification of intellectual activity. It tends to favor the reduction, the homogenization, of the many continua of intellectual activity within a multi-cultural society. In the face of institutional pressure toward *homogenization* and *stratification*, the recognition and protection of intellectual diversity is difficult. The challenge of multiculturalism demands that intellectual diversity be recognized; otherwise, it will perish. When a college applicant is deemed less than mentally fit for admission, the question must be asked, Is this applicant truly not (mentally) able, or is the applicant (mentally) unable according to a unicultural standard?

It may be that the diversity of intellectual activity, and even free thought, is becoming archaic, an anachronism. It may be slipping away in the same way grains of sand leave a hand—imperceptibly until enough is gone for an observer to finally notice the difference. As intellectual diversity (and, thus, free thought) leaves, there is an increasing lack of awareness regarding this loss. Perhaps the capacity to notice the difference between intellectual diversity and intellectual singularity has already been lost.

The connection between freedom of thought (and thinking styles) and the determination of intelligence is a complex one. It is made at the multiple levels of cultural, social, and political organization. It is at once painfully subtle and grossly concrete. A societal preference for, or recognition of, a singular model or gradient of intelligence suggests that only the thought processes that manifest that particular intelligence are intelligent thought processes. A university's preference for students who exhibit academic merit indicates a preference for a particular type of intellectual performance. When that university creates another admissions process for students who cannot win the standard academic merit competition (e.g., Tier 2 at U.C. Berkeley), we must ask: Is it really making room for alternate spectra of ability or merely responding to social pressure?

Perhaps the admissions policy, even when complemental, and the whole educational system exist to organize citizens along a continuum of intellect, one that contains the highest potential of a particular intelligence at one end and lesser degrees of that same intelligence down the line. If so, then the university and the encompassing society are selecting, in a Darwinian sense, what are deemed the most outstanding of those with thought processes best serving that continuum. People who think differently, to a small or a large degree, may actually think according to a different intellectual paradigm, with a separate continuum of its own. They will, nevertheless, be organized along the official continuum. They may not succeed in the university system. Freedom to apply alternative intellectual strategies, and to engage in free thinking itself, becomes alien to the academic and larger social order. Alternative forms of intelligence go unrecognized, unselected. They atrophy, suffocate, or die off. Individuals possessing these alternative forms of intelligence drop out of college or learn little of use while there.

Some advocates of American-style democracy suggest this reduction of intellectual freedom to be the case only in more politically repressive societies. Perhaps, however, the capability of bearing fair witness regarding steps in this direction is missing.

The following sections of this chapter describe two arenas in which the sociopolitical determination of intelligence proceeds, namely, the school system and the prevailing belief system; the systematic transfer of intelligence; and problems of definition in intelligence. The notions of intelligence and expression of intelligence are used interchangeably until the next chapter, when this discussion enters the arena of scientific definition.

SCHOOL AS AN AGENT OF SOCIAL STASIS

College admissions processes can be protectors of the sanctity of the status quo or promoters of new life on and around campus. The previous chapter looked at U.C. Berkeley's "mixed" admissions policy in terms of the balancing of tension between academic merit and fair representation. Such a policy offers a broader range of applicants an opportunity to acquire the worldly success that is expected to result from higher education. However, the link between worldly success and education is also influenced by factors outside the campus. Students admitted through the fair representation route are more likely to be, or to have been, negatively influenced by these factors than those admitted on academic merit. This influence begins long before college, in the years from kindergarten through Grade 12. In his book *A Place Called School*, Professor John Goodlad wrote the following:

> Most basic and difficult is whether we can change fundamentally . . . the widely held belief that a significant part of the population is destined to have serious difficulties in school, and at best can be prepared only for jobs requiring narrow programs of preparation. More formidable is the belief held by some . . . that this is not only the way things are but the way things have to be if the least desirable and lowest paying job slots are to be filled. There are those that believe these two beliefs to be so prevalent that . . . short of a revolution in the surrounding society, . . . schools will remain an institution from which students gain uncommon benefits that reflect fairly accurately their privileged or disadvantaged economic status. [4]

School is an institution that prepares students for participation in the encompassing society. School is designed to perpetuate and to direct the social order: Students must attend school or break truancy laws, and a high school diploma marks the completion of childhood. However, the most profound workings of the institution of school are so massive that it is difficult to take a view of society large enough to see them. Indeed, students are rarely trained to gain such a broad perspective of what they are doing in school.

Because education in primary and secondary school is a key part of the schooling process and because it prepares students for whatever higher education they receive, a substantial part of the following discussion must focus on the broadest ranges of schooling, from childhood into young adulthood.

School Perpetuates Social Order

That school conducts its preparation of students efficiently, thoroughly, and fairly is questionable from several theoretical viewpoints. Goodlad, in the statement just quoted, refers to the belief that school must and does prepare a significant proportion of the population to fill "the least desirable and lowest paying job slots." Anthropologist John Ogbu attributes this predicament to the existence of a social caste system that organizes and controls the schools. [5] From this perspective, instead of serving as the guarantor of equal opportunity as a great equalizer, school serves the function of perpetuating inequities of social class as well as of ability and opportunity. In Yale Professor Sternberg's view, "the conceptions of intelligence held and incubated by the school—the school's eye view of intelligence—will determine what is rewarded and what is punished, and ultimately, who garners society's rewards and who does not." [6]

Equality Is Complex

Yet the means by which school could make it possible for all individuals to garner society's rewards is not agreed on. Some contend that treating all students equally prepares them to garner society's rewards. Others disagree. On the con side of the issue, Arthur Jensen wrote the following in the early 1970s:

> Present educational programs are failing to provide all segments of our population with the knowledge and skills needed for economic self-sufficiency in our increasingly technological society. Literal equality of educational opportunity falls short of solving this problem. Inappropriate instructional procedures, often based on the notion that all children can learn best in essentially the same way except for easily changed environmental influences, can alienate many children from ever entering upon any path of educational fulfillment. [7]

The notion of equality is complex. The actual achievement of equality is still more complex. School has become the laboratory, the place to experiment with methods of changing the level of so-called "equality" within the social system.

Where the Order Is Questioned

While maintaining order within society is desirable to most all of its inhabitants, maintaining a specific social order may not hold such nearly universal appeal. Those who benefit least are prone to desire a change; those who benefit most tend to want to either preserve the status quo or to fortify it. Exceptions to this premise arise when the beliefs or perceptions of the citizens of the social order change.

In the case of some of those who benefit least, who are prepared to fill only the "least desirable and lowest paid job slots," a numb acceptance of the existing order may set in. Some of their numbers may be so well trained to take their places in the social order that they become intellectually unaware of their alternatives. This process, what can be described as "learning out," is discussed later in this chapter. The result of this change in perception among some of those who benefit least is that they no longer resist the status quo and even help to fortify it.

In the case of some of those who benefit most, who are best prepared to fill the most desirable, highest-paying, and dominant job slots, an awareness of externality may set in. In this discussion *externality* refers to the notion that undesirable conditions outside one's immediate milieu have an undesirable effect on that immediate environment (or that the good of others affects one's own welfare). [8] In other words, an undesirable effect on someone else can be undesirable for one's self. The perceived undesirable effect may take any of a number of forms, including economic and medical circumstances. For example, vaccination to stop the spread of a disease that is most prevalent among a subpopulation but threatens the entire population is publicly supported because of an awareness of externality. The result of this social sense of externality is that some of those who most benefit by the social order do not want to preserve the status quo. Support of a social order that denies opportunities or benefits to some segments of society may be perceived as dangerous, and support for an admissions policy that denies access to higher education for representative proportions of disenfranchised segments of society may be viewed as unwise.

School Serves the Dominant System

Regardless of changes in consciousness by some citizens, school continues to serve the dominant social system. This is because, as Ogbu explains, "schools are not usually set up to offer an education designed to change the basic organization of society, official ideologies to the contrary." [9] When a university admissions policy has as one of its goals the intent to help bring about a "genuinely pluralist society," it is not clear if the university has actually decided to reduce its role in serving the dominant social system or if it is in the process of redefining the dominant social system from unicultural to multicultural. Perhaps the pressures of externality are at work.

Below the college level, compulsory schooling for all citizens is considered desirable in that it ensures universal access to essential knowledge, or at least access to the possibility of learning it. This is an important building block of a democratic society if knowledge is indeed power. To distribute the power, the knowledge must also be distributed. Citizens have both a right to education and a responsibility to be educated in order to participate effectively in the social system. The first premise on which the concept of school has been built is thus described by Goodlad as follows:

> There are essential traits of mind, skills of communicating and accretions of knowledge that can be acquired only through deliberate, systematic, and sustained cultivation. Since these are unlikely to be acquired casually, the requisite learnings should be selected and made available in schools. [10]

Selection for Essential Traits of Mind

The determination of which traits of mind are "essential" is made by those who approve school texts; those who design school curricula; those who use the texts and implement curriculum design; and those who write, fund, and legislate education policy. The essential or "requisite learnings" made available in the schools are designed to support the social system in which the school exists.

Presumably, the individual members of this system are also supported by the school. When a citizen has been well schooled, he or she fits into and succeeds within the social system very well. Yet there is a fine line between the school supporting its individual student members, thereby enhancing the individuality of its members, and the school supporting the social system. A school system can go too far in either of these directions.

Channeling of Abilities

If it is indeed the case that school seeks to perpetuate and fortify the existing social order, then school channels the abilities and determines the ability levels of its students in order to meet the needs of the existing social order as set by those who dominate it. This is a dangerous process, as noted by author Sarah Lawrence Lightfoot:

> When schooling serves to accentuate and reinforce the inequalities in society, then it is not providing a viable and productive alternative for children. The message of ethnocentrism is conveyed to parents and children when socialization, acculturation, and learning within schools are defined in the narrow, traditional terms of the dominant culture. [11]

Rethinking School Failure

In the wake of the 1960s Civil Rights movement, the most recent decades have witnessed an increased concern for those who benefit least. School has been described by some of those who have this concern as a potential instrument of social change. Change in the manner in which school prepares its various students to participate in society has the potential to alter the social order. Professor William Labov emphasizes the importance of a change in perception on the part of the "dominant culture."

> Poverty and school failure are not the results of natural disabilities, but rather the result of a conflict in our society between two opposed cultures; . . . the conflict will not be resolved in any favorable way unless the dominant culture recognizes the values of the dominated culture, and changes its way of dealing with it. [12]

Labov places the onus on the sociopolitical environment. Poverty, school failure, even intelligence are not biologically based, they are environmentally determined. By attempting to mold the minds of the dominated culture to fit its own needs, the dominant culture renders what are perceived as school failures and learning disabilities. Language development specialist S. B. Heath reported in her comparison of language development in three subcultures in the United States that when children are raised with one view of intelligence and are then confronted with another in school, the results can be disastrous. [13] Young children may start off on the wrong track in school. They may be unable to participate in simple classroom procedures when these differ radically from the interpersonal interaction patterns of the homes and communities with which they are familiar. Children can appear unintelligent when they do not respond correctly to questions as simple as "What is your name?" or "Is John here today?" or when they do not follow directions. Heath found that these apparent disabilities frequently reflect entirely different cultural experiences. Children may come from subcultures where questions are not asked with the expectation of getting responses or where nicknames are always used and children never use or hear their real names. [14] Children who come from minority subcultures in which the more subtle interactive behaviors of the dominant culture have not been assimilated start out and continue to be at a disadvantage in the school system. The dominant culture labels children of such dominated cultures as being less intelligent. This is an expedient means of handling cultural differences. This also serves to ensure that the dominated intelligence cannot eventually become *selected for* and dominant, that it cannot take over.

BELIEF SYSTEMS IN CONFLICT

This tension between cultural systems reflects deep-seated conflict between different belief systems. Yet even this profound conflict between belief systems is taking place within and is guided by the encompassing dominant belief system. Even forward-looking, seemingly egalitarian admissions policy is guided by the dominant belief system. Perhaps fair representation admissions are an effort at appeasement, driven by a sense of externality, rather than a sharing of power among multicultural belief systems.

Lightfoot writes of what she describes as "the determining power and momentum of social and cultural imagery": [15]

> The individuals involved in negotiating the bridges and boundaries of families and schools are greatly influenced by the socio-historical and cultural forces that incorporate their lives. This is not to say that parents, teachers, and children are helpless victims of a predetermined fate or that individual initiative and interpersonal exchange are meaningless gestures, but rather that interpersonal and intrapsychic issues exist within the context of encompassing belief systems and enduring structures. [16]

Social Construction of Reality

Professor Carol Estes explains this "social construction of reality" in a somewhat different light:

The policies that social institutions produce reflect the dominance of certain values and normative conceptions of social problems and their remedies. These value choices and definitions of existing conditions are not derived from consensual agreement of the members of society, nor do they result from happy compromises among those persons most affected by them. Some individuals and groups bring greater resources of class, status and power to influence the definitions of social problems than do others. [17]

The encompassing belief system, or *system of social perception* (defined in the following section of this chapter), is a critical determinant of the reality in which schools exist and teaching occurs. The dominant system of social perception is the milieu in which human intelligence is developed, nourished, evaluated, and applied. Out of the dominant social imagery arises the socially preferred definition, or image, of intelligence and of who is, or can become, recognized as intelligent.

The Power of Social Imagery

Subtle but ever-present social imagery has a powerful and varied influence on the development of members of different subcultures. Its effects even extend to gender differences in the outcome of education. This is especially evident in studies of the outcome of education for women in lesser developed countries. The majority of analyses of the effects of education on citizens of these countries are gender-free analyses that mask differences in the different effects of schooling on men and women. [18] However, studies that focus on gender indicate that the student's socioeconomic subculture and social institutions (mainly the family and the school) operate in a symbiotic manner to affect participation in, achievement in, and long-range outcomes of the educational process. These effects differ substantially between the sexes. [19] For example, girls are socialized into domestic roles, especially in poorer regions of the globe. In many cultures the family–school interaction limits the intellectual options available to females. When parents rely heavily on girls for domestic help, their school attendance is poor, their academic performance is low, and they repeat grade levels and drop out more frequently, often by the end of their primary school years. [20] Social class has an increasingly powerful effect on women's education. In India the gap in university education between men and women from the higher social classes is closing much faster than the gap between the sexes in primary and secondary schools of all classes. [21] Of those enrolled at the university level in many African, Asian, Middle Eastern, and South American countries, more women than men have parents who are highly educated. [22] At the same time, in these countries, it is not uncommon to find that girls in rural and poor families are sent to school only until they are old enough for marriage. In instances where an increase in a girl's educational level would require a marriage to a boy of a higher educational level and thus a larger dowry from her family, girls are actually kept out of school past a certain age. [23]

In the United States the social imagery of women's liberation and of the upwardly mobile working woman has merged with economic demands placed on families. The resulting image impacts many subcultural and traditional views of women. As the encompassing belief system of the dominant culture shifts, the schooling system responds by changing its treatment of female students (e.g., by creating a special admissions category for older women returning to college, as mentioned in Chapter 5). The invisible tail of the dominant culture thus wags the monstrous body of the education system it has created.

The school system, in overpowering the structure of the individual family system, has the ability to promote or deny equality, whether it be gender equality or some other sociodemographic equality. Quite understandably, some members of minority communities resist the assimilation of their children into the academic system. This adds to the difficulties their children encounter in school. [24] College-age students, being young adults, may resist assimilation, or they may instinctively straddle the cultural and intellectual fence once they gain access to higher education. Adults of dominated subcultures resist the intellectual and social homogenization of their own and their children's minds.

As the powerful broker of educational opportunity for equality, school operates in several dimensions, including (1) *access*—enrollment or participation in school, (2) *survival*—completion of an educational cycle, (3) *output*—level of learning attained, and (4) *outcome*—job status or income level attained later. [25] Whatever belief systems are in conflict with the school, school prevails in that it is has substantial influence on the creation and perception of intellectual fitness of its graduates. If students do not conform to school's demands, they graduate less intellectually fit to participate and compete within the social system. At the university level, where opportunities for worldly success are most specifically generated, the concern regarding the intellectual fitness of the applicants is heightened beyond that experienced at younger ages. The activity varies with the sociopolitical and economic tenor of the times, but access to higher education of high quality is usually bestowed upon those deemed among the most intellectually fit and/or the most intellectually deserving.

CONFLICT BETWEEN BELIEF SYSTEMS REGARDING INTELLIGENCE

The conflicts between the school system of the dominant culture and the social system of dominated cultures occur in the context of far greater conflict: overarching conflict in beliefs about intelligence, that is, in the social imagery of intelligence.

The Perception of Intelligence

Sternberg has argued that research efforts to determine the controversial nature of intelligence "need to be complimented by efforts to understand how intelligence is perceived." [26] He maintains that there is a complex interaction between the objective construct of intelligence (inside the head, in the mind) and the subjective social construct of intelligence (outside the head, in the society) and that efforts to understand or alter the effects of schooling will always be limited if this interaction is overlooked. [27] In this view of intelligence, the internal and external constructs of intelligence interact and must be considered together.

Constructs of intelligence are embedded in belief systems, the social imageries in which they are founded. Herein lies the determining power of the social and cultural imagery of intelligence. Perhaps such social imagery is so omnipresent that it even determines much of what each individual mind perceives of its own internal thought processes and strategies. New developments in the science of cognition may eventually reshape the social imageries of intelligence. Since the early 1970s, research has been elaborating on "metacognitive processes." These are defined as being both "knowledge about cognition and the regulation of cognition." [28] Intellectual activity is increasingly viewed as having an executive control system, a meta-level that regulates activity within each ability area and its cognitive domain. [29]

Internalization of Social Stimulation

The existence of a metacognitive control system can be explained in terms of either innate capability (from the rationalist view) or environmental input (from the empiricist view). In terms of the latter possibility, metacognitive competence can be attributed to social stimulation.

Although it does not address metacognition per se, Vygotskian theory holds that the interpersonal exchange of ideas and concepts is transformed via experience to an intrapersonal internal process. It is this transformation that social and developmental psychologist Lev Vygotsky called "internalization." [30] A young person internalizes interpersonal experience, and this experience can mold the way he or she thinks. This theory would perhaps say that interpersonal exchanges within the environment enhance or even deliver not only explicit ideas and concepts but more implicit metacognitive abilities as well. Vygotskian theory would say that the ability to think about and control one's thought processes can be learned via internalization.

This view of internalization of basic cognition and even deeper metacognition can be extended to the issue of cultural dominance. While in Vygotskian theory internalization is essential and positive in intellectual development, it may also be detrimental and negative: it may facilitate the internalization or acquisition of cognitive and even metacognitive conflict. How? Young people who do not belong to the dominant culture, whose predominant social experiences occur outside the lingo of dominant social imagery, internalize the thought processes of their nondominant cultures, even the nondominant metacognitive processes. These processes are not in sync with the dominant thought processes. If a young member of a dominated culture experiences conflict between the metacognitive thought processes of the subculture and those of the dominant culture, he or she may internalize this conflict. Intellectual dissonance from the environment of conflicting cultures may be internalized, or transferred, into the deepest levels of the mind. The metacognitive programming, the entire knowledge structure, may become highly confused and severely weakened by disorganization. Both the transfer of knowledge and the expression of intelligence are delicate processes that are highly reactive to the cultural environment. Conflicting mental control systems, metacognitive structures, may obstruct the acquisition of knowledge.

The system of social perception is closely related to the monumental determining power of social and cultural imagery and its massive but usually invisible influence on all social policy. The next section of this chapter is devoted to a brief description of it.

THE POWER OF PREVAILING BELIEF SYSTEMS

Beliefs about reality determine perceptions of reality; beliefs about intelligence determine perceptions of intelligence. Philosophers have often insisted on this controversial view of the perception of reality. [31] As author Edward Newton wrote, "One of the laws of thought ought to be: the way in which a phenomenon is manifested depends on the way it is observed." [32] In a manual designed for government employees, a visual communications specialist concluded, "People in different periods and different societies *do not see in the same way at all* [Italics in original]." [33]

Receptivity to Knowledge

Indeed, the interpretation of sensory input is greatly influenced by social factors. According to anthropologist Franz Boas:

> A mass of observations and thoughts is transmitted to the child. These thoughts are the result of careful observation and speculation of our present and past generations; but they are transmitted to most individuals as traditional matter, much the same as folklore. The child combines his own perceptions with this whole mass of traditional material, and interprets his observations by its means. It is a mistake to assume that the interpretation made by each civilized individual is a complete logical process. [34]

This might be amended to read as follows: "It is a mistake to assume that the interpretation made by each civilized individual is a *complete process.*" Instead, there is a cross-file check. The process has already occurred, has already been experienced at a previous moment elsewhere in the culture or subculture, and need not be relived. Relatively few experiences are subject to naive or fresh perception and reaction. Relatively few naive perceptions would be acceptable within the context of cultural reality norms. Birth into a particular culture is an arrival into a predefined reality. Birth into a dominated culture is an arrival into a predetermined social reality that says, "Your ways of seeing and learning are not the official or dominant ways. The way your mind works, your intellectual activity, may not be typical of the dominant culture. Learn to think differently."

The Confines of Culture

Regardless of cultural background, an individual is a prisoner of his or her own personal learning and experience in addition to that of the surrounding culture. Information scientist Norbert Wiener commented, "In the case of the brain, there is no normal process, except death, that can clear it of all past impressions." [35] The brain is a memory bank of personal experience, all of which is subject to cultural sensitivity.

Culture is the storage cell for the impressions and learning experiences of generations of individuals. The individual is a recipient of this cumulative description of reality, adds to it during his or her lifetime, and passes it on to the next generation. There is, then, a traditional view of reality that evolves with the human mind within its culture. Dominated cultures feel pressure to evolve toward the views of reality held by the dominant culture. The school system, administrated by the dominant culture, exerts this pressure. And each individual, regardless of culture of origin, is pressured to accept the dominant culture's views of reality.

In his controversial book *The Closing of the American Mind*, Allan Bloom notes that "every educational system has a moral goal that it tries to attain and that informs its curriculum. It wants to produce a certain kind of being." [36] This kind of human being is one who will serve as a participant in and a vessel for the presiding culture. When families send their children to school, they are turning the cultivation of the minds of their children over to a social institution. Lightfoot describes the parents' feelings:

> All parents, of course, experience great anxiety when they must relinquish their dominant and pervasive control over their child and trust that he will thrive under the supervision of a stranger. Feelings of anxiety and threat are accompanied by deep feelings of competition and concern. . . . Feelings of loss and detachment are intense as mothers send their children off to school for the first time—to be publicly evaluated, judged, and categorized, and perhaps

to be abused and unappreciated. But, where there is almost perfect conso-
nance between the perspectives and goals of the communities and schools,
families experience less anxiety in relinquishing parental control. [37]

School–Home Conflicts

In contrast to the school–home match of upper-middle-class suburban communities, communities of the dominated culture find that "schools represent a
distant cultural perspective." The dominated culture finds that the schools

> force a direct confrontation with the peer-oriented society as they evaluate and
> rank neighborhood children by criteria that are meaningless and alien to the
> community. The message being conveyed by the school to community resi-
> dents is both humiliating and threatening, but parents painfully recognize the
> implicit bargain that they must make if their children are to be prepared for life
> in the world beyond the boundaries of their community. [38]

Between what Labov terms the "vernacular" culture and the school culture
are "profound differences" in "the way people deal with one another." [39] Labov
argues that "school learning is . . . a matter of individual study and competitive
display before the group" and that these activities are not those of the vernacular or
native culture, in which the skills that are favored and highly developed "depend
on close co-operation of groups." [40] Labov suggests that educators build on the
power of group interaction to encourage learning. Such cultural sensitivity may be
a critical component of effective education. Labov also notes that there is little
information on how cognitive skills develop in a vernacular setting [41], the implication being that cognitive ability is given the nature and power of its basic
characteristics by the subcultural setting in which the individual originates.
Cognitive ability is culturally sensitive, the expression of intelligence is culturally
sensitive, and yet policies that seek to educate intelligence may or may not be
culturally sensitive (even when they claim to be).

The Systematic Transfer of Cognitive Ability and Intelligence

The dominant culture systematizes the transfer of its knowledge in order to
remain dominant. Once members of the dominant culture establish a definition of
desirable knowledge, members of the dominated culture must live with this
definition. Yet they do not acquiesce without some resistance. Conflicts appear
between generations, among schools of thought and dogma, and across political,
economic, and cultural divisions. Power struggles result.

In the schools, the losers of these struggles and their children are subjected to
the winner's systematized definitions of cognitive ability and intelligence. Children's futures are created by the school system's understanding of these definitions. The most blatant example of this often detrimental dictation of potential

occurs when young people who are not mentally retarded are labeled as such because they do not "test well." [42] A few years spent erroneously placed in a class for retarded youth can seriously curtail the intellectual functioning of a student. Another and less visible example occurs when a student regarded as bright within his or her own subculture is not admitted to, or is admitted to but flunks out of, the university.

This hints at a host of issues surrounding the definition of intelligence, some of which are addressed in the next section of this chapter. While the mislabeling of an individual of normal intelligence as retarded is indeed disastrous, it is not alone among the misfortunes of the war for dominance in the definition of intelligence. Any inappropriate labeling on which academic tracking, curriculum, and flunking are based can be detrimental.

Misunderstanding of students' knowledge structures abounds. This is especially true for knowledge structures evolved in subordinate cultures. However, research conducted in the 1970s and 1980s offers a new understanding of underlying knowledge structures and intelligences. Knowledge is increasingly understood to be interactive with environment. The expression of intelligence is highly environmental; it is context dependent. Whether or not intelligence is innate or is something entirely independent of the context in which it is developed and expressed, intelligence is of no use unless it is applied in some fashion. It is the expression of intelligence that educators address. As education science improves the technologies required to teach students to learn, it will gain greater power to strengthen mental ability and increase the expression of intelligence. Higher education may have the potential to go beyond the transfer of knowledge to the deeper transfer of mental ability and intelligence. Consider some of the research in the area of transfer, context dependence, and metacognition.

Intelligence as Transferable Metaknowledge

In this rapidly changing world, today's youth must be prepared to absorb new knowledge and quickly apply new patterns of thought. Although modern curricula are stuffed with a host of specific topics, what students need most is the ability to transfer knowledge and training from one problem, one domain, to another. This view of essential knowledge is expressed as follows: "If we think that basic broadly transferable knowledge and skills are learnable and teachable, then we will aim our courses at such knowledge and skills, without too much concern for 'covering' any specific information, topics or techniques." [43]

The Case for Teaching Heuristics

There are those who claim that a strong case can be made for the explicit teaching of problem-solving heuristics, of an overarching or meta-level of knowledge. [44] This teaching of heuristics increases the applicability and transfer value of what is being learned. Increasing research regarding this metalevel of cognition creates new possibilities for educators. It also suggests a new view of intelligence as a sort of executive control system that is educable. Students can be taught to think about *how* they think; they can then improve the methods of thinking and problem solving that they choose to apply to particular problem sets. On a basic level, students can learn to approach mathematical word problems in a more algebraic manner; they can learn to better outline their thoughts when writing an essay; and, similarly, they can learn to consciously improve their other, more complex and abstract, metacognitive processes. As the technology of teaching general and specific problem-solving heuristics advances, the possibility of teaching intelligence, or what might be defined as intelligence, is being created. If heuristic skills are defined as intelligence, then intelligence can be raised. If students from dominated subcultures can be effectively taught to transfer heuristic skills from one cultural domain to another, perhaps they will have a greater advantage in the social system without relinquishing their individual and sub-cultural characteristics.

Intelligence as Context Dependent

Research on cognition has been criticized for its reliance on experimental settings and its lack of attention to cognition in its natural context. Problem-solving behavior differs between experimental settings and settings that are not prefabricated. [45] An extension of this notion is that problem-solving behavior may vary in different social settings as well.

Learning Depends on What Is Already Known

It is not only the mind and the environment that are interactive. There is also what psychologist Ann Brown describes as "headfitting" or an "intimate relation-ship between what is currently known and what can be readily acquired." [46] Existing knowledge and the subject matter to be learned are highly interactive. An individual's expressed intelligence may be the product of a series of such inter-actions, rather than a distinctly separable item. An extension of this notion is that children from dominated subcultures build an entirely different knowledge base than do children of the dominant culture. The result of interactions of school subject matter with their existing knowledge will have differing results.

The environment, or context in which learning occurs, extends well beyond the physical environment. The *learner-in-context* is only the learner and not the whole of the learning process. In this sense, it can be said that no mind is an island. Components of the learning process include the learner (with the learner's knowledge base and metacognitive state), the learning activities, the materials to be utilized in learning, the teacher–student dynamic, and the essential "criterial task" or tasks. [47] Differing interactions of these elements result in differences in the learning of knowledge, in knowledge structures, and perhaps in intelligences.

Intelligence Is Acquired on the Basis of Adaptive Value

Another facet of context dependence in learning is the perceived utility of the skill to be learned or assimilated. Perceived adaptive value is, in itself, a context. Again, learning is context dependent. Research in the areas of animal behavior, ecology, and animal cognition suggests that "animals are active investigatory creatures who mine the world for information on a need-to-know basis." [48] Perhaps humans also mine their environments, developing intelligence on a perceived *need-to-know* basis. Within their home cultures young members of the dominated culture may perceive a need to have a particular type of intelligence not favored in the schools. They may develop these knowledge structures, intelligences, before arriving in the school system. The school system instills, or attempts to instill, the "official" (i.e., dominant culture's) set of adaptive values in the minds of these students, thus encouraging them to mine the so-called "appropriate" social context for knowledge as well as for metaknowledge. Their nondominant cultures' expressions of intelligence are not likely to be recognized as having adaptive value when expressed in the environment of the dominant culture.

Learning Develops from Specific to General

Learners exhibit varying degrees of sophistication in their development of metaknowledge. Generalization and flexibility are characteristics not of knowledge but of learners. [49] What a learner can do, or learns to do, with learned knowledge may determine the perceived intelligence or "maturity" of that individual. Consider Brown's observation that it is the range of applicability indicated by any particular learner that "forms the diagnosis of expertise or cognitive maturity." [50] Apparently, expert, mature learners find particular processes to apply in a greater number of contexts than do novice, immature learners. Brown adds, "The less mature, less experienced, less intelligent suffer from a greater degree of contextual-binding, but even the expert is bound by contextual constraint to some degree." [51]

Brown views cognitive development as a process that proceeds from "specific context-bound" toward a more "general context-free" state. [52] This again suggests that learners can be helped to mature by teaching them transfer skills in order to extend applicability. Imagine a university that makes this intellectual "maturing of its students" one of its stated goals. Grounds for admission might shift dramatically there. A new sort of value-added approach might be taken perhaps along the lines discussed in Chapter 3. A knowledge structure can be trained, educated; it can be amplified. When learners become highly adept at transfer, their intelligence is less context dependent. While context dependence always limits the development and expression of intelligence, learners are increasingly released from its limitations as their meta-level transfer skills are enhanced. Unfortunately, some learners continue, in Brown's words, "to suffer from a greater degree of contextual binding." [53] Is this a result of their inabilities or the educational system's insensitivity to their preexisting knowledge structures?

Recognizing Opportunities to Restructure Students' Intelligences

Attributing contextual binding to individual differences relieves the educational system of the pressure to address its role in the matter of intellectual limitation. Although some cognitive theorists report that certain architectural units of the brain—including its capacity, durability, and efficiency (or encoding speed)—are resistant to change, many of these same scientists do not claim that control processes and memory strategies are also resistant. [54] It appears that metacognition can be educated. Whatever the innate degree of intelligence as determined by brain architecture, there is ample opportunity for training individuals to develop, express, and even restructure their intelligences. As the knowledge base in the area of human information processing expands, it is important to become increasingly sensitive to individual differences and needs in the development and application of metacognitive skills. [55]

Intelligence as Learning Out

The term *learning out* has been applied to those members of society who are so well trained to take their places in the social order that they become intellectually unaware of their alternatives. In this way, they are rendered unable to resist the powerful channeling pressure of the educational system. How deeply does this process of learning out reach into the heart of an individual's knowledge structure? Perhaps metacognitive competence is "learned out" along with specific information and skills. Perhaps those who suffer most learn out the empowering transfer skills or the ability to acquire these skills. These possibilities raise larger questions about intelligence: How much of the expression of individual intelligence, or intelligence itself, is being learned out in the social system? How much does the system encourage this learning out?

Intelligence as a Valued Metastrategy

It has been suggested that metacognition is not distinct from cognition. [56] Whether or not a clear delineation of these mental processes is possible, the use of the term *metacognition* at least permits consideration of heuristic and other processing capabilities independent of specific content. The possibility that even some individuals consciously use their metacognitive capabilities opens up the possibility that many other individuals can learn to use the capabilities. Apparently, most individuals engage in some degree of conscious but passive (i.e., undirected and unmanipulated) metacognition. Research reveals that even pre-schoolers report metacognitive awareness in the areas of memory. When presented with a memory task, they can talk about the difficulty of the task with respect to the number of items to be remembered, the distractions from remembering, and numerous associative cues. [57]

Enhancing Metacognition

Given the appropriate training, metacognitive power might be enhanced; however, it has been demonstrated that "children who acquire a potentially useful strategy often fail to utilize that strategy" [58], owing, at least in part, to what are called their attributional beliefs. [59] These are beliefs regarding the relationship between their level of effort and their successes in solving problems. Children who view increased effort as positively related to problem-solving success are more likely to engage in meta-level mental activity. [60] They are more likely to do the extra work of thinking about their thinking because they believe this work to be related to success. Here again is evidence that beliefs and belief systems affect the expression of intelligence. Intelligence transfer and the building of applicable knowledge structures is a delicate process. The teaching of metacognitive skills may be complicated by the strength of students' beliefs. Effective metacognitive instruction may actually involve the building of beliefs that make it possible for students to *believe* that they *can* utilize the heuristic processes they learn.

THE FLOW OF THEORY

Throughout this chapter the terms *expression of intelligence* and *intelligence* have been used. This largesse of definition has allowed a discussion of the socio-political determination of intelligence without the problem of having to argue that intelligence is environmentally influenced or determined. The notion that the environment may influence the expression of intelligence is one step removed from the notion that the environment influences intelligence itself. Having now arrived deep in the world of theory regarding mental ability and intelligence, the discussion will remain at this level in order to continue to examine the implicit undergrid of explicit university admissions policy.

The Swing from Nature to Nurture and Back

It has been suggested that, over time, the pendulum swings back and forth between the extremes of the nature (genetic) and nurture (environmental) views of intelligence. In a research article written in 1974, which concluded that the effects of IQ on economic and social status are minimal, economists Samuel Bowles and George Nelson wrote the following:

> The growing disillusionment with compensatory education and other anti-poverty programs has given new life to an old theme in the United States social theory: the poor are poor because they lack mental skills. Their poverty is particularly intractable because it is rooted in the genetic structure inherited from their parents who were also poor and "mentally deficient." An explanation of transmission of economic status from one generation to the next is thus found in the heritability of I.Q. The idea is not new: an earlier wave of genetic interpretations of economic and ethnic inequality followed in the wake of the failures of the purportedly egalitarian educational reforms of the early 20th century Progressive Era. [61]

However, Professor Richard Herrnstein, emphasizing the genetic aspects of IQ and social performance, explained the swing of the pendulum somewhat differently. He noted that Darwinism began going out of style in the United States after World War I. It ran against the American grain, challenging egalitarianism. Herrnstein wrote in the early 1970s:

> But Darwinism was not only disagreeable, it could also be dangerous, as a rationalism for individual or class or racial advantages. And then, in the 1930s, Nazi Germany proved how lethal the idea of group superiority could become in malevolent hands.
>
> Today we have mostly grown up in an intellectual climate dominated by extreme, unrestrained environmentalism. . . . Virtually all influential political and social theories since the 1930s assume that society, as well as the individuals composing it, are shaped mainly by social forces. Change those forces, the theorists promise, and man in society will change accordingly. [62]

Predetermined Stages of Intellectual Development

Although the degree to which intelligence interacts with experience (to affect psychosocial and socioeconomic characteristics such as academic performance, income, and occupation) is debated, it is rarely argued that intelligence does not interact with experience at all. In fact, research in the area of behavior genetics indicates that the effects of environment on intelligence vary at different stages of development. Genetic inheritance is able to explain the smallest proportion of the variation in IQ; heritability has the smallest effect during infancy, increases through middle childhood, wanes in early adolescence, and increases again in adulthood. [63]

The older field of developmental psychology further substantiates the developmental perspective on ability. However, the field also provides the theoretical foundation for the nature–nurture tension. On one end of the spectrum, stages are viewed as being innate developments. Swiss psychologist Jean Piaget contributed a great deal to this view of cognitive development. According to Piaget, intelligence develops from the inside outward. His model includes specific and predetermined successive periods of intellectual development (Table 6.1 indicates the order in which these periods proceed). [64]

In the Piagetian model a child acquires cognitive capacity by (1) fitting new environmental inputs into existing mental structures and (2) adapting his or her cognitive structures to assimilate input from the environment. These are the Piagetian mechanisms of accommodation and assimilation. [65] For Piaget, the mind interacts with the environment but in a manner predetermined by the individual's stage of development.

Environmentally Determined Intellectual Development

Vygotsky, as discussed earlier, took a different approach to the development of the individual, postulating that intelligence develops or is set in motion socially from outside the individual and is acquired by the inner self. Because young children internalize social processes, they are able to do later what they at first are able to do only with help or guidance. The gap between the potential manifested by the child and the latent potential of the child can be measured by watching the child perform with the guidance of an adult. Social processes unlock and confirm the potential, the intelligence of the individual. [66] The social system has a powerful impact on the development of intelligence.

Contradictory assumptions about mental ability are often at work alongside each other. Although the Piagetian rigidity of specific and innate stages has been criticized for its unrealistic qualities, the thinking of Piaget has filtered into curriculum design from preschool through high school: Three-year-olds are not taught calculus, but adolescents are expected to be able to learn three-dimensional

Table 6.1. Piagetian Stages of Development

Period	Approximate age range (in years)	Development
Sensorimotor	Birth to 2	Child interacts with environment in simple sensory and motor modes.
Preoperational	2–7	Child acquires advanced symbolic capacity; is able to let one object represent another that is out of sight.
Concrete operational	7–12	Child learns to apply mental operations to concrete objects.
Formal operational	12–	Child is able to apply mental operations to abstract or formal objects, i.e., to think by analogy.

geometry when it is depicted on a two-dimensional chalkboard. The tension between the internal (predetermined-stage) and external (internalization-of-environment) models of intelligence is not dissipating. This tension has long been foreshadowed by the philosophical tension: rationalism versus empiricism (Tension 4 of the tensions identified in Chapter 1).

TESTING FOR INTELLIGENCE

IQ Testing

In this century the definition of intelligence has undergone a fascinating evolution, one organized around the changing understanding and measurement of human abilities. In 1904 Alfred Binet, the inventor of the prototype for the most widely used psychometric test, was hired by the city of Paris to design a test that would predict children's performance in school. [67] Early in this century Charles Spearman developed not only the notion of a general ability (Spearman's "g") factor but also a statistical procedure to measure it. [68] Decades later, by means of a more sophisticated statistical procedure, Louis Thurstone, one of the pioneers in the development of factor analysis, discovered seven primary abilities. In the mid-1930s evidence developed indicating that Spearman's "g" was actually two factors; Thurstone's second-order analysis of primary abilities indicated that more than one primary factor existed among them. [69] Spearman's "g" was eventually separated into two factors: fluid (g_f) and crystallized (g_c) intelligence. [70]

The Dichotomization of Intelligence

Cattell defined fluid intelligence as that intelligence "unconnected with cultural skills, which rises at its own rate and falls despite cultural stimulus . . . which has the 'fluid' quality of being directable to almost any problem." Crystallized intelligence, by contrast, is "invested in particular areas of crystallized skills which can be upset individually without affecting the other." [71]

This measurement-based division of intelligence into two factors makes it possible to think of intelligence as both innate *and* environmentally influenced, as originating both inside and outside the individual, as both rigid and educable. Research in the field of behavior genetics supports this division. Behavior geneticists are, in fact, finding that, on average, about half of the individual differences in intelligence are explained by inheritance and half are explained by environmental factors. [72] This leaves a great deal of room for the sociopolitical imagery of intelligence to work its differential influence on the expression of intelligence among members of the dominant and dominated cultures.

Cultural Bias in Testing

In response to the resurgence of the nature–nurture controversy in recent decades, the matter of measurement and test bias has been examined. Do tests favor members of the dominant culture? Is there cultural bias in test items? Cultural bias refers to differences in the amount of opportunity the test subject has had to become familiar with both the subject matter of test items and the process of testing. [73] Whether or not tests have been and continue to be culturally biased is the focus of disagreement and action. [74] The very definition of intelligence has been taken over by test designers. As a result, new tests and even new models of intelligence have been proposed. For example, Howard Gardner, professor and director of Harvard's Project Zero, explains that there are multiple intelligences and that they are not always found together in the same proportions. [75] The impact of ability testing on the lives of citizens is becoming so great that the social consequences of testing are now being formally examined. The National Commission on Testing and Public Policy, founded by the Ford Foundation in 1986, was charted to conduct "a systematic, policy-oriented analysis . . . of the role that standardized tests—as measures of individual merit and as predictors of future classroom and workplace performance—play in the allocation of educational training and employment opportunities." [76]

Testocratization

An effort to determine the social consequences of testing is especially critical in the current era. The widespread use of ability testing establishes what U.C. Professor Bernard Gifford calls the "testocracy," for admission into educational and employment opportunity is increasingly test based. Unless the impact of test-based ability measurement on citizens is clearly understood, there will be little opportunity to control it. Insofar as testing measures both internally (innately) and externally (environmentally) derived mental ability and then dictates access to opportunity on the basis of this measurement, tests serve as gatekeepers to status within the socioeconomic system. Insofar as the expression of intelligence is, at least in part, potentiated by opportunity, the test determines the expression of intelligence. Whether or not the test claims that it measures intelligence, it has a profound influence on the perceptions of its existence.

CONSTRUCTING SOCIETY AROUND INEQUALITIES

As explained earlier in this chapter, education from kindergarten on is in the main an instrument of social control. The dominant culture relies on the educational system to preserve the dominant knowledge structure. In turn, the educational system is funded by the dominant system of social perception that it supports.

Intelligence, when defined as a meta-level cognitive activity, may be learnable; however, this learning, the application of this learning, and the transfer of this learning are highly context dependent. The sociopolitical environment is the ultimate medium, or context, in which intelligence flourishes or fails to develop. It is also the arena in which public policy, such as public university admissions policy, develops. Even admission to the transfer of higher learning done in higher education is dictated by sociopolitical definitions and manipulations of intelligence.

It is within the context of the dominant culture that academic merit, ability, intelligence, and the top percentages of high school graduates have been and are being defined. It is also within this context that the tension between academic merit and fair representation has been supposedly "balanced" in explicit admissions policy. Unfortunately, contextual sensitivity may result in this culture being unable to see things that threaten to disprove its prevailing and supposedly fundamental notions. As long as intelligence is sociopolitically determined, what it really is— or what it really can become—cannot be determined.

In the meantime, admissions policy uses tests of various sorts to measure academic achievement and to infer abilities and intelligences of various sorts. As even Richard Herrnstein, co-author of *The Bell Curve*, acknowledged, against the background vision of the classless society "the main significance of intelligence testing lies in what it says about a society built around human inequalities." [77]

All societies have in some way been built around perceived human inequalities, whether depending on them or compensating for them or both. If the sociopolitical environment can create within itself an environment more favorable for the development of everyone's intelligence, then specific environmental influences on differences in mental ability should decrease. With this decrease may come the increase of genetic influence on intelligence, because this will be the only remaining influence, as Herrnstein has explained. [78] It is doubtful that any political system is planning for this development. However, were this to occur, this would be the ultimate in the sociopolitical determination of intelligence; a reality would be created where biology alone could be responsible for the problems of society now taken to the halls of Congress in the hope that legislative intervention will be the solution. The next chapter examines scientific theories of intelligence, including theories pertaining to the biology of mental ability.

7

Academic Aptitude
versus Achievement
Scientific Interpretations of Intelligence

> Science must be understood as a social phenomenon, a gutsy human enter-
> prise, not the work of robots programmed to collect pure information.
> STEPHEN JAY GOULD [1]

The tension of academic merit versus fair representation and the tension of intelligence versus education as the key determinant of worldly success basically reflect differing stands on the importance of aptitude versus achievement. Either students have the ability or they achieve the ability. Either students come equipped with intelligence or they acquire intelligence. Mixed admissions policies imply a belief that students *can* acquire the ability to succeed at the university and go on to worldly success.

Even if it can be described as purely objective, much of the scientific litera-ture pertaining to intelligence and mental ability can be interpreted as evidence of either the aptitude (nature) or the achievement (nurture) side of this basic di-lemma. Some findings suggest that intelligence is largely inherited, some suggest that it is largely determined by environment, and still others break the influence of nature and nurture down to a 50–50 split. Whatever their stance on the matter, findings continue to fuel the discussion regarding the most realistic balance between nature and nurture and the most reasonable means of allocating educa-tional opportunity. Nevertheless, research scientists are seldom directly involved in formulating or implementing social policies. They do not write admission policies, for example. Instead, their research may be applied by nonscientists who are usually less knowledgeable on the obscurities of statistical analysis. Misunder-stood or misused research findings may serve to buttress implicit assumptions in ways never intended by the researchers. This chapter looks at a sampling of these many pieces of relevant literature. How society chooses to define and apply definitions of intelligence is, to a great extent, based on subjective assumptions and theories regarding mental ability, as is indicated in the latter sections of this chapter concerning testing and the research on sociological aspects of intelligence.

TESTING

Cognitive testing serves more than the process of identifying levels of mental ability, intelligence, and giftedness. It serves as a gatekeeper of opportunity. A meter of ability sits at the gate and opens it for those with what are deemed "appropriate abilities."

Early Intelligence Testing Policy

Policies pertaining to the use of mental ability testing are excellent examples of the influence of assumptions about intelligence on policies and their impacts. Researcher Lewis Terman published the Stanford-Binet intelligence test in 1916, culminating over 25 years of many researchers' efforts in Europe and America on the nature of intelligence and the means of measuring it. [2] Terman was called upon by the American Psychological Association to aid the war effort when the United States declared war on Germany in 1917. The group intelligence tests developed by Terman and other psychologists were used to test and classify 1.7 million recruits over the next 2 years. [3] The application of these tests was viewed as being "of great value to army efficiency" [4], and the tests were expected to find, in Terman's words, "universal use in the schoolroom," a development Terman claimed was essential if schools were to achieve "educational efficiency." [5] By 1919 Terman had helped create the National Intelligence Tests for schoolchildren, which were based on the army tests. [6] By 1925 over 75 tests of general mental ability had been developed. [7] Ability grouping and tracking became the rule rather than the exception, and in the decades since the 1920s the testing of students in order to group them has become standard practice. [8] This testing has inspired sharp and continuing controversy since its inception. [9]

Conflict Regarding Intelligence Testing

In 1987 the Commission on Testing and Public Policy, headed by U.C. Berkeley Professor of Educational Policy Bernard Gifford, began the study of the effects of tests on individual opportunity. Gifford interpreted the controversy over testing as being fundamentally a dispute about politics. [10] He found that the use of standardized tests as a means to allocate significant opportunities to individuals is "an increasingly ubiquitous feature of American life." [11] Gifford contended that in an environment of unlimited wealth the issue of "allocative fairness" might not arise but that in the real world, where resources are limited, methods of allocation such as testing are devised to serve as distributive mechanisms. [12] According to Cattell's view of the supply of and demand for intelligence, times of economic surplus result in a greater demand for a broader range of intelligence levels. If, as Gifford says, testing serves as an "allocative mechanism" in the distribution of opportunity, then in times of anything but unlimited wealth testing will be more heavily weighted and applied.

Admissions and other forms of testing become gatekeepers in a technocratic civilization. Gifford placed the problem of the emerging "testocracy" [13] in the context of the political system, a system "where both skepticism and dogma are essential to the stability and cohesiveness of the polity and to the capacity of the polity to tolerate dissent and guarantee minority political rights in a majoritarian political culture." [14] Allocative fairness is an issue central to political inter-actions and the source of much political conflict. Allocative fairness is thus "the focus of both skepticism and dogma"—dogma in that advocates of standardized testing see testing as the actualization of logic and science over speculation and prejudice [15] and skepticism in that critics of testing distrust it in the areas of fairness, objectivity, and application procedures. [16] What a double bind!

Opportunity Allocation

Opportunity allocation can be described as a political and nonscientific variable, one that measures the degree to which individuals *perceive* that tests are fair as allocation mechanisms, perceptions that "may determine the success of testing policy." [17] Whatever the cause, test result disparities have been recognized for some time. African-Americans and Hispanics generally do not perform as well as whites on tests that emphasize mastery of the dominant culture. [18] Women do not perform as well as men on tests that emphasize certain mechanical and physical skills. [19] That these differences in results exist is rarely debated; however, their causes (such as cultural bias in testing [20]) and their implications in decision making are controversial.

Whether it be the disproportionate placement of African-American children in EMR (educable mentally retarded) classes based on IQ tests [21]; the tracking of schoolchildren based on IQ along with IQ-correlated tests [22]; the labeling of certain students as gifted or genius; or the test-based determination of an individual's suitability for a job, admission to college, or immigration into a nation, testing policies continue to challenge the tender balance between dogma and skepticism.

Misconceptions Regarding Aptitude Tests

The use of the aptitude test to measure innate capacity has long been separated from the use of the achievement test to measure the outcome of education and the effects of learning. [23] While the former is traditionally used to predict future performance (e.g., in college or on the job), the latter is used to measure acquired ability, to determine what has already occurred. Aptitude tests are further differentiated from achievement tests in that they do not measure the results of a seemingly controlled and specified experience, such as a high school education containing basic preset subjects. Instead of specified achievement, aptitude tests measure ability that results from what Fordham University psychology professor Anne Anastasi describes as "uncontrolled and unknown conditions." [24] Anastasi explains that the differentiation between aptitude (or innate capacity) and achievement (or effects of learning) is a misconceived distinction: both tests measure learned as opposed to innate abilities. [25] The problematic differentiation nevertheless persists and is especially relevant in this examination of implicit intelligence policy.

It is in this gulf, and concurrent overlap, between the notions of aptitude and achievement that the nature–nurture and related tensions are most explicit in education. The sociopolitical ramifications of this polarity are especially clear in higher education admissions policies; those who appear to have the "aptitude" to succeed in college and beyond will be awarded the most potent and prestigious educational opportunities.

Standardized Test for College Admissions

The confusion between aptitude and achievement is perhaps most explicit in higher education admissions practices, where the standardized Scholastic Aptitude Test (SAT) is a major determinant of admission. As manifested by its very name, the SAT is considered a predictor of academic success in college. The SAT and the ACT (American College Testing Program) are the most commonly used entrance tests and have increased in popularity over recent decades. There are now 1.25 million people taking the SAT each year and 1 million taking the ACT. These tests are key factors in admissions, in the course of study available, and in non-college-based scholarship funding. [26] The increased emphasis on test scores for college entrance has been controversial. The utilization of standardized entrance examinations was once applauded for its fairness in comparison to the frequently biased process of case-by-case selection, which permitted favoritism and prejudice in the allocation of educational opportunity. Case-by-case selection also fueled what Christopher Jencks, professor at the Center for Urban Affairs and Policy Research at Northwestern University, calls the "old-boy network," which recognized and admitted students from known families and/or big-name schools.

[27] However, the use of standardized tests was also faulted for its bias against educationally disadvantaged students [28] in that the SAT, although called an aptitude test, is actually a measure of learning acquired from the social and educational environment. A student from a deprived environment would have less opportunity to learn what was required to test well.

What has been repeatedly described as "the continuing tension in our society between egalitarianism and meritocracy" [29] is reflected in the aptitude-versus-achievement question. The force behind the drive for equal opportunity is egalitarian. It entails the acceptance of two premises: (1) that differences in ability levels reflect inconsistent environmental influences and (2) that the allocation of higher education opportunity should not be based on assumptions that attribute differences in ability to anything other than environment. By contrast, meritocracy reflects social opportunity. Buried within its tenets are notions of relatively unalterable individual differences that support the social hierarchy awarding the merit. This tension between meritocracy and egalitarianism—or, as it is also described by some writers, the "tension between quality and equality" [30]—is pervasive and is buttressed by conflicting assumptions regarding intelligence and mental ability. Continually fueling the application of these assumptions are economic considerations. It is argued that it may be more costly to admit many students by means of a more egalitarian "open admissions" policy that does not factor in aptitude-type entrance test scores because the dropout rate may be higher. Highly selective admissions standards factor in these test results to cut the number of dropout students. [31] What this line of argument suggests is that in times when economic efficiency is emphasized, admissions policies may be driven in a more meritocratic, selective, aptitude-oriented, test-based direction. In times of economic largesse, admissions policies may be driven in a more egalitarian, fair-representation, open, nonaptitude, non-test-based direction. It is also reminiscent of the model of the shifting demand for intelligence proposed by Cattell.

INTELLIGENCE

Within scientific research on intelligence there is, as elsewhere, a fundamental tension. Is intelligence innate or environmentally determined? If it is some of both, how are these influences balanced? The adequacy and fairness of the use of a representation of a unitary core intelligence, an intelligence quotient ("IQ"), as a measure of intelligence has been hotly contested, and many alternative definitions have been suggested. The nature–nurture (or what could be called aptitude–achievement) dilemma has been obscured but not eliminated by differing interpretations, sometimes implicit but more often explicit, of the data.

Howard Gardner, responding to the constraints of the unitary intelligence model, described his theory of multiple intelligences. This theory undermines theories of a single, general innate mental capacity, a capacity that is measurable in everyone. Gardner suggested that it is more appropriate to measure multiple intelligences. He wrote, "I have taken some pains . . . to avoid pitting genetic against cultural factors." [32] However, he did note that "social scientists need a framework that, while taking into account genetic predisposition and neuro-biological factors, recognizes the formative role played by the environment." [33] As much as the genetic–cultural or nature–nurture polarity can be avoided in discussion and in research, it is not eliminated. Even when the discussion allows for the cofactoring of nature and nurture, which it usually does, there is still the question of which elements of mental ability are contributed by each and to what degree. The balance of nature and nurture continues to be debated.

The theory of multiple intelligences, as Gardner suggests, "challenges the classical view of intelligence that most of us have absorbed explicitly (from psychology or education texts) or implicitly (by living in a culture with a strong but possibly circumscribed view of intelligence)." [34] Note how Gardner describes a process of explicit and implicit absorption of theories of intelligence.

To understand the various conceptions of intelligence Robert Sternberg posed a comprehensive framework that incorporates competing theories of intelligence into a series of levels and interactions. [35] In so doing, Sternberg integrates otherwise competing notions of intelligence. This can be viewed as an ecological or systems model of the loci in which intelligence is influenced, manifested, and observed, a system of phenomena or of definitions of intelligence. The ideas about intelligence listed in the Sternberg framework are operative as either explicit or implicit components of many programs and policies. (See Table 7.1 for a condensed version of the Sternberg model.)

Intelligence Quotient

The literature on intelligence draws on research in a number of fields. Both within and across participating fields there is great tension regarding human intelligence. [37] The scientific hereditarian stance on intelligence is that intelligence is primarily determined by genetic inheritance and that environment has less significant or little, if any, effect on it. [38]

In the 1920s Spearman contributed the concept of a "general factor" or "g" that is common to all items on a cognitive test. This "g" was contrasted with the "specific factor" or "s," which was unique to a particular item on a cognitive test. Therefore, "s" is content related and "g" is not. This is Spearman's two-factor theory of intelligence. [39] In the two decades following Spearman's proposal, various writers, including Thurstone, contended that intelligence is multifactorial rather than bifactorial. [40] Cattell, who listed various elements of "g" rather than a single "g," built his construct of intelligence around a model positing two basic general factors. Cattell differentiated between innate, or "fluid" ("g_f"), and

Table 7.1.   Loci of Intelligence (Excerpted
from Sternberg Framework—Foundation
for Further Conceptual Organization [36])

I.   In Individual
   A.   Biological Level
      1.   Across Organisms
      2.   Within Organisms
      3.   Across-Within Interaction
   B.   Molar Level (Mental Functioning)
      1.   Cognitive
         a.   Metacognition
         b.   Cognition
            i.   Processes
               (a) selective attention
               (b) learning
               (c) reasoning
               (d) problem solving
               (e) decision making
            ii. Knowledge
         c.   Metacognition–Cognition Interaction
      2.   Motivational
   C.   Behavioral Level
      1.   Academic
      2.   Social
      3.   Practical
   D.   Biological–Molar–Behavioral Interaction
II. In Environment
   A.   Level of Culture/Society
   B.   Level of Niche Within Culture/Society
   C.   Level X Sublevel Interation
III. Individual–Environment Interaction

acquired, or "crystallized" ("g_c"), intelligences. He claimed that "fluid ability is conceived as a power which is a function of the total, effective, associative, cortical cell mass and of certain parameters of efficiency in those cells. The efficiencies are concerned with metabolic rate, biochemical qualities, . . . and freedom from too high a burden of memory storage." [41] Crystallized intelligence is, by contrast, connected and responsive to cultural stimulation and not to overall cortical mass or efficiency. [42]

    Spearman's general factor, or "g," nevertheless became known as "general" intelligence. Although Spearman's analysis focused on statistical relationships among answers to test items and not at all on the heritability of intelligence, Spearman's "g," or what it was understood to be, became the basis for the perceived implication that basic or core intelligence is innate. Racial differences in cognitive tests scores were studied and became the focus of great controversy.

As early as 1927 Spearman proposed differences in intelligence between African-Americans and whites. [43] In 1969, in a controversial article published in the *Harvard Educational Review*, U.C. Berkeley Professor of Psychology Arthur Jensen suggested that compensatory educational programs failed to increase the IQ scores of African-American students because the programs focused on environmental variables when genetic factors (particularly within-race heritability) were, he felt, actually the primary determinants of IQ differences. [44] Numerous studies have concluded that African-Americans score one standard deviation (15 points) lower than whites on IQ tests. [45] However, there has been great disagreement about the reasons for this difference and about the use of IQ and other traditional tests to measure intelligence and differences in intelligence [46], the argument against them being that simply finding racial differences in test scores does not speak to the matter of the heritability of these differences.

Jensen writes that "educational performance is highly but not perfectly correlated" with "g"; that "g" is the "main source of variance in educational achievement"; and that this is true "in any setting at any age," whether it be early school, higher education, or work life. [47] Educational achievement and educational outcome are among the key concerns of education policies such as university admissions policies, which are the focus of the latter chapters of this book. Sociopolitical explanations for differences in academic achievement, especially in the area of ethnic differences, counter Jensen's argument with contentions that discrimination, cultural differences, poverty, and other factors actually account for these differences.

Heritability

Proof of the heritability of intelligence is viewed by some as the counterpoint to the sociopolitical arguments in favor of its environmental origins. The degree to which intelligence is innate, or inherited, has been and continues to be the focus of a large body of behavioral and genetic research. Because they are of the same genetic composition, identical twins reared in different environments have provided great opportunities for heritability research. Studies of identical twins suggest a strong genetic component to IQ, with average correlations on IQ tests being quite high—.86 (with the highest possible correlation being 1.0 and no correlation being 0). [48] Studies of the statistical relationship between identical twins' differences in birth weight and their differences in IQ suggest that differences in birth weight may explain much of the variance in their IQs. Identical twins frequently display marked disparity in birth weight, averaging about 10% of their total birth weights [49], and birth weight has been positively correlated with IQ. [50] Controlling for this systematic variability in twins' weights, their IQ correlations have been measured as statistically significant. [51] These and other studies of identical and fraternal twins reared apart and together provide a large body of data that weighs in the direction of the heritability of intelligence or of some aspect of intelligence.

Many studies of first-degree relatives also suggest that IQ is driven by heredity. [52] Adoption studies indicate significantly lower correlations in IQ between adoptive family members and the adopted children. [53] Although adoption studies suggest that IQ is not strongly influenced by environment, other studies indicate that various elements of environment—such as prenatal environment [54], mother–infant relationship and communication, sibling order [55], family size [56], parental age, among numerous other factors [57]—contribute to the influence of family environment on IQ. [58]

Yet the family environment does not exist in a vacuum. It exists within the overarching society. Although they suggest that inherited traits explain a significant portion of measured intelligence, pro-heritability findings do not maintain that environment has no effect. Pro-environmentalism findings contend that the environment, especially the encompassing sociopolitical environment, is a profound determinant of measured mental ability. Social-level explanations of intelligence that form arguments against the pro-heritability interpretations of twin, relative, and adoptee studies are discussed in one of the following subsections. Of course, the definition of intelligence that is applied mediates all discussion of its determinants.

GIFTEDNESS

No discussion of intelligence policy can overlook the notion of giftedness. Giftedness is excellence of some sort, and excellence is a prized commodity. Excellence serves as a model for individuals, a symbol for nations, a meter of possibility for humanity. This thing called excellence can manifest itself in almost any area of human endeavor. However, if the culture in which the excellence is manifested does not place value on that particular area, the excellence will remain unrecognized. This oversight can cost a society a great deal, especially in the area of creativity. In the words of philosopher Arnold Toynbee, "To give a fair chance to potential creativity is a matter of life and death for any society." [59]

The Difficulty of Defining Giftedness

It is particularly disappointing and damaging when there is an oversight of talent or giftedness in a child. [60] Oversights occur at all grade levels but most easily in the early years, before a child's intellectual functions consolidate into the set of cognitive skills that are functionally related to adult intelligence. [61] One of the greatest challenges in the identification of gifted children is to recognize them at an early age. [62] When giftedness, even in conventional subject areas, is not detected early, it may never be developed to its fullest potential. Worse yet, it may never be detected at all.

Schools, quite naturally, are most likely to identify giftedness when it appears in conventional subject areas such as science, mathematics, writing, or athletics. However, giftedness even in these areas can be overlooked. [63] This oversight can be the result of the inadequacy of assignments, tests [64], or other obscuring factors in drawing out the giftedness.

As early as 1874, Sir Francis Galton, who invented the correlational method that underlies psychometric analysis, attempted to study giftedness in the domain of intellectual activity. The characteristics he identified were vivid imagination, fluent mental association, high energy, good health, independence, purposefulness, and a powerful enough drive to overcome internal and external constraints. [65] Four decades later, in the 1920s, Terman, chief author of the Stanford-Binet intelligence test, defined a gifted person as one who has a high level of general intelligence, as measured by conventional intelligence tests covering language development, reasoning and classification skills, perceptual syntheses, and decision-making processes. Terman also described a gifted individual as being highly creative, having an extraordinary ability to adapt to new situations, exercising sensitive judgment in solving problems, and learning from experience. [66]

The early definitions of giftedness tended to focus on what was presumed to be innate intellectual ability (perhaps of origin *within* the mind, as the philosophical rationalists would have said). More recently, definitions of giftedness have been expanded beyond the "core" intelligence ("g") assessed by traditional IQ tests to include other modes of giftedness. For example, gifted education specialist M. M. Piechowski named five modes in which giftedness can be expressed: the psychomotor mode, the sensual mode, the intellectual mode, the imaginative mode, and the emotional mode. The actual expression of giftedness in any of Piechowski's five modes occurs when an individual is both highly talented and highly excitable. He or she reacts intensely to experience and expresses this reaction in one of these modes. [67]

Research regarding the specific characteristics of the creatively gifted has indicated that these individuals are indeed subject to greater intensity of feeling and do react more strongly to stimuli. [68] A frequently cited model of giftedness is that designed by psychologist Joseph Renzulli. His theoretical model consists of a triad composed of above-average ability, task commitment, and creativity. These components of giftedness are brought to bear on general performance areas such as mathematics, language, and visual or movement arts and on specific performance areas such as cartooning, microphotography, film criticism, musical composition, and city planning. The result is gifted performance. [69]

Another iteration of giftedness is offered by Sternberg, a major contributor of new ideas in the field of intelligence (and author of the full version of Table 7.1).

Sternberg emphasizes the ability to perceive a problem along with the ability to learn how to solve it. The importance of problem posing is not to be overshadowed by the emphasis placed on problem solving. Sternberg views problem detection as being a valuable contribution made by the gifted. Posing and solving a problem is a process composed of all of the following components: the metaperformance, acquisition, retention, and transfer. [70]

The definition of giftedness has changed with the temperament of the times. Controversy regarding the innateness of intelligence has been answered with new definitions of intelligence and of giftedness. [71] Some of the opposition to gifted education is that it appears to arise "from the mistaken belief that gifted and talented children automatically shine," resulting in their almost automatic success and social approval [72], and from the fact that special gifted programs are closed to those who do not shine so automatically but who require educational opportunities at least as much. Today, the task of defining giftedness is complicated by both political and theoretical difficulties. These issues are frequently blended, primarily because educational research and programming are highly dependent on asocietal resources, usually in the form of public funding.

Policy Struggles with Definition

A large body of international literature on giftedness has emerged in recent decades, especially since the First World Conference on Gifted and Talented Children in London in 1975. [73] The literature on giftedness contains various and often conflicting characterizations of the gifted. As a step above this conflict and perhaps with an eye toward policy and program enhancement, Sternberg suggests that evidence of "differential efficacy" in a number of areas can be used to differentiate the gifted from the nongifted. He says that the gifted show "accelerated acquisition" of knowledge and constructs; "accelerated automatization" (i.e., they perform rote mechanical operations and process information more quickly); more responsive and more "automatic activation" of componential thought processes; a greater tendency for emotive alignment (perhaps "passionate involvement" is a better phrase) with the subject under study; a higher level of sustained inquisitiveness; and more higher-order insight, abstraction, and meta-analysis. [74] The gifted are also characterized as being able to juggle more than one idea at a time, as preferring complexity to the obvious [75], as thinking more independently and therefore being less "syllabus bound" [76], and as being better able to operate on an interdisciplinary basis. [77] These criteria are more complex than those that have defined IQ, but they make room for a wider variety of individuals. The following are basic definitions of giftedness that have emerged in the literature on gifted education: superior intellectual potential and ability (approximately 120+ IQ) [78]; high ability to achieve in areas ranging from the "3 Rs" to art, leadership, and music [79]; and an interaction among three basic clusters of human traits, namely, above-average general ability, high levels of task commitment, and high levels of creativity. [80] The latter two definitions make room for a wider range of abilities and the individuals exhibiting them.

The growing body of literature on giftedness includes descriptions and evaluations of the components of educational programs for gifted students. A review of hundreds of evaluations of gifted programs in the United States reveals broad heterogeneity in admission standards, program design, curriculum, outcome measures, and overall outcome. [81] While this heterogeneity offers diversity and the potential of meeting a broad range of educational needs, it also results in great disparities. [82] This profound lack of consistency and cohesiveness in gifted education is representative of the low priority gifted education receives and the decentralized approach to gifted education typical in the United States. To be sure, gifted education suffers from the same low social priority and incoherent policy associated with all public education in the United States. However, advocates of gifted education argue that gifted education has low priority among educators themselves [83] and that when it is time to allocate the resources earmarked for education, gifted education is budgeted for with reluctance and great reservation. [84] Perhaps this reflects societal inhibitions and ambivalence regarding the definitions of mental ability.

SOCIOLOGICAL ASPECTS OF INTELLIGENCE

The foregoing discussion of testing, definitions of intelligence, and giftedness brings us to the broader consideration of sociological aspects of intelligence.

Environmental Influence on IQ

The 20th century has witnessed a continuing increase in comprehensive IQ test scores. [85] Whether or not similar increases occurred in previous centuries remains unknown because comprehensive IQ tests are a 20th-century product. The broad improvements in health and nutrition of the 20th century suggest that environment does indeed influence IQ. However, there is considerable argument against the conclusion that environment accounts for the majority of the increase in IQ. The timing of health trends, such as advances in neonatal care and the use of particular vaccines and antibiotics, does not correspond to a rapid rate of IQ growth. [86] And yet it has been argued that certain exceptional abilities that are displayed among various ethnographic subpopulations and that neither develop nor dissipate over a single generation do develop more rapidly over a smaller number of generations than population genetics can explain. [87] Some combination of deterioration or improvement in environment and genetic–environmental (GE) interaction is offered as an explanation. [88] Even so, modest improvements in environment may not be enough to produce a powerful GE interaction. For example, it has been estimated that to generate a 5-to-7-point increase in population IQ, two-thirds of all current home environments would have to improve enough to surpass the top third of all such environments. [89]

Cultural Discontinuity

Those who argue against heritability as the dominant determinant of intelligence maintain that cultural disparity and discontinuity are powerful determinants of variations in measured intelligence. [90] Ethnic groups who have not been full participants in the dominant culture and who suffer persistent economic and social discrimination develop communication and social styles in opposition to the dominating culture. These are "secondary cultural discontinuities," as Ogbu describes them [91], and they must be recognized by university admissions policies. These discontinuities develop in response to a disadvantageous contact situation and then survive as a means of identity preservation for the minority group. While primary cultural discontinuities, such as the discontinuity between home and school, are experienced by everyone, the secondary discontinuities are reactive in nature, limited to disadvantaged subgroups, and much more difficult to overcome in the school environment. These secondary discontinuities are frequently too great to *want* to overcome in the school environment.

Ogbu categorizes social minorities into three groups: autonomous, immigrant, and caste. [92] Caste, or subordinate, minorities have been involuntarily co-opted into society via mechanisms such as slavery or colonization. They are denied the opportunity to assimilate into the dominant culture, are relegated to menial tasks, and are generally perceived to be inferior to the dominant culture. While formal education is viewed as the means of ascending the social ladder by members of the dominant culture, caste-like minorities do not necessarily expect that a given level of education will have the same value for them that it has for members of the dominant culture. [93] Ogbu argues that current IQ tests measure skills that are critical in schools and in jobs, that these skills and jobs are largely unavailable to African-Americans, and that African-Americans do not tend to acquire as much IQ-type intelligence as whites or demonstrate it on standard IQ tests because it is a symbol of the oppressive culture and has no functional value in their lives. [94] This raises a question of the value of fair representation university admissions in the absence of other major changes in university curricula and occupational structures.

Difficulty Measuring Macroenvironmental Impacts

The sociopolitical determination of intelligence may be so massive that its greatest mechanisms cannot be seen. Princeton University Professor Leon Kamin, a strong defender of the environmentalist position, argues that "the careful examination of the studies of heritability of IQ can leave us with only one conclusion: we do not know what the heritability of IQ really is. . . . The question of IQ is irrelevant to the matters at issue." [95] He also notes that genetic differences between the races are "negligible as compared with the polymorphism within each group" [96] and that "human 'racial' differentiation is, indeed, only skin deep." [97] Kamin maintains that the heritability of a trait such as IQ only tells us "how much genetic and environmental variation exists in the population *in the current set of environments.*" The power of environment in a different set of environments cannot necessarily be predicted. [98]

Technological Opportunities for the Redefinition of Intelligence

Given Kamin's contention, it is possible that there are social changes or even technological innovations on the horizon that may increase the power of environment in determining intelligence. For example, metacognitive training [99], the teaching of thinking skills, the mechanisms of intelligent thought, may alter the power of education to bring students into the fold of the dominant intelligence (whether they find the experience desirable or not). Education, the knowledge structure offered by the dominant culture, is to a great extent engaged in conflict with highly prevalent "alternative" or "less desirable" knowledge structures. [100] In physics and in other domains, education confronts, disassembles, and reshapes "inappropriate" knowledge structures. [101] In young children such educational intervention can take place before the "wrong" knowledge structures are deeply embedded. However, as students mature, the "wrong" structures can become deeply embedded. High school and college may be too late unless we develop new teaching methodologies. [102] Learning what makes knowledge structures assemble within the mind may lead to assembling more viable and more powerful knowledge structures within more minds, with the possibility of raising the average mental ability of the population.

THE PLATFORM OF COGNITIVE SCIENCE: A CONCEPTUAL BRIDGE?

While much of the research and professional literature on mental ability can be organized around the nature–nurture dilemma, modern cognitive science and its offshoot, metacognitive science, offer a bridge between the poles of the perceived dilemma. Perhaps science will make it possible to teach a mind to improve its ability to think, to raise its intelligence. If intelligence can be altered by scientists, then it can be made accessible to most students. Nature recedes as a new technology of nurture emerges, one that is more powerful, technically more competent, better suited to modern human goals. Gardner writes that "the triumph of cognitivism has been to place talk of representation on essentially equal footing with those entrenched modes of discourse—with the neuronal level, on one hand, and with the sociocultural level, on the other." [103]

In a sociopolitical environment of increasing technology, increasing competition, and increasing disparity of opportunity, differences in measured mental ability may increase. Proponents of environmentalism may argue that this is the result of environmental disparity. Proponents of biological determinism may argue that this is the result of the disproportionate growth of particular segments of the population. Whatever the reasons for the disparity, the problem of disparity may not be insurmountable. The science of cognition may advance far enough that new educational interventions can improve mental processes and ability. Both nature and nurture can then be superseded. This line of thinking was discussed earlier from a sociopolitical standpoint; now it can be viewed from a research standpoint.

New developments in cognitive science are especially important in the consideration of education policies that affect adults, such as university admissions policy. Cattell claims that crystallized intelligence (g_c), which is, by definition, the acquired form of intelligence, remains level or even increases from age 20 to 65 whereas fluid intelligence (g_f), which is, by definition, physiologically innate, declines steadily (with age) beginning between the ages of 20 and 25. [104] Thus, it may be the educability and consequent utilization of young adults that is especially affected by new developments in cognitive science. Which abilities can be developed in college and which will decline? Can these paths of mental development be altered?

Cognitive scientists use the term *metacognitive activity* for higher-order thinking, or control-level thinking, that is, for the mental processes involved in thinking about thinking itself. [105] A mental suprastructure exists within the mind. In the words of Gardner,

> The major accomplishment of cognitive science has been the clear demonstration of the validity of positing a level of mental representation: a set of constructs that can be invoked for the explanation of cognitive phenomena, ranging from visual perception to story comprehension. Where forty years ago . . . few scientists dared to speak of schemas, images, rules, transformations, and other mental structures and operations, these representational assumptions and concepts are now taken for granted. [106]

Cognitive science thus opens the door to new (or asks again the old) questions about the mind. Once these mental structures and operations are believed to exist, there is cause to wonder where it is that they originate. In light of evidence that the head houses a powerful biocomputer [107], there is new emphasis on the biological basis of intelligence: The brain is more readily accepted as being the originator and director of mental activity and of the mental structures that organize and operate on that activity. For many, the new scientific view of the brain renders the genetic explanation of intelligence more palatable than ever: The brain is complex enough to give rise to thoughts from within itself, with or without environmental (external) stimulation. So the argument goes: *If the complexity of the brain is inherited and if it affects the intelligence of the individual who inherits that complexity, then intelligence is somehow affected by genetic makeup.*

Cognitive Science Can Deflect the Dilemma

Whether or not the effectiveness and the ultimate origin of any one individual's cognitive schemata are entirely or even partially biologically determined is a controversial matter. Yet, according to Gardner, most cognitive scientists no longer care whether the rationalists or the empiricists win the debate. [108] Cognitive scientists find the cognitive schemata to be so very important in themselves that notions regarding their ultimate origin take a back seat. Knowledge structures and the mental abilities based on them can arise in a variety of contexts, but once they exist it is important to handle them well. Regardless of their origins, knowledge structures may be susceptible to the intervention of educators. This means that university admissions policies may be able to bring in students who need special training in intellectual skills and expect these students to do well.

Cognitive scientists focus on the special significance of higher or "meta" cognition, the level of cognition that structures, organizes, and operates on basic cognition. Consider, for example, mature reading skills. There are specific ways in which knowledge structures affect reading ability. The reader must be able to organize "schemata" (knowledge structures) in sufficient amounts and of enough general ability so that they can be applied to many different texts. The reader must then be able to select from among his or her repertoire of schemata or knowledge structures, the ones most appropriate to the understanding of the reading material. In applying the selected schema, the reader must be able to modify or adapt them to best understand what a given text is about. [109] The ability to apply, access, and adapt appropriate knowledge structures is metacognitive ability. Academic performance is dependent on sufficient acquisition and application of appropriate knowledge structures; it is dependent on metacognition.

Thinking as a Process

Today, the acquisition of knowledge is viewed as an elaborate system of processes. Thinking is viewed as a "complex but understandable *process.*" More than ever, an emphasis is placed on the mental process itself. [110] This new model of knowing about reality assumes a process or set of processes that are highly responsive to and reflective of experience. Processes are more malleable than cerebral hardware, which seems to be more permanently configured.

Educators Interact with Preexisting Mental Structures

Caution must be exercised in educators' efforts to mold students' mental structures. Educator and physicist diSessa contends that "education is an interaction with the thinking process and can influence it best by respecting the present structure of the process." [111] The student arrives in the classroom with a host of previous experiences; the slate is not blank (if it even was blank at birth!). These experiences affect, if not determine entirely, students' thought processes, their abilities to learn, their apparent intelligences. Whether or not they realize it, educators interact with the preexisting notions of reality maintained by their students. Educators come face to face with the mind as empiricist. In this sense, educators seek to retrain the empiricist minds of their students. When classrooms contain a multicultural cross-section of the population, educators can face a complex array of conflicting knowledge structures.

Recent research demonstrates that education that teaches to students' preexisting mental contexts is more effective than education that proceeds as if students' minds were either devoid of all previous impressions or filled with identical impressions. [112] All too often, a teacher is tempted to assume that the reason for a student's incorrect answers is low intelligence. [113] While this is an understandable assumption, it is frequently incorrect. This assumption is based on the teacher's lack of information about the alternative knowledge structures of students. For example, there is a growing body of research regarding the development of knowledge and reasoning in physics and related subject areas. [114] Among its findings is the fact that students' naive theories of physics affect their understanding of the laws of physics. [115]

Misconceptions Are Not Signs of Low Intelligence

The science of physics is a study in which a huge superstructure of mental theory, conceptualization, and mathematical abstraction is superimposed on empirical data. A student's naive understanding of physics is also based on empirical data. However, the mental superstructure that processes the data is not trained in the science of physics. Students arrive in their first physics class not as "blank slates" in the areas of force and motion [116] but with, in the words of physicist-educator Michael McCloskey, "remarkably well-articulated naive theories of motion." [117] (Descartes said that dreaming illusions formed out of sensory data is preferred over acknowledging the truth.) Although these theories describe and provide causal explanations for the behavior of moving objects, they also buttress a host of misconceptions that run counter to the laws of physics. (Perhaps these are the pleasant illusions described by Descartes or are indications that Descartes's rigorous system of methodic doubt is not in use by humans in their daily lives.)

Some of these misconceptions are similar to medieval explanations of force and motion [118], and many have, in the eyes of physicists, what seem to be childlike qualities. Most of these naive explanations of force and motion are shared by many people who have not studied physics. [119] What does it mean when misconceptions based on allegedly empirical ways of knowing are shared by many people? Does this indicate that many share the same naive version of external reality because many minds are structured to process a rather fictional external reality in the same way?

Whatever the specific misconceptions of childlike (i.e., untrained and therefore "naive") physicists, they are resilient and highly resistant to change even in the face of contradictory evidence. A noted physicist suggests that these misconceptions have become "embedded into the system" at the perceptual-motor ('gut') level rather than at an abstract level." [120] What people "know" about present reality on the basis of interpretation of sensory experience from the past is not always correct. Bombs do not drop directly down from moving planes even though that is expected (they curve downward). Water does not gush from a coiled hose in a spiral (it shoots straight out). Yet many people who have had several courses in physics will continue to provide reasons why the bombs drop straight and water gushes in a spiral. Their reasoning is based on what they believe they have seen rather than on what they later mentally imposed on their previous mental schemata of what they experienced.

Old belief systems die hard, when they can be put to rest at all. The process of changing one's mind, changing one's mental processing, may require a great deal of what educator and computer scientist Michael Ranney terms "coherence-enhancing reorganizations among naive beliefs." [121] These require activities that provide individuals with experiences that are "incoherent," or incompatible with their naive beliefs, as well as with alternative predictions, feedback, and new explanations for physical events that they have previously explained naively. [122] Coherence-enhancing activities can be provided by educators who understand the notion of conflicting knowledge structures. The delicacy and adeptness of such an educational intervention, a reformulation of mental schemata, calls for careful training of the educators who attempt to reach into their students' mental programming.

Mental Schemata Are Malleable

What seems to be low intelligence may actually be the expression of intelligent but naive experientially developed assumptions that have been woven into schemata (or knowledge structures). [123] Whether or not intelligence is learnable, the mental schemata it designs can be modified, adapted, and even rebuilt. If the mind is a learning organ, it can learn to revise its knowledge structures. What does it take to bring about such a revision? How fixed and exclusive do the intuitive schemata become in the early years? How early do they mature, and does their growth end? Can higher education intervene in this process? Can preexisting schemata of childhood be reformulated as late as early adulthood?

The Structure of Knowledge

To answer such questions, researchers are reaching deeply into the fabric of the mind. The very structure of knowledge is the subject of current research in the areas of cognition and metacognition. Perhaps following the footsteps of earlier philosophers on both sides of the debate, diSessa delineates two basic purposes of knowledge: [124]

- *Material knowledge*, the purpose of which is to be "directed externally, toward the structure of physical events or abstract relations"
- *Control knowledge*, the purpose of which is to be "directed internally toward personal functioning and the structure of thinking itself"

It is tempting to suggest that these definitions fall along the empiricist–rationalist axis. It is tempting to say that material knowledge is primarily empirical and that its purpose is to know about the environment whereas control knowledge is primarily rational and its purpose is to know knowing. Yet beyond the clarity of theoretical delineation, these purposes of knowledge intertwine; they overlay and support each other. Material knowledge is "directed externally," and control knowledge is "directed internally." Whence comes the direction? There must be some director that directs these.

In addition to these basic and relatively dichotomous purposes of knowledge, diSessa identifies two basic forms of knowledge: [125]

- *Knowledge-of-procedure*, in which there exists "an explicit surface structure which is step-by-step procedure" containing "explicit reference to purpose and what circumstances make the procedure usable"
- *Knowledge-within-process*, in which "the purpose of the knowledge is only evident in the control structure that evokes the process, or in the function it serves; indeed, the actual subject of the knowledge may be quite invisible"

Knowledge-of-procedure is a map of how to proceed in transactions with the phenomenal world, which is generally called material. Knowledge-within-process is difficult to detect. However, it controls the thinking process; it requires the mind to apply particular forms and procedures to its thoughts. Knowledge-within-process maps mental functioning for the mind; it is *meta*cognitive, overseeing cognition.

Such a clear delineation of the forms of knowledge is comforting. Yet before being tempted to organize these forms of knowledge along the rationalist–

empiricist axis, one must acknowledge that, upon close examination, the boundaries of these two basic forms of knowledge fade. Knowledge-of-procedure may rely on knowledge-within-process for direction, for executive control. Knowledge-within-process may be quite invisible but may be affected by the interaction of material knowledge with the environment; therefore, it can perhaps be manipulated by a corresponding manipulation of the environment.

Clearly, knowledge-of-procedure is the more likely of these two to be explicitly learned. But what of the more mysterious, elusive knowledge-within-process? Could this actually be core intelligence, the seemingly heritable "g" factor? Could it be influenced by the neurological competence that other lines of research suggest to be biologically determined? Does metacognition operate independently of mental hardware? Or can it mold and direct the development of mental hardware? How plastic is knowledge-of-procedure?

As research suggests [126], if naive and alternative knowledge structures can be displaced, modified, or reformulated, they have probably been learned in the first place.

Policy Implications

Cognitive science may succeed in moving beyond the struggles between merit and representation, aptitude and achievement; however, this same struggle continues in education and in overarching social policy. Whether it be special supportive services at the college level, mainstreaming, special education, gifted programs, teaching to the test, or testing to track, these educational "interventions" are all acting on students' minds—which are alternately viewed as being either entirely, partially, or barely malleable. Educational programs and policies continue to masquerade as programs and policies when they are actually experiments on involuntary human subjects in the social laboratory. If the mind is the originator of knowledge, can it be guided by educators toward the realization of higher mental competence and intelligence? To be fair, it must also be asked whether the mind guides itself from within, independently, in spite of external stimulation. Is the environment the source of all knowledge and are the senses its analog transmitters—or not? What can educators really do with their students' minds? Is the sky really the limit? Is anything possible? *Is intelligence learnable?*

Unresolved and provocative questions such as these reflect deeper, unresolved philosophical questions regarding the source of knowledge. These questions continue to be the root of the intellectual tension in modern education policy and programming. Because these questions and tensions are permitted to lurk invisibly behind the scene, they upset, obscure, and manipulate the very definitions of knowledge and intelligence on which admissions policy and other educational decision making is based. It is as if an invisible tail is wagging a visible monster.

8

Rationalist versus Empiricist Views
The Philosophical Backdrop on the Learnability of Intelligence

A freeman ought not to be a slave in the acquisition of knowledge of any kind.

PLATO [1]

Issues surrounding knowledge acquisition inspire unending discussion and heated debate. Because philosophy is "the oldest of the cognitive sciences," [2] there must be a dialogue with long-deceased as well as living philosophers when intelligence is discussed. Yet too frequently a deep engagement in this dialogue remains in the unconscious, especially as modern education policies are developed. Consider the following frequently cited comments by Socrates and Glaucon:

SOCRATES: Citizens, we shall say to them in our tale, you are brothers, yet God has framed you differently. . . . Such is the tale; is there any possibility of making our citizens believe in it?

GLAUCON (*in reply to Socrates' question*): Not in the present generation; there is no way of accomplishing this; but their sons may be made to believe in the tale, and their son's sons, and posterity after them. [3]

Centuries ago, Socrates and Glaucon discussed the concept that God has framed every person differently, that each is born with significant individual differences. Although Glaucon doubted that this concept would be accepted by his own countrymen, he did not doubt that future citizens could be made to accept this view of divine involvement in class and capability distinction. Even when this notion is debated in this modern era, it is as if this divine involvement is accepted on some very deep level.

And, at the same time, it is denied just as deeply. Many centuries after Socrates posed the dilemma as a political one, social philosopher John Dewey placed the determination of the social order not in God's predetermining hands or in the perpetuation of such a belief but in the hands of the environment—including the schools:

> Schools thereby do take part in the determination of a future social order; accordingly, the problem is not whether the schools should participate in the production of a future society (since they do so anyway) but whether they should do it blindly and irresponsibly or with the maximum possible courageous intelligence and responsibility. . . . The existing state of society, which the schools reflect, is not something fixed or uniform. The idea that such is the case is a self-imposed hallucination. [4]

Although philosophical division lines have long been drawn, education still plays on a field of doubt regarding the source of mental ability. So deeply embedded in education policy is the confusion regarding the acquisition of mental ability that the organization of education is molded by it. What appears to be a marvelous feat of political compromise may be the official incorporation of confusion.

The tension between academic merit and fair representation policies, between the view that intelligence predicts worldly success and the view that higher education predicts worldly success, and between measures of aptitude and achievement—all were foreshadowed by a basic philosophical dilemma. This age-old philosophical debate has always been quite simple. *Rationalists* have maintained that the mind imposes its powers of reasoning on all incoming sensory experience and that the mind is best suited to *know* when it relies on its internal rationality rather than on sensory data from the environment. *Empiricists*, on the other side of the argument, have maintained that to "know" is to have ample foundation on externally induced sensory impressions and that there is no correct knowledge without full use of these impressions. Although various mixes of rationalism and empiricism have emerged over time, they have not diffused the essential conflict between these two diametrically opposed views.

Why journey into such a basic philosophical dilemma in an examination of social, specifically educational, policy? Because policy makers continue to struggle between the two positions, sometimes consciously but usually without acknowledging or even realizing they are doing so. Rationalist and empiricist perspectives have subtle but powerful influence on modern views, on the interpretation of modern data, and on the understanding of genetic and behavioral research regarding what can be called the *learnability* of intelligence and mental ability. (Because the very definition of intelligence depends on the philosophical perspective in which it is borne, this discussion does not attempt to define intelligence here; rather, the focus is on its philosophical encasement.) These perspectives have filtered their ways into education and even dictate many of the political views regarding it. These perspectives are powerfully operative, even in the formulation of such critical policy as that of college admissions. The politics of opportunity allocation, which is reflected in college admissions policies, is built on largely philosophical assumptions regarding the learnability of mental ability. There must be an effort to recognize and trace the impact of policies built on these assumptions, no matter how unspoken or implicit they may be.

THE LEGACY OF RATIONALISM

In order to unravel the network of assumptions regarding intelligence that influences social policies, it is necessary to look at the origins of these assumptions. While many are familiar with the various philosophers cited in this chapter, a review of their comments is valuable for policy implications. (The philosophical view of the mind is graphically depicted as Continuum a in Figure 4.1.)

Ancient Notions of Knowledge and Intelligence

The legacy of rationalism can be traced back to the 4th and 5th centuries B.C. in ancient Greece. The works of Plato inspired a family of philosophical movements that embraced his belief in the existence of an absolute knowledge that is rooted in the realm of eternal realities that are independent or even generative of the world perceived by the senses. [5] This model of knowledge has persisted through time.

Knowledge and intelligence, in the form of intellect, were confluent in the philosophy of Plato. He viewed the intellect as the dominant and most important part of the soul. He did not concern himself much with individual differences in intelligence or the environmental influences that might cause them. However, in *The Republic* Plato did distinguish between certain types of people, namely, philosophers, warriors, and artisans. This suggestion of individual differences was one of the earliest formulations of ability differences and of a hierarchy of mental functions. It was also an occupational hierarchy. For Plato, the mind, being part of the soul rather than of the material body, was not subject to individual differences beyond those given in occupations, and if it had been, the differences would not have been explained primarily by environmental influences; in the rationalist model, the mind exists independently of and precedes any experience of the external world. [6]

Also central to Platonic rationalism is the great value placed on the mental domain. Plato's emphasis on reason as the highest of human activities, a reason that distinguishes man from animals in that it lies within the domain of the soul rather than the flesh, lingers to this day. Intellectual and educational achievement are highly prized. The mental domain is considered to be the source of all innovation and continuity.

It was Plato's student Aristotle who helped secure the honored place of intelligence by bringing its definition into existence. Aristotle revised Plato's originally threefold view of the soul into two parts: (1) the dianoetic (cognitive) functions and (2) the oerectic (emotional) and moral functions. Following Aristotle, the Roman orator Cicero translated dianoetic into the Latin word *intelligenta*, from which the word *intelligence* is derived. [7]

Although the modern notion of *levels* of intelligence was slow to emerge, the differentiation of *types* of mental ability is quite ancient. Early Greek and subsequent Roman philosophers went so far as to consider the social utility of the different types of mental abilities. Centuries later, the Christian Scholastics, led by 13th-century theologian Thomas Aquinas, returned to the general notion of differences in mental abilities [8], although they did not focus on differences among individuals in the manner that modern psychology does. The conceptual level on which the Scholastics focused was the abstract philosophical and theological level, where the functions of the mind were divided into intellectual and appetitive functions, with the intellectual functions further divided into sensation, perception, memory and reproductive imagination, and reasoning and creative imagination. [9]

The threads of rationalism continued on through intellectual and cultural history. Some 400 years after Aquinas, 17th-century philosopher René Descartes expounded the age-old rationalist position that experience is not the path to knowledge. [10] Descartes's struggle to construct his own particular epistemology of rationalism was a precursor to the continuing but now more implicit struggle to develop an epistemology of intelligence, and thus of education. He therefore warrants extended attention here.

Descartes looked upon the senses as the source of biases and misinformation; the external world could not teach truth. He therefore undertook the task of developing a methodology that would enable a disciplined and reliable construction of true knowledge without dependence on sensory input. Descartes considered it feasible to extrapolate the formal logic of order and measure inherent in mathematics to nonquantitative spheres of thought. [11]

Only gradually did Descartes see the inadequacy of such a purely formal methodology and come to recognize the necessity for metaphysical doctrine in this regard. Mathematical schemata would not provide for validation in the nonquantitative spheres of thought. On a new tack, Descartes next incorporated into his method of proof his basic method of doubt. He then focused his method of doubt on the foundations of accepted knowledge. This allowed him to question the senses, the powers of imagination and memory, and even intellectual capability. Through this process Descartes arrived at the notion that the thinking self, independent of its physical reality, was undoubtedly existent, real, regardless of the status of its environment. [12] This logic can be extended to postulate that the ability of the thinking self to think rigorously is not determined by the environment.

From his lofty vantage point, Descartes devised a logical path to the notion of God. Metaphysical explanations buttressed the epistemology of Descartes.

Of the soul, Descartes eventually wrote: "What is required principally and primarily for knowing the soul is immortal is that we formulate as clear a concept of the soul as possible." [13] For a rationalist, a very clear, methodologically sound idea of something, even something as intangible as the immortal soul, establishes its reality and then the mind is the ultimate source and test of all knowledge, even knowledge of the soul. Great faith in the human mind permeates rationalism.

Transforming Ideas

According to Descartes, the mind permits the denial of the truth about reality. There is a preference to dream of illusions formed out of sensory data than to acknowledge the truth. Even of himself, Descartes said, "I am not unlike a prisoner who might enjoy an imaginary freedom in his sleep. When he later begins to suspect that he is sleeping, he fears being awakened and conspires slowly with these pleasant illusions." [14] There is a responsibility for the illusions created. What does this say about efforts to educate the human mind? Perhaps much of what is learned in the laboratory is an illusion, too dependent on the senses and a physical world, at best. Being a good rationalist Descartes concluded, "Modes of thinking—which I will call sensations and imaginations—insofar as they are only modes of thinking, are within me," [15] and not environmentally determined.

For a rationalist, anything learned experientially and constructed from what is obtained with the ears, eyes, and other senses is not valid. It is empirically set. Anything learned from existing nonsensual knowledge is a thinking of the mind and is, as rational thought, a mental production from initial source to final apprehension.

After Descartes, rationalism was developed further by 17th-century philosopher Benedict Baruch de Spinoza, but in a somewhat different direction. Spinoza was both heir to and critic of the Cartesian philosophy. The improvement of knowledge, according to Spinoza, lies in *transforming* confused ideas into adequate ones, in taking the distinct ideas already possessed as markers. [16] This notion of transforming ideas at first sounds as if it calls for external intervention. Yet the legacy of rationalism held its ground in Spinozistic thought. For Spinoza, there was no question that the improvement of an idea is accomplished *only* by a detachment from external natural causes and an attachment to or deeper understanding of the laws of one's own inherent nature. [17]

Highest Knowledge of God

A religious tone entered the history of the perception of the mind. Both Descartes and Spinoza included God in their discussions. The connection between highest knowledge and God is strong in Spinoza's epistemology: the mind is able to form a clear and distinct idea of itself, by viewing itself intuitively and a priori in its eternal essence, as constituted by the eternal power and attributes of God. Intuitive knowledge is consummated in an intellectual love of God, *amor Dei intellectualis*. [18] Thus, one becomes a partaker of God's love of Himself. Spinoza's God loves man only in the sense that He loves Himself, and so He makes *amor Dei intellectualis* a part of this infinite love for His own nature, in all its aspects. Furthermore, God is the only substance; there is no other. [19] In this case, rationalism dictates that everything—the perceived external world and the human mind—is a mode of divine substance. The emphasis on the connection between the intellect and the divine again surfaces. Again the great esteem for mental ability surfaces.

Analytical Reduction of Composite Ideas

The legacy of rationalism is one that places great emphasis on intuitive ideas possessed without external intercourse with a physical (including societal) environment. It does not allow for the possibility that the mind is blank until filled with sensory data. Besides declaring the existence of fundamental intuitive ideas, rationalism emphasizes the analytical reduction of composite ideas in the mind to their purely simple natures, the attainment of clear and distinct ideas that separate the confusion of imagined objects built from sensory input, and the mental methodology by which proofs are obtained. In all this resides the implication or primary intuition that the mind, acting upon and within itself, without environment, is obliged to articulate toward the attainment of intellectual truth. This view of the mind as being so very capable, so godlike, was, of course, made manageable by an acceptance of the existence of such a supreme possibility as God, with the result that the God referred to by the rationalists was ultimately fashioned by their rationalist-metaphysicist minds.

Special Esteem for Rational Intellect

In this rationalist channel, the production of intelligence, or the improvement of the mind, acquires a particular context, with a special esteem for the relationship between the highest intellectual activity and God. In these very complicated modern times, society often operates from within the rationalist context, driven by great esteem for the relationship between the mind at the height of its performance and the God that it most closely approximates when at this height. Yet today science is constructing a view of mental activity that is many steps removed from the old metaphysical schools.

The Hardware of Human Thought

Until the 20th century, to assume the existence of a core intelligence contained within the mind, independent of environment, would have been to assume a largely rationalist perspective regarding a God-given characteristic. However, with the advent of highly technical biochemical and neurological research, that perspective has been obscured. It is increasingly difficult to distinguish the mind from its own hardware and biochemical environment, that is, to separate thinking from the machinery of thinking. It is increasingly difficult to detect the presence of God within that machinery; at the same time, the machinery is so amazing that there are those who suspect that a higher power had a hand in its design. Whoever or whatever the original architect of the mind, a biological basis of intelligence may be unearthed as the brain is probed.

It has been argued that there is a core intelligence that is detectable in psychometric and behavioral genetic studies. [20] It has also been argued that there is a neurological level to intelligence and that as measured intelligence in the form of IQ increases, there are corresponding changes in the speed and duration of signal transmission throughout the brain. [21] These controversial conceptualizations of intelligence assume that there is a required hardware of human thought: genes, molecular neurotransmitters, brain cells.

THE SURGE OF EMPIRICISM

Recall that Dewey was quoted earlier in this chapter as saying that schools take part in determining the social order. Schools exist outside the mind, in the physical environment. Dewey thus awarded schools almost godlike power.

Undermining Rationalistic Causality

The rationalism of Descartes inspired fervent responses on the part of a group of British philosophers who argued that the only basis of reason and knowledge was experience. Among this group was 18th-century philosopher David Hume, whose work undermined the applications of the notion of causality that he saw as prevalent in rationalism. Of causality, Hume, almost more a skeptic than a philosopher, claimed that "experience only teaches us, how one event constantly follows another, without instructing us in the secret connexion, which binds them together, and renders them inseparable." [22] But observed sequence is not causality, Hume argued. The mind cannot be trusted when there is no empirical proof of causality. The notion of causality exists in the mind, in the absence of experience (in this case, the specific experience of causality), and knowledge without experience is not knowledge. In this way, Hume attacked the centrality of the rational mind.

It is important to note here that empiricism did not entirely abandon the concept of causality. The natural selection hypothesis set forth by 19th-century naturalist Darwin is a brilliant example of empirical work that included causality.

[23] The construct of evolution depends on causality (and was, of course, based upon empirical observation).

Mind as a Blank Slate

It was philosopher John Locke, writing in the 17th century and actually preceding Hume, who maintained that it is necessary to be content with a small degree of empirically based certainty and to hold all other views that lack empirically derived causality as matters of probability or belief. It was also Locke who said that all knowledge comes from two sources, sensation and reflection, but that there exist no innate ideas. According to Locke, all knowledge is founded on experience and the mind is a *tabula rasa*, a blank tablet, at birth. The tablet is filled with impressions via the senses. [24] Such a view places a great emphasis on the power of education.

In traditional empiricism there is no internally determined mind and therefore there can be no internally determined differences among minds. Although Locke and other empirical philosophers did not concern themselves with intelligence per se or with individual differences in intelligence, they would have seen the source of all individual differences in mental ability as being the result of individual differences in experience. [25]

More can be understood about the concept of the mind by seeking the origin of the concept of causality. Locke claimed that an individual's idea of the relationship between cause and effect is based on experience. Ideas come to be only after sensory experience. Before this experience, an idea is not present in the mind. Locke said that although new thoughts can and do appear, such a beginning among ideas occurs when the environment triggers mental operations. This is cause and effect; in other words, cause can exist outside the mind. But although even substance can exert cause, the resulting observed changes, according to Locke, belong entirely to the field of ideas. [26]

This is the field of ideas where educators dare to walk: the field of the inner workings of students' minds. Education can indeed be the cause of a mental event such as learning. It can be the cause of a redesigning of mental structures within students' minds. Locke would have advised that only education can accomplish this, as it is only in acts of remembering, combining, and relating ideas, as well as in voluntary decisions to move one's bodily members, that action can be brought into the realm of experience. [27] This may indicate that mental operation, reflection, is an independent source of objectively valid ideas and that sensation without operations upon it is not alone among the sources of experience. [28]

Acquisition of Knowledge

While the mind, in Locke's view, is a blank tablet before experience, the acquisition of knowledge involves mental activity on the data drawn from experience. Locke described knowledge as "the perception of the connexion and agreement, or disagreement and repugnancy of any of our ideas. In this alone it consists. Where this perception is, there is knowledge, and where it is not, . . . although we may fancy, guess or believe, . . . we always come short of knowledge." [29] The acquisition of knowledge depends on empirical experience, such as that found in daily life or in classroom projects.

Empricism has within it that which strongly suggests the nurture concept. If, after all, ideas come to be in the mind only after sensory experience, then the character and/or arrangement of that experience determines the specificity of the ensuing ideas. If such is the case, then a shift in sensory experience can be depended on to bring about a like shift in ideas. From this, only a small step is required to posit that an educational process can be used to bring about a related shift in the ideas of each student. According to Locke, before the sensory experience, an idea is not present in the mind. Thus, before the educational process, the ideas of the teaching environment are not present as academic elements in the student's mind. Furthermore, what is given in the teaching situation is the substance of a student's transformation, and so ideas desirable to society can be made ideas of the student body. Knowledge, on this ground, can be a nurturing of the youth. Since sensory experience is the sole source of ideas, there is no quarter left for elements of rationalism, and the nurture side proceeds without recourse to the nature side.

Causality Is Habitual Association

Hume continued this examination of knowledge and reasoning. He explained that the workings of imagination are accepted as real and existentially credible only when they are guided systematically by the principles of association. All reasoning consists in a discovery of the relations that objects bear to each other. [30] This is even true of moral reasoning, which attempts to go beyond what is presented in sense perception and memory in order to discover something about the existence or action of objects that lie beyond experience. [31] But such inferences concern matters of fact and must submit to the limitations placed on moral reasoning; in the realm of matters of fact, whatever is may also not be. As Hume wrote, "The contrary of every matter of fact is still possible; because it can never imply a contradiction, and is conceived by the mind with the same facility and distinctness, as if ever so conformable to reality. Nothing we imagine is absolutely impossible." [32]

For Hume, the expanse of the mind was limited by its range of experience. Moral reasoning in general can never yield more than a high degree of probability or moral certitude, and causal reasoning can never surpass this intrinsic limitation. A necessary connection between two objects is affirmed, joined in the natural relation of cause and effect, because they are experienced in constant, or rather frequent, conjunction. Again, the foundation of knowledge is experience. The leap from a sensorially perceived conjunction of events to the establishment of causality is made by the mind, acting involuntarily under the force of habitual association. [33]

Sensory Reduction of Complexity

The complexity of the self and the mind can always be reduced via sensory data. Hume described the mind as merely an abstract name for a series of experience-based ideas. In fact, "all our ideas are nothing but copies of our impressions." [34] Even complex thoughts are built out of simple thoughts that are based on experience:

> Complex ideas may, perhaps, be well known by definition, which is nothing but an enumeration of those parts or simple ideas that compose them. But when we have pushed up definitions to the most simple ideas, and find still some ambiguity and obscurity; what resource are we then possessed of? By what invention can we throw light upon these ideas, and render them altogether precise and determinant to our intellectual view? Produce these impressions or original sentiments, from which ideas are copied. These impressions are strong and sensible. They admit not of ambiguity. [35]

Empiricism says, "Trust the senses." They produce unambiguous impressions. The senses have the capacity, the mandate, in fact, to reflect the environment. Without the strong and sensible impressions, the vivid sharp images gained from the environment, there can be no ideas, no knowledge, no intelligence.

The Unit-of-Analysis Problem

Recall that critics of the nature side of the nature–nurture debate have noted that some theoretical approaches appear to be sound until they are examined on other levels of analysis; genetic explanations for individual differences in intelligence are viewed as being too narrow. In this vein, rationalist explanations for the origin of knowledge may focus too narrowly on the mind, overlooking the critical dependence of the brain on its environment at least for sustenance. Even the limits of what can be called biological rationalism are readily detectable on the sociopolitical and environmental, or *ecological*, level of analysis.

The Environment Is Essential

Regardless of the importance of the genetic and cellular hardware found *within* the organism, survival independent of the external environment is impossible. Survival requires learning how to forage environments for food, protection, and other essentials—including information. The world has to become the source of information because such information is essential to life. This means that in order to survive, there must be a reliance on sensory inputs coming from outside the mind and on a consequent knowledge that is believed to represent an outside world pragmatically.

This reliance occurs on many levels. The human individual interacts with his or her specific environment, deriving information and behavior possibilities.

Human (and other) species respond to the biological, the geological, and the overall ecological environment. Human families and other organizations respond to economic and sociological environments in the same way, namely, information is erected on an empirical equivalent of the environment and then a reaction is formulated. (Empiricists are usually aware of the fact that sensory input comes first and then it is followed, perforce, by a construction of information on the intellectual plane.)

Information about the Environment Is Essential

What could be called "ecological empiricism" is a worldview that considers information derived from the surrounding environment as being critical and as being the only source of an accurate knowledge of reality. The more information derived from the many levels of the environment, the greater the survival value of the body of information amassed. At this stage in the evolution of life, reliance on the internal workings of the mind in isolation—if there *are* any thoughts independent of external reality—is deemed dangerous for individuals and for the species. According to philosopher Gregory Bateson, one of the earliest contributors to ecological reasoning:

> Any biological system (e.g., ecological environment, human civilization, and the system which is to be the combination of these two) is described in terms of interlinked variables such that for any given variable, there is an upper and lower threshold of tolerance beyond which discomfort, pathology, and ultimately death must occur. [36]

Ecologists argue that the survival of life on earth depends on a respect for the ultimate truths about reality that are found only in information derived sensorially from the environment. [37] Unlike Descartes, who articulated the notion that one sleeps in the world of illusion to avoid reality, ecological empiricists suggest that we are sleeping in a bed of *partial* empirical knowledge to avoid the greater empirical truths arrived at through more complex environmental knowledge. Such sleeping, such denial of external reality is death to the species according to this line of thinking.

What does this broad view of species knowledge, ecological empiricism, have to do with individual knowledge and intelligence? A great deal. In the empirical understanding of knowledge, human intelligence is environmentally determined. When humans think they can survive, can know and act on reality, without data derived from the environment, they operate with lesser intelligence. Some would argue that this is, in fact, unintelligent. The moral imperative underlying ecological empiricism is clear: mental workings that attempt to define reality without data from the surrounding environment are dangerous and irresponsible. [38]

Ecologists maintain that the environment and all its inhabitants are threatened. [39] It is implicitly expected that there will be no intelligence without an environment in which it can exist. Ecologists are confronted by philosophical extremes: at one end, the genes, the neurotransmitters, and the brain cells form the equipment for the rational process, and, at the other end, the semisleeping empirical edifice we call reality forms knowledge of the environment. In this extraordinary set of deceptive extremes, essential truths carried in by ecological empiricism must be environmental truths.

Evolving Intelligence

Within the constraints of new understandings of the human brain, ecological empiricism views knowledge acquisition as a plastic, malleable process, something that must occur continuously within a rapidly changing environment. Philosophical empiricism has merged with modern environmentalism to imply a model of what might be called "species intelligence." This model opposes the view that core intelligence exists within the mind and is primarily independent of environmental influence. Ecological empiricism and biological determinism are not highly compatible. If intelligent thought was ever purely within the mind, it can be that way no longer. Ecologists imply that species intelligence has become, by desperate necessity, ecologically empirical. Now intelligence itself must evolve. And policy makers may not have enough information to enable them to accurately predict which forms of mental ability and intelligence should be promoted by society. As naturalist Loren Eiseley suggested, it is difficult to say which abilities may be essential to the survival of life in the future. Eiseley, quoted in the frontispiece of this book, asked, "Who is to say without foreknowledge of the future which animal is specialized and which is not?"

The standards of ecological empiricism are strongly influenced by the Western democratic ideal. If intelligence is indeed forged by the environment, then access to intelligence and the social power it awards can be made available to all citizens. Policy that seeks to provide broad access to higher education leans in this direction. Although knowledge can be restricted to elite portions of the population, it may be that the survival of the species depends on the enhancement of the environmentally determined intelligence of a critical mass of its members. Fair representation university admissions policies may be implicitly addressing the need to raise species intelligence. If so, this is something deeper than a mere moral or political imperative. It is survival.

This chapter has painted an age-old philosophical backdrop onto the three modern tensions described in Chapters 5, 6, and 7. There is no claim that the connections are precise, merely that the tensions are parallel. While one tension exists within policy, one within sociopolitics, another within scientific research, and another within philosophy, each of these reflects a basic tension regarding the impact of the environment on the shape of the intellect. Part III develops a map of the impact of these parallel tensions on university admissions policy.

9

The Illusory Faces
of Implicit Intelligence Policy

> When three [now five] billion people are in a space ship hurtling into an
> unknown space in which dark stars may be on collision courses, with another
> ice age as the least of their impending domestic troubles, it behooves them to
> achieve some understanding and control of their environment as early as
> possible. The question is no longer the sybaritic one: "What balance of
> distribution of intelligence makes for a comfortable society?" but rather,
> "How do we increase our resources of top-level intelligence to ensure man's
> eventual survival?"
>
> RAYMOND B. CATTELL [1]

The preceding chapters have initiated a search for truth regarding the influence of
assumptions about intelligence on social policy. As is common among quests in
which a singular truth is the goal, the discovery is made that the truth being sought
is, in reality, multifaceted, complex, mercurial, controversial, and, above all,
highly elusive. In keeping with this truism, implicit intelligence policy has many
faces, although they are usually well-masked.

Given the obscure and relatively intractable nature of the true relationships
between implicit assumptions, explicit policies, and their outcomes, why should
any attempt to unearth these relationships be made? Why not leave unexamined
the implicit assumptions that drive social policy? If truth is so elusive, so illusory,
why invest so much energy in chasing it? Perhaps some stones are best left
unturned. If the truth, once revealed, may be dangerous, why seek it?

When it comes to exposing assumptions regarding the educability of human
intelligence, a truth seeker risks the imposition of ignominy, either upon himself or
upon others. No one wants to be caught saying the "wrong thing" about human
intelligence. Yet this fear is ludicrous given the conflicting and unsettled states of
the science of intelligence and the various definitions of its subject matter.

Nevertheless, in an egalitarian climate few people feel comfortable stating that some people are more intelligent than others and that they are thus entitled to special opportunities denied to others. Who would want to say such a thing in a society that considers itself to be democratic? On the other hand, who would want to deprive those with a high degree of intellectual talent of opportunities to develop and apply that talent? Much of the fear surrounding definitive statements about human intelligence is determined by the prevailing style or political sentiment of the times rather than by truth. And, if anything, such fear is validated by whatever is the dominant truth of the time rather than invalidated by the ultimate truth—elusive, intractable, and unprovable as it may be.

The truth seeker, engaged in some form of policy analysis, especially an analysis of the assumptions behind a policy and its outcome, is treading on dangerous ground. The truth seeker upsets people merely by engaging in the process of examining the driving assumptions about intelligence. Why? Because he or she is not simply asking some people to risk saying the wrong thing about intelligence but to risk appearing as if they "do" the wrong thing about intelligence by building and implementing policies upon dangerous, obscure, unprovable, and maybe even politically dubious assumptions.

If the policy-analyzing truth seeker is looking at college admission policy, he or she may find that policy makers and their supporters increasingly assume that the mental ability affecting college performance is highly malleable at the college level. He or she may perceive admission standards based on this assumption to include increasingly lower mental ability requirements as measured prior to admission. How might one go about detecting the veracity of this perception? Can one unearth the truth from such perceived or actual trends? And why would one wish to identify such a truth?

SEEKING TRUTH IN POLICY

Key reasons for seeking truth behind policies can be addressed briefly here. First and foremost is the matter of theoretical integrity in social policy. Integrity is not necessarily the end result of the search for truth, however, but the process of searching for the implicit undergrid (as modeled in Chapter 3) can introduce a greater integrity into the design, implementation, and evaluation of social policies. But why integrity? Any discussion of the characteristics of intelligence hints at the nature versus nurture debate. Most such discussions seek to avoid an open and objective examination of the research and of the decisions made that claim to be based on it. Too many programs and policies fall short of their intended outcomes as a result of reluctance to openly examine the assumptions about intelligence that drive them. Perhaps the intended outcomes are unrealistic. Or perhaps another policy would better achieve these intended outcomes. The process of seeking to identify, acknowledge, specify, and then clearly connect underlying assumptions to policies can force integrity into the system through an open examination of the motives and beliefs that are permitted to shape policies.

Another reason for seeking truth behind policy is that this search forces a level of intellectual discourse into the debates over policy, a level essential to the preservation of a self-aware democracy in a modern institution-based world. This sort of inquiry is the individual's chief defense against institutions and institutionalized systems of belief. A political system that seeks to preserve what it claims are the inalienable rights of its citizens has no excuse for the lack of dedicated examination of the assumptions, even the most implicit ones, that drive it. Without such an examination, an implicit intelligence policy remains backstage but is always directing the play of policy and policy outcome. Whatever masks the actors wear, they only disguise the many faces of implicit intelligence policy, not replace them.

Yet another reason for seeking truth behind policy is that this search can be contagious: it models a method of inquiry that can inspire other searches. And these searches are essential. Although this book focuses on college admissions policy as its chief example, the effects of implicit intelligence policy on the mechanism of selection and other aspects of social policy, in all its variations and polarizations, are virtually omnipresent. The very fact that the nature–nurture ratio is the subject of continuing controversy, both overt and covert, influences almost all social policy in some fashion. The danger in failing to probe and question could lead to extreme policy mandates. For example, if the prevailing view held that mental ability was in no way affected or altered by environment, policies affecting genetic breeding could become the only recognized mechanism of intelligence promotion and maintenance. This absolute extreme is, however, rarely suggested, even by those who argue that IQ is predominantly determined by inheritance.

THE ENVIRONMENTALISM FACE

As discussed earlier in this book, one of the more extreme nature-biased definitions claims that IQ is 80% heritable; that leaves 20% to be influenced by environment. As teaching technology increases its power to stimulate mental ability by environmental influence, the power of that 20% strengthens. Most findings, however, indicate that the heritability of intelligence is at approximately the 50% level. Thus, even the defined versions of intelligence that claim some effect of genetics allow for significant environmental influence. Most social policies that aim to select, train, educate, employ, or otherwise utilize human intelligence imply that there is a significant degree of environmental influence on intelligence.

THE DEFINITIONAL FACE

Implicit intelligence policy is always a reflection of the prevailing views and conflicts regarding both the degree to which environment can raise levels of intelligence and the characteristics of environment (including specific aspects of education) that can raise levels of mental ability. But implicit intelligence policy is more than this. In addition to the difficulty of defining intelligence in terms of the degree to which environment affects it, there are numerous other strands of implicit intelligence policy—fragments of research analysis that affect the thinking of policy makers and educators and are then transmitted to the minds of the lay public. These include the following:

• *The matter of single versus multiple intelligences.* What form of intelligence is being discussed? IQ? Forms of intelligence that must be measured in ways other than IQ tests? In ways other than heavily "g"-loaded tests that have buried within them entire IQ tests or IQ-test-type questions?

• *The question of how to define multiple intelligences, if indeed they exist.* Who should decide which forms of ability are intelligences and which are talents of some other sort? If and when there is a consensus regarding the existence of several forms of intelligence, such as those proposed by Howard Gardner, should a measure of intelligence, an IQ or "g," be developed for each of these intelligences? Would it be better to have a verbal IQ, a math IQ, a spatial IQ, a musical IQ, and so on, instead of a single measure of IQ? Would these measures have increased utility? At what point would IQ become divided into so many categories that it would become meaningless?

• *The controversy regarding the measurement of IQ differences among races.* If multiple intelligences do indeed exist, is IQ a satisfactory measure? Is there any value whatsoever in the use of "g"-loaded selection tests? What of significance is being measured when racial differences in "g" are detected—cultural bias built into IQ tests or actual racial differences in a particular form of mental ability? Would it be more realistic to write an IQ test for each race and then generate a race-specific IQ measure for each? How many IQ or "g"-loaded tests would be needed to address the many subcultural factors influencing the IQ scores within each race? And what would several different IQs reveal about ranking applicants for academic or work positions in a racially diverse society where members compete for the same opportunities?

• *The unclear value of IQ or "g."* Does "g" measure a particular form of mental ability that is essential to high functioning and, as suggested in the Cattell quote opening this chapter, even to the preservation of society and all mankind? Is something missing if policy is allowed to downgrade, dilute, and disregard the potency of the traditional measurement of purportedly innate "g"? Or is policy that emphasizes the value of "g" politically dangerous?

THE ECONOMIC FACE

Cattell has expressed great concern regarding the lack of emphasis on the preservation and promulgation of the higher levels of human intelligence as measured by innate "g." [2] He depicted the economic (supply and demand) relationship behind the shifting of the demand for mental ability. No matter how objective they are claimed to be, standards regarding mental ability may merely be highly subjective reflections of the demand for mental ability and the availability of opportunity for its utilization. Cattell states that when opportunity (be it in the form of university admissions policy, elite educational opportunities, or hiring and promotion policies) is scarce, the desirable level of mental ability rises in response to this diminishing demand—and diminishing demand means increasing competition for fewer opportunities. When spaces are scarce, requirements for admission into them are much more stringent. When spaces are plentiful, requirements for admissions into them are less narrow and less stringent. As has been explained in Chapter 7, these requirements are frequently heavily "g" loaded. We can say then that, conversely, as abundance increases, the "g" loading of selection instruments or the emphasis on "g"-loaded selection instruments decreases.

The economic force that drives the demand for mental ability not only affects the degree to which its definition is "g" loaded but the overall definition of mental ability as well. Whether or not policy makers choose to officially acknowledge the role played by economic fluctuations in the policy process, they must admit that even the most basic characteristics of intelligence can appear differently in various economic climates.

THE SELECTION-TESTING FACE

Implicit intelligence policy thus manifests itself in the use of "g"-loaded tests as mechanisms of selection. Tests of mental ability place a heavy weight on the single definition of core intelligence, using IQ or "g." In most intelligence tests (including the Stanford-Binet and Wechsler Adult Intelligence Scale), in most scholastic aptitude tests, in most military placement tests, and in many employment agency examinations, "g" accounts for a significant portion of the score variance. Tests that involve some form of verbal or mathematical reasoning tend to have a higher "g" loading than those involving mainly visual motor skills or simple memory of previously learned material. [3]

The outcome of this emphasis is that the most popular mechanisms of selection, namely, tests, select for particular definitions of intelligence. Testing for a particular and very restricted form of mental ability continues to be implicit in many selection processes. So the implicit policy is to favor—to select for—this form of intelligence. And this form of intelligence continues to be "g."

Allowing admissions officers and employers to knowingly select from a pool of applicants via a mechanism that guarantees a certain percent error on a regular basis is another implicit policy. The National Commission on Testing and Public Policy offers an excellent example of this typically accepted error:

> For example, consider the case where 800 people out of a group of 1000 could perform successfully on the job or in school. If a test with the typical power to predict performance is used to classify them into two groups—likely or unlikely to succeed—about 66 percent of the 200 who "fail" the test barrier could actually perform successfully; and of the 800 who "pass" the test about 17 percent would be unlikely to perform successfully. [4]

And yet tests, despite their accepted limitations in the realm of performance prediction, are increasingly popular. All age groups are being tested, and tests are being used more and more frequently to make such critical decisions as entry into and exit from kindergarten, promotion from grade to grade, graduation from high school, and placement in remedial and special programs. Teachers and other professionals are credentialed through test scores, and once they are hired, they are held increasingly accountable for their students' and clients' test scores. Initially modeled by the military, the use of test scores in making hiring, placement, promotion, and training decisions is on the rise in other areas. And, of course, college admission continues to be heavily reliant on tests to rate applicants.

This emerging dependence, even fixation, on standardized testing as the mechanism of opportunity allocation is expensive, with taxpayers picking up much of the tab. Estimates of the annual direct cost of state and local testing to taxpayers range from $70 million to $107 million. If the indirect costs of test administration and preparation are added on, the cost to taxpayers ranges from $725 million to $915 million annually. [5]

The effects of implicit intelligence policy are a complex web of issues to be unraveled, sorted out, and, hopefully, acted on. First, many tests are "g" loaded, selecting for a particular type of mental ability, the traditional single or core intelligence usually depicted as IQ. Second, prediction error in testing is accepted, with selectors knowingly selecting applicants who may not have the ability to perform and knowingly rejecting applicants who do indeed have the ability to perform.

As the 1990 Report of the National Commission on Testing and Public Policy summarizes, increasing emphasis is being placed on high school students' test scores as determinants of college admission and on job applicants' scores as evidence of their ability to perform on the job. [6] After some 50 years of use, it is evident that there is no elaborate or simple test that can precisely predict the tested individual's performance in school or on the job. [7] A number of factors not represented by questions on a test influence performance. As noted by the Commission, these include the tendency of individuals to seek help from others when needed, their day-to-day study or work habits, their ability to cooperate with other people, and numerous institutional factors, including disciplinary measures and efforts to counteract systemic racism. [8]

The commission agrees that "the general problem of the fallibility of test scores in predicting real-life performance has long been known to specialists in testing." [9] However, insists the Commission, "because test scores are increasingly being used as absolute arbiters in the allocation of opportunities," the problem of mislabeling people and selecting them for academic and occupational opportunities on the basis of this mislabeling must be addressed. [10]

The commission thus suggests that new mechanisms for ensuring the relevance and accuracy of selection tests be instituted, to determine both how many of those who fail can indeed perform acceptably and how many of those who pass cannot actually perform acceptably. [11] The commission also says that the questions it raises become increasingly important as the number of new applicants to the job market declines. The percentage of the total U.S. population (all races combined) under age 35 is projected to drop from over 55% in 1990 to 48% in 2000, 46% in 2010, and 41% in 2030, while the population of what were once clearly minority races is expected to increase (across all age groups); the population of African-Americans is expected to increase by 50% by the year 2030, while the combined population of Asian-Americans, Pacific Islanders, and American Indians is projected to triple by 2040. [12] As the overall population under 35 is decreasing, its diversity is increasing.

THE ABILITY-SHIFT MODEL IN SELECTION POLICY

How can the findings of the National Commission on Testing and Public Policy be related to the ability-shift model posed by Cattell? A brief overview of the commission's breakdown of test error groups will facilitate the response to this question. A diagram provided by the commission (included here as Figure 9.1) illustrates the errors involved in classifying applicants by test score cutoff levels. This figure breaks down the applicant pool into four groups [13]:

GROUP 1: Those who "*pass*" the test and can perform well in the position for which the test selected them.

GROUP 2: Those who "*pass*" the test but cannot perform well in the position for which the test selected them.

GROUP 3: Those who "*fail*" the test but can perform well in the position for which the test failed to select them.

GROUP 4: Those who "*fail*" the test and cannot perform well in the position.

If the test is "g" loaded, the shift in the IQ requirement to pass the test and thus be selected for the position changes the number of persons in each of these

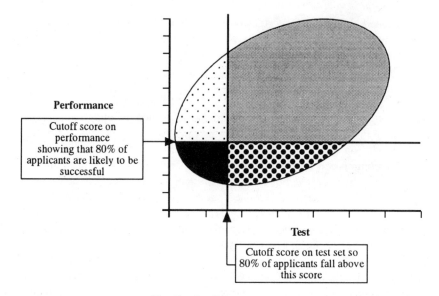

Performance

> Cutoff score on
> performance
> showing that 80% of
> applicants are likely to be
> successful

Test

> Cutoff score on test set so
> 80% of applicants fall above
> this score

Classification Key

	Above cutoff score on both test and performance	Correctly classified	= Group 1
	Above cutoff score on test but unlikely to succeed according to performance indicator	Misclassified	= Group 2
	Below cutoff score on test but likely to succeed according to performance indicator	Misclassified	= Group 3
	Below cutoff score on both test and performance	Correctly classified	= Group 4

Figure 9.1. Imperfect classification based on test scores and performance. [14] *Note*: The data illustrated represent test scores with typical power to predict performance (i.e., a correlation of 0.35 between test scores and indicators of performance).

groups. When a very high IQ is required to pass the test, there will be fewer people in the selected group than when an average IQ is required. These outcomes are the natural result of what is deemed the "normal" statistical distribution of IQ throughout the population. There are more people who test average on IQ tests than test high. (The group selected is always composed of those in Groups 1 and 2, regardless of the IQ being tested for either explicitly or implicitly via hidden g-loading.)

Using Figure 9.1 to expand on Cattell's concept of the shift in demand for intelligence as a result of economic fluctuation, one can see how an upward shift of the "g" load in a selection test may be required when there is a scarcity of positions or opportunities available. (The vertical line in Figure 9.1 would move to the right.) Conversely, a downward shift of "g" load in a selection test would, in Cattell's terms, reflect the abundance of positions or opportunities available. (The vertical line in Figure 9.1 would move to the left.)

All this is based on the assumption that "g" is a good predictor of performance for whatever position the "g"-loaded test aims to fill. If, however, "g" load is not a good predictor, Groups 2 and 3 are going to be large. In fact, the more the predictor errs, the larger these groups become.

Predictor error is compounded by economic fluctuation. Referring to Cattell once again, there is a distortion based on broad economic pressures, fluctuations from abundance to scarcity. To restate, in times of abundance, the cutoff point or passing score on a "g"-loaded selection test will be lower than in times of scarcity; "g" will be treated as a relatively inconsequential predictor of performance, and the potency of test error related to "g" loading will be lower than in times of scarcity. Test error can still occur, owing to other reasons, but it will not necessarily be viewed as a critical error, given the abundance of opportunity and the small proportion of applicants rejected.

In times of scarcity, however, the cutoff point or passing score on a "g"-loaded test will be higher. Moreover, the rate of error of the "g"-loaded test will be increased if "g" is for some reason an invalid predictor of the desired performance level. So, ironically, in times of economic scarcity the use of selection mechanisms loaded with measures of "g" is very fragile, all the more untrustworthy, even though it is emphasized more. In times of scarcity, perceptions of the value of intelligence are the strongest but the most shaky. When "g" is most emphasized, test errors related to "g" are most common. There is the potential for backlash: pressures may emerge to invalidate "g" almost entirely. The danger of such philosophical backlash lies in resultant failing to select for a critical human trait by denying focus on it and by purposefully refusing to allocate key opportunity to it.

The future of intelligence selection is a puzzle. As the Commission indicated, the number of new applicants to the job market is expected to decline. Based upon Cattell's model, this situation may create the *illusion* of abundance, where there are more positions open than applicants to fill them. However, Cattell's model was designed prior to our postmodern multicultural era. Today, supply and demand are even more politically confounded. A new mediation of the definition of mental ability and its relationship to "g" may evolve. The applicant pool will be more racially diverse than ever, and the mix of abilities across this pool may be more disparate than ever. The problem of finding qualified applicants may take on new urgency. If the relaxation of "g" requirements typical of abundant times continues, what will be the new mechanisms of selection? What implicit intelligence policy will drive these mechanisms? It may be that the trend in admissions policy at the University of California at Berkeley, as analyzed in my case study, holds some answers to these questions.

III

The Impact of Implicit Intelligence Policy on Explicit Policy

10

The Potential Value of Impact Analysis on Intelligence Policy

The move from general principles to concrete policies is not an easy one.
U.C. Berkeley Committee on Admissions and Enrollment [1]

Given that there exists an extensive web of underlying implicit intelligence policy, it is likely that this web has extensive impact on explicit policies. But how can this impact be traced? How can the relationships among the elements of implicit policy and the elements of the explicit policy it drives be analyzed?

It is quite natural that some form of impact analysis be applied here. Chapters 10, 11, and 12 model the general theoretical tenor of such an impact analysis. Although the factors of implicit policy are elusive, existing methods of policy impact analysis and a thematic analysis of the effects of implicit intelligence policy on higher education admissions policy can be adapted and combined. In this chapter, conceptual and theoretical areas central to this adaptation of a general policy impact analysis to intelligence policy analysis are reviewed. These conceptual and theoretical areas are general policy analysis, ecological rationality, and impact analysis itself. Further discussion regarding the specific development of the thematic impact analysis is developed in Appendixes A and B.

POLICY ANALYSIS

The literature on policy analysis provides a theoretical backdrop for the objectives of this book and offers a useful general definition of "implicit" policy, namely, that aspect of explicit social policy that is informal, unarticulated, unspecified, often unspoken, and sometimes even officially denied. [2] The relatively nascent and fascinating science of policy analysis has opened the door to

149

an objective understanding of the design, implementation, outcome, and effectiveness of public policies.

Not only is implicit policy hidden and difficult to identify, but it tends to be rigid and difficult to recast. So many assumptions, biases, and belief systems rule the specification of policies. Unless these are unearthed, there can be little understanding of the reasons for particular policy designs. Heavy doses of skepticism and dogma congeal to generate the powerful force of implicit intelligence policy. The brilliant political scientist Aaron Wildavsky described the science of policy analysis as one that requires "learning to draw the line between skepticism and dogma" and "balancing social interaction against intellectual cogitation." [3]

Impact analysis can identify problematic and potentially problematic impacts of policy. Although policy scientists' efforts at impact analysis have thus far been focused on explicit policies, implicit policy can also be analyzed. The identification of problematic impacts is a task central to any impact analysis. Wildavsky, one of the founders of policy science, noted that a large part of policy analysis is indeed problem-finding: "Problem-finding is analogous to inventing or theorizing. . . . In policy analysis, the most creative calculations concern finding problems for which solutions might be attempted." [4] He stated that the spirit of problem-finding should encompass all policy analysis: "Instead of thinking of permanent solutions we should think of permanent problems in the sense that one problem always succeeds and replaces another." [5] In line with this thinking, the effect of implicit intelligence policies on individuals, groups, and society must be viewed as a permanent, ongoing problem. A methodology for continuous detection of the effect of such policy is essential.

Supporting this train of thought, Parts I and II of this book first identified the problem of implicit intelligence policy. Now, Part III proposes and demonstrates a thematic methodology for analyzing the impact of incorporating the issue of human intelligence in policy, program design, and implementation, with the specific problem of admissions policy as the example. Precedents for such a thematic and, hopefully, anticipatory methodology or what is called "prospective" impact analysis can be found in the literature on environmental, urban, and societal impact, as explained in Appendix A.

Readers will note that in order to accomplish its primary objectives, this book has brought together information from a number of fields of research, ranging from economics to behavioral genetics to political science. Policy analyst Richard Nathan emphasizes the importance of this sort of interdisciplinary approach to policy problems. [6] C. West Churchman, a leading systems analyst and founder of the Peace and Conflict Studies Institute at U.C. Berkeley, claims that "when one is considering systems it's always wise to raise questions about the most obvious and simple assumptions." [7] Such inquiry about even the simplest assumptions was demonstrated in Chapter 3, which described the underlying assumptions about intelligence as a class of phenomena to be questioned and studied. Low recognition of the potential impacts of these assumptions on policy and policy outcome can be corrected. The form of problem-finding suggested by Wildavsky requires an understanding and synthesis of the literature and theory from many disciplines, as this book demonstrates.

ECOLOGICAL RATIONALITY

Because the body of implicit policy emerges from so many different socio-political, scientific, and psychological arenas, this body must be recognized as an extensive and complex, albeit mostly hidden, *system*. Ecological or systems thinking must necessarily be part of any study of implicit policy. It is not surprising, then, that the justification for and the rationale behind a systemic and interdisciplinary approach to policy analysis has surfaced in many fields. The first strand of ecological thought came to the forefront when environmental ecology became a political issue. "Ecological rationality" appears in much of the litera-ture on natural and environmental resources policy, where it is described as "a rationality of living systems, an order of relationships among living systems and their environments" [8] in which "relationships are seldom unidirectional, linear, or simple." [9] Fundamental to the notion of ecological relationships is the view that there exists an *intricate web of interrelationships that comprises the whole system*. Ecological rationality is process oriented, deriving its logic from natural processes such as feedback, oscillation, entropy and "negentropy," and evolu-tion. [10]

Because it was born in environmental ecology, the foundations of ecological rationality are as much ethical and philosophical as scientific; substantial ecologi-cal rationality is exhibited "when a decision or action takes account of the possibilities and limitations of a given situation and recognizes it so as to produce, increase or preserve a good." [11] In the case of environmental ecological rationality, this "good" is "the capacity, diversity and resilience of the biotic community, its long-term life-support capability." [12] The scope of the "good" is extended to other policy domains, to what is called "social rationality," which includes technological, economic, and other social conditions as well as physio-logical, geographic, and environmental conditions. [13] An analysis of the impact of implicit intelligence policy should naturally spring from such social rationality. This rationality wavers, however, in the face of conflicting "goods," that is, when competing social groups desire different policy outcomes. The case study of college admissions policy in this book offers a superb demonstration of the wavering of social rationality when it is pulled in opposing directions by compet-ing social "goods."

IMPACT ANALYSIS

It comes back to impact analysis. Social rationality, tempered by competing "goods," must permeate the application of impact analysis to intelligence policy. A fluid and creative approach to impact analysis is essential because social rationality is fraught with conflict and then implicitly tied to various components of policy. Chapter 11 demonstrates an impact analysis that is fluid and creative, as well as thematic and qualitative, while Appendixes A and B elaborate on concepts, theories, and literature relevant to the development of this special approach to impact analysis. When the policy being impact-analyzed has implicit components (such as the elements of implicit intelligence policy), the impact analysis must go beyond being qualitative and must become creatively heuristic, even intuitive, in linking implicit policy with the potential long-range and unpredicted impacts of the explicit policy it drives. Impact analysis of implicit policy must take on a brainstorming characteristic.

Ideally, it is social rationality that drives the examination of the implicit assumptions behind explicit college admissions policy and its outcomes. Concern for the "good" (as defined earlier) calls for policy makers to examine the actual and potential effects of their policies from the standpoint of what is good for the whole of society as well as for specific socioeconomic constituents. When these policies are driven by implicit assumptions, concern for "good" must take into account these assumptions as roots and precursors in the chain of causality that leads to policy design and policy impacts. Such a conscientious analytic procedure can be used to create more effective and more enlightened policies, in this case, college admissions policies designed to drive desirable outcomes in a heterogeneous society and an ever-changing world.

As far as the actual utility and popularity of the application of impact analysis to implicit policy, as demonstrated in the following chapter, is concerned, only the real-world application over a long period of time will yield the most reliable evaluation. Also, as is true of most interdisciplinary endeavors, the strength of the weave between the relevant disciplines and the potential for theoretical synthesis, and the application of essential concepts will determine the power and the limitations of the findings and consequent recommendations of such analysis. Above all, the pull of competing social "goods" must be respected, explicitly acknowledged, and formally related to specific components of specific policies. Such an effort is initiated in Chapter 11.

11

The Impact of Implicit Intelligence Policy on Explicit University Admissions Policy

If you do well in language and logic you will do well on IQ tests and SATs, and you may well get into a prestigious college.

HOWARD GARDNER [1]

Although most of the country's leading educators understand the direct correlation between intelligence (as presently measured) and SAT and similar test scores, few would willingly bring that information to the public's attention. Informed politicians also know of this strong relationship. . . . Educators realize that they would be publicly condemned for focusing on the correlation of the test scores with intelligence. Most people are unwilling to acknowledge the linkage between SAT and similar test scores and intelligence, even though their common sense makes the connection.

GUY R. ODUM [2]

Opportunity is a key to what may be an otherwise locked door. What could be more democratic than to distribute that key to everyone? Yet when the keys are limited in number, universal distribution is not possible. Some seemingly logical means of deciding "who gets what" must be devised, a means that can withstand the scrutiny of an increasingly diverse polity. Enter selection policy, the mechanism of allocation. In higher education this mechanism is admissions policy.

With the goal of injecting a new analytic perspective into the analysis of all social policies but particularly selection policies, this chapter models that perspective by mapping the impact of intelligence policy on one of the most, if not the most, powerful mechanisms of selection—college admissions policy. Once again the University of California at Berkeley is used as the case in point. To accomplish this task, simple and almost obvious (but usually implicit) connections are drawn between the four basic tensions explored in Part II of this book and the fundamental elements of the admissions policy of U.C. Berkeley (described in Chapter 5).

THE UNIVERSITY OF TOMORROW

The admissions policy of the University of California at Berkeley offers a significant opportunity to develop the methodology for an analysis of the impact of implicit intelligence policy. U.C. Berkeley has been described as "the university of tomorrow" [3] in that the evolving mix of its student body and the mounting social, political, intellectual, structural, and economic pressures it faces represent trends that many other institutions of higher education will encounter in the coming years. In fact, most colleges and universities have already begun to experience the democratic tug of fair representation and the curricular and policy questions it raises in light of current and growing financial restrictions.

U.C. Berkeley, long considered one of the leading universities in the world, was founded in 1868 in the city of Berkeley, California, which has become a densely populated and racially mixed urban environment. The ethnic mix of the more than 20,000 full-time undergraduate students attending U.C. Berkeley, is as follows:

- 31% Asian-American
- 7% African-American
- 39% Caucasian
- 15% Hispanic
- 1% American Indian
- 7% Other [4]

Ninety-three percent of all undergraduates attending U.C. Berkeley are California residents. [5]

Comparing the same data on ethnicity with several other institutions of higher education reveals that the makeup of the student body at Berkeley is indeed distinct, especially in terms of the proportion of Caucasians to Asian-Americans in its undergraduate student body. Consider the variation in racial composition of the 1992–93 freshman classes at the public institutions listed in Table 11.1. [6]

Note that the University of Hawaii at Manoa, admitting 10,774 freshmen for the 1992–93 academic year, registers a racial composition distinctly different from the others, a composition relatively reflective of the state's population. Next lowest in terms of Caucasian admissions is U.C. Berkeley, which admitted approximately twice as many freshman as the University of Hawaii in the same academic year but whose racial balance was distinctly different from that of the statewide population of California, which was 9.1% Asian-American, 7.1% African-American, 57.2%

Table 11.1. Racial Composition of Freshman Class at Selected Public Institutions in the 1992–93 Academic Year (in %)

University	Asian-Americans	African-Americans	Caucasian	Hispanic	American Indians	Other
California, Berkeley	*31*	*7*	*39*	*15*	*1*	*7*
Georgia Institute of Technology	12	8	76	3	—	—
Louisiana State (Baton Rouge)	3	8	85	2	—	2
Ohio State (Columbus)	3	6	85	1	—	4
Michigan State (East Lansing)	3	8	84	2	1	2
Colorado (Boulder)	6	2	82	6	1	4
Florida (Gainesville)	5	6	78	7	—	4
Hawaii at Manoa	56	1	16	1	—	26
North Carolina at Chapel Hill	4	10	83	1	2	1
Texas at Austin	9	4	69	14	—	4
Washington (Seattle)	19	4	65	3	1	8
Wisconsin-Madison	3	2	85	2	—	8

Caucasian, 25.8% Hispanic, 0.8% American Indian and other during about that same period. [7]

The contrast between the ethnic mix at U.C. Berkeley and at private universities is also distinct. Consider the same data for these private universities shown in Table 11.2. [8]

Ethnic diversity and racial balance is but one characteristic outcome of admissions policy. Competition is another. Of the 20,281 applicants for admission to the 1992–93 freshman class at U.C. Berkeley, only 8,700 were accepted. The entering class averaged 563 on the verbal portion and 654 on the math portion of the SAT. [9] Ninety-five percent of this class ranked in the top tenth of their high school class and 100% ranked in the top quarter. [10] Table 11.3 lists the same data for the 1992–93 academic year for the institutions presented in Tables 11.1 and 11.2.

It is apparent that U.C. Berkeley has a large number of applicants for admission, the largest applicant body among all the institutions being compared in Table 11.3. Although Berkeley is a large public university (with an undergraduate student body of 21,841 during the 1992–93 academic year), it was only able to admit 43% of the 20,281 applicants for the 1992–93 academic year. This makes the admissions policy of U.C. Berkeley among the more restrictive in the nation in terms of applicant-to-admission ratio and among the most restrictive of the public institutions. Therefore, when combined with the unusual balance of ethnic groups actually admitted, the sheer turnaway rate at U.C. Berkeley renders an important

Table 11.2.   Racial Composition of Freshman Class at Selected Private Institutions in the 1992–93 Academic Year (in %)

University	Asian-Americans	African-Americans	Caucasian	Hispanic	American Indians	Other
California, Berkeley	31	7	39	15	1	7
Brandeis	8	4	82	3	—	3
Brigham Young	2	1	88	2	—	7
Brown	15	7	72	6	—	—
Columbia	19	10	64	9	—	—
Dartmouth	9	7	63	5	3	13
Duke	8	8	79	4	1	—
Georgetown	6	7	68	5	1	13
Harvard/Radcliffe	18	7	61	8	1	5
Johns Hopkins	20	5	67	2	1	5
Princeton	10	7	77	5	1	—
Stanford	20	8	57	10	1	3
Yale	15	8	71	6	—	—

Table 11.3. Admissions Data for Freshman Classes (1992–93)

University	Total applicants	Total admits	Admits' verbal SAT	Admits' math SAT	% in top tenth of high school class	% in top quarter of high school class
California	*20,281*	*8,700*	*563*	*654*	*95*	*100*
Brandeis	3,827	2,752	—	—	36	74
Brigham Young	7,365	5,402	—	—	48	82
Brown	12,194	2,953	620	670	87	95
Columbia	8,014	2,546	—	—	75	—
Dartmouth	8,076	2,107	622	681	85	98
Duke	14,528	3,859	—	—	88	97
Georgetown	10,116	2,973	—	—	68	90
Georgia Tech.	6,970	4,321	541	655	68	92
Harvard/Radcliffe	13,029	2,135	—	—	90	100
Johns Hopkins	7,820	3,390	610	685	72	93
Louisiana State	6,707	5,266	—	—	26	54
Michigan State	18,407	14,871	461	525	26	69
Ohio State	16,158	12,759	—	—	26	56
Princeton	12,716	2,026	640	700	90	100
Stanford	13,530	2,715	—	—	91	98
Colorado	13,761	10,473	—	—	28	66
Florida	12,444	8,273	—	—	50	85
Hawaii	3,664	2,896	440	539	—	—
North Carolina	16,580	5,735	530	592	76	94
Texas	14,235	9,319	521	600	48	84
Washington	12,516	6,969	—	—	54	91
Wisconsin	14,002	10,237	—	—	35	76
Yale	11,054	2,455	—	—	95	99

example of what many institutions of higher education, especially public institutions, may be confronting now or in the coming years. Other data, such as average SAT test scores for admittees and their rank in their high school class, are included in Table 11.3 in order to allow readers to make their own general comparisons among the various institutions.

All of the issues and tensions elaborated in this book are relevant to the admissions process of all colleges and universities. Moreover, they are consistent with such work force issues as selection for hiring, promotion, and training. Keep these consistencies in mind as the following discussion focuses on the example selected for this book, U.C. Berkeley admissions policy.

THE DIFFICULT ISSUE OF MATCHING

Any examination of admissions policy must carefully consider the issue of matching and its relevance to admissions. Even if it were possible to universally distribute admission to higher education at U.C. Berkeley, the additional challenges of distribution would remain, the chief of which has been central to the argument against affirmative action in admissions, namely, the problem of graduating all students who have been admitted. Critics of the Berkeley policy to accept half of all freshmen on a mix of criteria, the majority of which are other than academic, point to the gaps in graduation rates among racial groups. They note that the graduation rate for Hispanic and African-American students, the majority of whom enter Berkeley via Tier 2 (see Chapter 5), is only a little over half that of the graduation rate for whites and Asian-American students. [12]

Thomas Sowell, senior fellow at the Stanford University Hoover Institute, contends that "minority students with every prospect of achieving success [have been] turned into failures by being mismatched with institutions preoccupied with its minority body count." [13] What is the meaning of the "mismatching" referred to by Sowell, a process that turns what he calls "prospects of success" into "failures"?

According to critics of affirmative-action-type admissions, students who cannot perform at the level of U.C. Berkeley are nevertheless admitted in the name of fair representation. However, it is improbable that policy would encourage admission without the institutional and individual goal of graduation. It is more likely that the underlying assumptions that drive Tier 2 and Special Action admissions policies are that these students either are properly matched in the first place or can be made to match University of California standards subsequent to admission. In the latter case, some form of postadmission matching is indeed expected by means of a general acculturation to the academic environment of the university. [14] More directed postadmission matching is the goal of supportive services, such as those called for in the *Karabel Report* (see Chapter 5). [15] What might be called postadmission matching of Tier 2 and Special Action admits is expected to help ensure their graduation.

It is around the concept of matching that the tensions described in this book align. To say that matching *can* be accomplished after admission means to assume that the university environment can influence the mental ability or utilization of the mental ability that drives academic performance. To say that matching *cannot* be accomplished after admission to a demanding educational environment, such as that at Berkeley, means to assume that the mismatching generated at admission cannot be corrected. Several related assumptions may support the latter side of this debate. One assumption is that it is too late in life (young adulthood) for the environment to have such an effect, that the elementary school through high school years are the times when societal matching must take place. [16] Another is that the educational technology, such as high-power metacognitive training, necessary for the university environment to have such influence is lacking. A third general assumption, one that appears to be quite active in debates regarding admissions policy, is that mental ability and the level at which it is expressed are immutable and that intelligence cannot be learned.

These assumptions, which are posed as conjecture rather than as fact, either encase or address the assumption that matching of some sort, either before or after admission, is essential in the face of Berkeley's two-tiered policy. It has been argued that adequate matching has not occurred. Nevertheless, during the 1980s, while affirmative action admissions were at work, the overall academic merit of the student body increased rather than decreased. The average SAT score of all entering students has gone up over the past decade. Although the Asian-American and white average GPA is currently 4.0 and the average SAT is 1260, the average underrepresented minority high school GPA is 3.5 and the SAT is 1040. [17] While there is a gap between the two (GPA and SAT) averages, the lower of the two is certainly not a poor academic presentation.

Policy is based and amended on the interpretation of such data. While for some these data are evidence of the inadequacy of what appears to be differential admissions policy across racial groups, for others they are evidence of how very high the quality of incoming freshman is despite differential admissions. While for some the difference in dropout rate among racial groups is evidence of mismatching, for others it is evidence of differences in economic support, motivation, and acculturation. [18]

AN UNDERCURRENT OF TENSION

As discussed earlier, there is a positive relationship between the level of societal investment in the development of intelligence and mental ability and the prevailing perceptions regarding the malleability of intelligence and mental ability. The admission of, supportive services for, and eventual graduation of students who do not meet Tier 1 criteria can be considered a societal investment. Admissions policy, which manifests societal investment, is tremendously influenced by strong but entirely or substantively implicit notions of mental ability and its educability. The tension between competing assumptions regarding mental ability is also relatively unacknowledged in the context of policy. This tension manifests itself in political and legal conflict and in explicit policy; however, policy rarely explicitly traces, in a specific and detailed manner, its formation to underlying implicit tensions. Citizens served by policy are vaguely aware of shifts in policy and related social conflict, but they are not fully educated as to the multitude of relatively unspoken factors influencing such shifts. The societal inhibition regarding the in-depth debate of issues of intelligence as they pertain to policy development perpetuates this lack of understanding.

This reality is exemplified in the several investigations (still under way at the time of this writing) conducted by the Office of Civil Rights of the U.S. Department of Education of what has been called the "aggressive" affirmative action policy in admissions at U.C. Berkeley. [19] The press suggests that this study will find that the policy amounts to a form of reverse discrimination against white and Asian-American applicants. [20] The impact of such a decision may reach far beyond admissions policy to many other policy areas, including hiring practices, school desegregation policies, and judicial decisions. The media has given coverage to the net effect of this policy but not to the many forces that mold it and generate the tensions regarding the measurement, education, expression, and utilization of intelligence and mental ability.

What has been described as implicit intelligence policy is a running undercurrent to contemporary social thought and social policy. Were the undercurrent and its inherent tensions fully articulated, made entirely explicit, the impact of these undercurrents and inherent tensions would be more obviously related to and, consequently marshaled, in policy development and implementation. Citizens impacted by such policies as college admissions policy can be educated as to how their own implicit assumptions regarding mental ability as well as those of their legislators and other policy makers can drive policy. This chapter thus seeks to relate the inherent tensions in implicit intelligence policy to college admissions policy development and impact and to model, in abbreviated form, a suitable impact analysis. Recall that the four basic tensions having impact are the following:

TENSION 1: Academic merit versus fair representation
TENSION 2: Intelligence versus higher education as a determinant of worldly success
TENSION 3: Aptitude versus achievement
TENSION 4: Rationalist views versus empiricist views of knowledge acquisition

THE IMPLICIT UNDERGRID

Implicit intelligence policy forms an implicit undergrid, an invisible regulator that controls the content of explicit policy. This regulator is a web of unresolved theoretical and sociopolitical controversies containing the four basic tensions just mentioned, as well as other issues. Figure 11.1 shows a model of the flow of implicit tensions into explicit policies and their impacts. This flow diagram is based on the one designed by the author in Appendix B (see Figure B.1 for further clarification of Figure 11.1). As support for one side of a tension waxes or wanes, the elements of policy being influenced wax and wane as well. These tensions exist absent a resolution of the conflict between the assumptions that define them. Open resolution of these tensions or conflicts of assumption would be relatively explicit and would be one way to move intelligence policy into the realm of the explicit. Yet ongoing debate of major social questions is healthy in an intelligent democracy. Resolution, even if explicit, may not be ideal.

In fact, in 1992 Vice-Chancellor for Admissions and Enrollment Patrick Hayashi said of the debate regarding Berkeley's admissions policy, "I like the fact that the debate has become more intense. . . . When the state pays formal attention to race, [there is an added responsibility for] the people who carry out these policies to be very thoughtful. Everything we do should be analyzed and criticized." [21] Indeed, everything done in the name of social policy should be publicly examined. This bend toward social rationality might be taken a step further, however, by examining, via a more formal impact analysis, the implicit intelligence policy behind everything done in the name of social policy.

Ironically, it is the implicit and ongoing irresolution of the four major tensions that forms the core of implicit intelligence policy; however, the fact that the irresolution of these controversies regarding the malleability of intelligence and mental ability is implicit is far more of a problem than the question of whether or not implicit intelligence policy exists. Although some acknowledgment of these implicit tensions is made by the media—when it reports on policy decisions and student protests—these reports are but the tip of the iceberg. There is so much more to implicit intelligence policy than meets the eye. Although the "much more" seems amazingly obvious, it is rarely traced from the stages of policy development through policy implementation and on to policy impact. Why is it that thinking as basic and simple as this is not done as a matter of course?

Given that resolution of the dilemmas regarding intelligence may not be possible or even considered desirable, a potential and more readily achieved approach to moving implicit intelligence policy from the realm of the implicit to the realm of the explicit must be considered. *Instead of resolving conflicts and expecting them to remain resolved, the tensions could be made explicit, tied to corresponding elements of policy, and continuously monitored for their impacts in the form of policy outcome.* This suggests that policy makers should make an

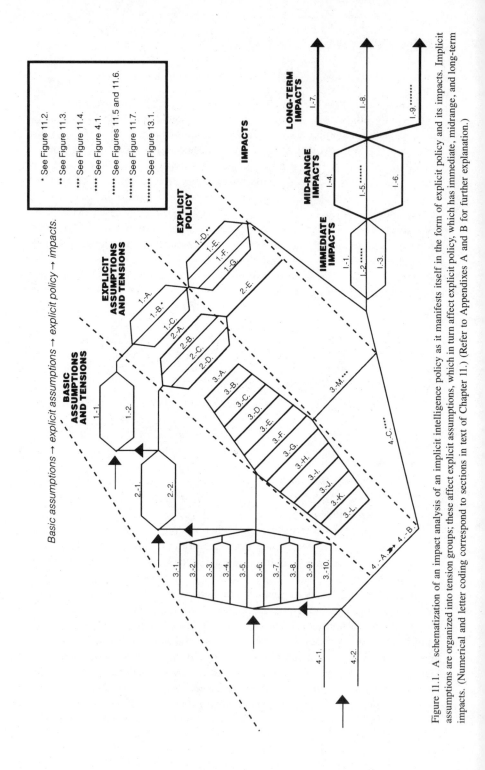

Basic assumptions → explicit assumptions → explicit policy → impacts.

BASIC ASSUMPTIONS AND TENSIONS

EXPLICIT ASSUMPTIONS AND TENSIONS

EXPLICIT POLICY

IMPACTS

IMMEDIATE IMPACTS

MID-RANGE IMPACTS

LONG-TERM IMPACTS

* See Figure 11.2.
** See Figure 11.3.
*** See Figure 11.4.
**** See Figure 4.1.
***** See Figures 11.5 and 11.6.
****** See Figure 11.7.
******* See Figure 13.1.

Figure 11.1. A schematization of an impact analysis of an implicit intelligence policy as it manifests itself in the form of explicit policy and its impacts. Implicit assumptions are organized into tension groups; these affect explicit assumptions, which in turn affect explicit policy, which has immediate, midrange, and long-term impacts. (Numerical and letter coding correspond to sections in text of Chapter 11.) (Refer to Appendixes A and B for further explanation.)

explicit and detailed specification of, and admission of the relationship of policies to, the tensions that drive the composition and amendments of these policies. Figure 11.1 is a schematic of such a specification. (All assumptions and tensions have been labeled with one of four basic tension numbers, 1 through 4, followed by a hyphen and a specific numeral or letter for a specific assumption or set of assumptions. All impacts have been labeled with an "I" followed by a hyphen and a specific impact number. See Figure 11.1.)

Impact analysis of implicit policy must be of a primarily theoretical nature because it concerns the examination of a massive yet invisible regulator built on a web of assumptions, theories, and the conflicts among them. Such an impact analysis must also be a combination of retrospective, prospective, and concurrent considerations. The following four sections of this chapter propose a conceptual framework for such an analysis. *Basic assumptions* are tracked to the *roots of the tensions* they generate as they undergo *translation into explicit assumptions and tensions* and eventually into *policies*. Each of these transformations of the basic assumptions are in themselves impacts of the basic assumptions. The final section then suggests various impacts of the combination of the four tensions. Although the impacts enumerated are in no way exhaustive, they serve the purpose of modeling impact analysis of implicit policy. (Note: Because many of the sources of information contained in this chapter have been referenced in earlier chapters, they are not referenced here.)

TENSION 1: ACADEMIC MERIT VERSUS FAIR REPRESENTATION

Of the four basic tensions, Tension 1 has the most obvious ties to explicit policy. (The one least clearly related to policy is Tension 4, the rationalist versus empiricist tension.) The basic assumptions underlying this tension are the following:

- *Academic merit*: Students should be admitted based on academic merit as indicated by academic achievement and test scores. This will best serve the students, the university, and the society (**1.-1.**).
- *Fair representation*: Students should be admitted based on their representation of the socioeconomic makeup of the encompassing society. This will best serve the students, the university, and the society (**1.-2.**).

Substance of the Tension

Competition for space at U.C. Berkeley is fierce. In 1975 there were 5,035 applications for admission; by 1988 there were over 22,000. About the same proportion of applicants were accepted both years. [22] Simply put, there is not room for everyone. Selection becomes increasingly selective, but not necessarily according to a single criterion. Academic merit admission narrows access to higher education to a limited number of high achievers and those with high test scores. Many applicants do not qualify. Fair representation admission, by contrast, provides access for a broader range of students more accurately representing the range of socioeconomic groups within society. These methods of selection are perceived to be in conflict in that students admitted through one route are not likely to be admitted through the other. Moreover, entry into the university by the fair representation route results in students who have had a different preparation for a university education than those who are admitted on the basis of academic merit, and the two groups may therefore perform differently.

Translation to Explicit Assumptions and Tensions

Academic merit and fair representation tend to be viewed and implemented as competing approaches to admission. At prestigious universities where space is limited, the number of students admitted under one of these approaches will be limited by the number of students admitted under the other approach (**1.-A.**). As space in the university comes into greater demand and becomes scarce (due to increasing population size and an increasing number of applicants from across that population), pressure from some sectors of society and some members of academia to select the top students from an academic standpoint increases (**1.-B.**, as shown in Figure 11.2). Note that the curve in Figure 11.2 is reminiscent of the curve drawn by Cattell to explain his ability-shift theory (Figure 2.4). Recall that Cattell's model indicated that a shift in demand for various levels of intelligence occurs in response to changing economic conditions: In times of scarcity, when opportunities for employment are more limited, the average "g" level of the population of employed people shifts upward. In times of abundance it shifts downward, with more people being employed at all "g" levels. This shift apparently occurs whether or not "g" actually corresponds with an explicitly identified criterion. The direction of economic and political pressure on merit-based admission policy is similar to that in Cattell's ability-shift model. Especially in times of scarcity, the tension between merit-based and fair representation admission approaches can become more profoundly explicit if the effects of merit-based admission standards are experienced as increasingly discriminatory when increasingly larger proportions of various applicant subgroups are rejected (**1.-C.**).

Translation to Explicit Policy

Figure 11.3 shows how a cutoff point can leave out subgroups who do not rank high by traditional measures of academic merit (**1.-D.**). In the case of U.C. Berkeley admissions policy, the response to competition between merit-based and

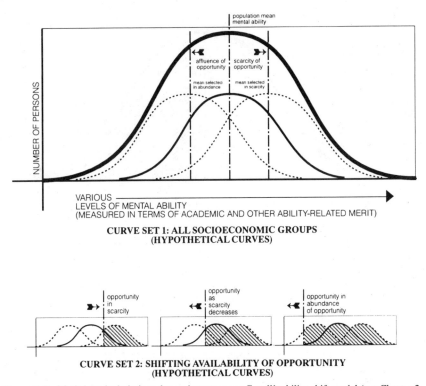

CURVE SET 1: ALL SOCIOECONOMIC GROUPS (HYPOTHETICAL CURVES)

CURVE SET 2: SHIFTING AVAILABILITY OF OPPORTUNITY (HYPOTHETICAL CURVES)

Figure 11.2. Merit-based admissions demand curve as per Cattell's ability-shift model (see Chapter 2 and its figures).

fair representation approaches to admission has been to allocate a percentage of admissions to each. In 1991 this percent allocation was the "50–50 criterion" (**1.-E.**). This percentage allocation shifted in 1991 from 40–60 to 50–50, increasing the proportion of merit-based admits. This is the element of policy that most definitely and explicitly responds to shifting political and economic pressures.

Other, more detailed, elements of policy stem from this basic tension. Among them is the influence of the statewide requirement that even students admitted via the Tier 2 route, which emphasizes flexible targets to bring about fair representation, must be U.C. eligible (in the top 12½% of California's high school seniors). This means that although Tier 2 has a lower merit base than Tier 1, it remains merit based (**1.-F.**). Other levels of detail appear in policy within the specification of special categories of secondary review, such as rural, older female, and economically deprived applicants. It is explicitly stated that these applicants will not be fairly or even reasonably represented if they must be admitted through academic merit standards (**1.-G.**). [23]

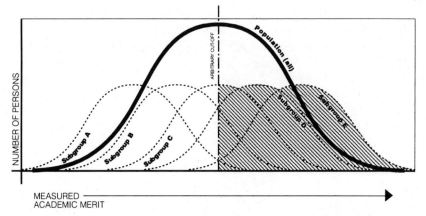

Figure 11.3. Variation among socioeconomic subgroups in academic merit admissions (as traditionally measured). Various socioeconomic subpopulations (with Subgroup A representing the lowest socio-academic group and Subgroup E representing the highest) are impacted differently by a single, often arbitrary, cutoff point.

TENSION 2: INTELLIGENCE VERSUS HIGHER EDUCATION AS A DETERMINANT OF WORLDLY SUCCESS

Debates regarding merit-based versus fair representation admissions involve the following basic assumptions regarding the role of intelligence and mental ability in determining the outcome of college education:

- *Intelligence in the form of mental ability* is (1) a primary determinant of the level of academic performance required to succeed in higher education and therefore (2) a primary determinant of worldly success (**2.-1.**).
- *Higher education* is (1) a primary determinant of the level of academic performance required to succeed in higher education (educational experience prior to higher education being also a primary determinant) and therefore (2) a primary determinant of worldly success (**2.-2.**).

Substance of the Tension

Merit-based admissions are predicated on precollege academic achievement. The choice of this approach to selection does not necessarily imply that academic achievement is officially viewed as being dependent on intelligence. Expressions for whatever is thought of as being intelligence—expressions such as *mental ability* or *cognitive ability* or even *academic achievement* itself—are frequently used, perhaps to diffuse reactions to the application of what may actually be a standard of inferred intelligence in admissions. Yet intelligence, or one of its milder expressions, is viewed as being either the precursor or the by-product of academic experience and achievement prior to college and thus implicitly connected in some way to success in higher education and later to worldly success.

Several arguments have been made from the standpoint that intelligence is indeed the precursor of academic and consequent worldly success. One of the most basic arguments states that tests of academic ability, whether aptitude or achievement tests, are "reasonably good measures of g." [24] Speaking of the link between "g" (or traditionally defined intelligence), academic success, and worldly success, Jensen referred to the "differing amounts of g-demanding educational requirements of various occupations." [25] These are, essentially, demands for intelligence made by both the occupational functions and the educational requirements of those occupations. Discussing the link between intelligence and job performance, Jensen explained that not everyone can do a given job, that "the threshold for successful performance . . . differs markedly for various occupations." [26] Professor John Hunter contended that learning is the key to job performance and that this learning is predicted by "general cognitive ability," which in turn "will be the key predictor of job performance." [27] Although psychologist James Crouse warned that academic ability is largely one-dimensional, at least for predicting life chances, he nevertheless concluded that "the most highly g-loaded tests were the best predictors of later success." [28]

The fabric of the argument that intelligence, in the form of mental ability, is the first and most important element in the sequence leading to worldly success begins to unravel when intelligence is perceived as being interpreted by, malleable within, and sensitive to environment. Crouse himself raised the possibility that the general academic ability that he linked to what he defined as intelligence "need not be linked to success and that its predictive validity may depend on existing practices among educators and employers that reward academic ability." [29] Given that existing interpretations of intelligence and its link to academic ability can shift, educational opportunity can move to the forefront as the primary determinant of worldly success. If higher education itself can affect the outcome of higher education, then fair representation admissions is a sound approach to admissions. Matching, in the form of standard supportive services and future versions of support that may actually work on the deepest metacognitive levels, is conceivable.

Translation to Explicit Assumptions and Tensions

The aforementioned implicit assumptions are potentially contradictory. The notion that intelligence is a determinant of worldly success tends to include within it the assumption that intelligence is a precursor of academic performance. On the other hand, academic performance may not be dependent on intelligence or on traditionally measured intelligence. Instead, one determinant of academic performance may be education, including higher education. If the assumption that intelligence is a precursor of academic performance is favored in admissions but is incorrect, many admitted students may do no better in college than those of a lower measured academic merit who are rejected (**2.-A.**). If the latter assumption that education is a determinant of academic performance is favored but is incorrect, many admitted students may be mismatched and may never graduate nor do well enough in college to achieve worldly success (**2.-B.**). That is, unless matching can remedy the mismatch. Many colleges have developed special programs (including remedial programs and motivational counseling) to ensure the graduation rate based on the assumption that postadmission matching is possible. [30]

When a public university such as U.C. Berkeley is taxpayer and voter supported, it must offer the promises of higher education to the citizens who support it. Restricting access to the promises of higher education to those who achieve and test high prior to admission at the university would offer these promises only to those perceived as the individuals most likely to realize them (**2.-C.**). However, if higher education, rather than mental ability or intelligence (regardless of their sources), is the key to worldly success, it should not be restricted to those with the most academic merit (**2.-D.**).

Translation to Explicit Policy

Admissions policy at U.C. Berkeley has, for the time being, settled on a 50–50 format. Whether or not this is an explicit attempt to address implicit and explicit tensions, it is a policy that serves both sides of the dilemma (**2.-E.**). Preadmissions matching is expected of the merit-based half of admissions (**2.-F.**), and postadmissions matching is expected, based on students' needs, for at least some of the other (**2.-G.**).

TENSION 3: APTITUDE VERSUS ACHIEVEMENT

Many basic assumptions contribute to the aptitude-versus-achievement dilemma. They are generally concerned with the perceived malleability of intelligence and mental ability. Again, the potential effects of higher education will be greater if intelligence and mental ability are malleable during the college years. Malleability supports broad and mixed admissions standards. In this view, aptitude itself is malleable and is readily transformed into achievement. The conflict between notions of aptitude and achievement can be broken into a number of conceptual dilemmas. A few of the relevant conflicting basic assumptions are as follows:

- *Aptitude versus achievement*
  - ○ Aptitude predicts educational and occupational performance (**3.-1.**).
  - ○ Achievement itself, rather than aptitude, is an appropriate predictor of later achievement (**3.-2.**).
- *Innate capacity versus learned ability*
  - ○ Intelligence is an innate capacity, primarily inherited and therefore relatively static. In former times the heritable quality of intelligence would have most likely been interpreted as "God-given" (**3.-3.**).
  - ○ Learned ability is ability acquired as a result of interaction with the environment (**3.-4.**).
- *Static, immutable, intelligence versus dynamic, mutable, intelligence*
  - ○ Static, immutable, intelligence, regardless of its origin in the nature–nurture scheme, is relatively rigid (**3.-5.**).
  - ○ Dynamic, mutable, intelligence, regardless of its origin in the nature–nurture scheme, is changeable, educable, moldable (**3.-6.**).
- *Measured ability versus the effects of socioeconomic status on measured ability*
  - ○ Measured intelligence indicates actual intelligence (**3.-7.**).
  - ○ The socioeconomic environment affects both the development and the measurement of intelligence; measured intelligence is merely an artifact (**3.-8.**).
- *One intelligence versus multiple intelligences*
  - ○ There is a single continuum of intelligence along which everyone can be arranged (**3.-9.**).
  - ○ There are several types of intelligence, and individuals vary in the set of intelligences they exhibit (**3.-10.**).

Substance of the Tension

Aptitude is generally considered a static ability, while achievement is generally viewed as dynamically determined by educational and environmental interaction. These notions are held in opposition to each other when it is argued that aptitude determines achievement or, in response to that argument, that achievement is independent of aptitude (if aptitude exists at all). The other basic assumptions listed in this section tend to result in similar polarization.

Translation to Explicit Assumptions and Tensions

Innate capacity versus learned ability is a tension that is guaranteed to exist between the poles of the contrasting beliefs in a relatively unchangeable social hierarchy versus a highly malleable one (**3.-A.**). In this polarization of models is housed the nature–nurture debate. The innate capacity model holds that intelligence is determined primarily by the genes. In previous eras the opportunities awarded on the basis of perceived innate capacity were viewed as God-given birth rights. In a more democratic era, tension builds around the pull of the opposing implications of the learned ability and innate capacity models (3.-B.).

Students who test low or appear less than bright are not encouraged to alter their mental abilities when these abilities are defined as relatively static (3.-C.). Compared to students who test high, they are assigned to a level at which they are expected to learn—at a slower pace—less challenging concepts and skills (3.-D.). However, when intelligence is viewed as being trainable, educational interventions such as metacognitive training are applied to students who test at all levels (3.-E.).

The conflict between the notion that measured intelligence is representative of actual intelligence and the assumption that socioeconomic factors influence the measurement of intelligence permeates much of education policy (3.-F.). This conflict is so omnipresent that it tends to remain undiscussed (and implicit) as policy is organized around it. Thus, tests are often "g" loaded but not labeled as such (3.-G.). The conflict becomes explicit when disputes emerge regarding the placement and labeling of students based on IQ test scores (3.-H.).

The single, unified intelligence model allows for what is a unidimensional classification of people along a single continuum of ability (3.-I.). This necessitates the distinctions among high, low, and average intelligences. Where educational and occupational opportunities are affected by this narrow linear definition of intelligence, there runs a deep tension (3.-J.). From the standpoint that advocates equal opportunity, measures of a single intelligence are viewed as myopic, restrictive, unfair, and imposed by a dominant culture (3.-K.). The multiple intelligence model allows recognition of other abilities, aptitudes, or intelligences and of alternatives to a unidimensional organization of intelligence (3.-L.).

Translation to Explicit Policy

The impact of this web of assumptions reaches in many directions. However, these effects can all be summarized by the following concept: The more mental ability is perceived as being malleable, the broader the range of mental ability in demand by universities and employers (3.-M.). This concept is drawn as a direct and positive relationship in Figure 11.4. Of course, one limitation is the cost of providing services to students who may not test or grade as high as traditional high achievers but who can be raised to a higher level if funds are available.

TENSION 4: RATIONALIST VIEWS VERSUS EMPIRICIST VIEWS

Although the rationalist–empiricist philosophical dichotomy took root long before the emergence of modern social issues, it persists today and extends its

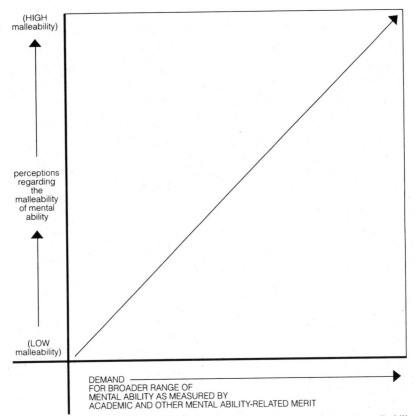

Figure 11.4. General demand for mental ability as it relates to perceptions regarding its malleability. Although there is no ascertainable direct relationship between the factors on the horizontal and vertical axes, a positive relationship of this sort is postulated.

tendrils into policies that affect, utilize, or categorize intelligence and mental ability, as college admissions policies do. The qualities of mind are no longer generally argued to be God given but are argued instead, with a modern rationalization for a new biological rationalism, to be gene given, or biologically determined. Modern empiricism opposes this modern biological rationalism. The opposing basic assumptions are as follows:

- *Rationalist view*: Knowledge originates within the mind (**4.-1.**).
- *Empiricist view*: Knowledge is acquired by the mind from the environment (**4.-2.**).

Substance of the Tension

The perceived power of the environment in the acquisition of knowledge is emphasized or diminished when influenced by one or the other of these basic philosophical stances, which run so deep that they have become inculcated without much conscious recognition of their influence (**4.-A.**). Nevertheless, their influence has trickled down through the ages into education policy, the most likely place for ancient speculation regarding the acquisition of knowledge to surface. After all, this is the arena in which public policy wrangles with the transfer of knowledge from teachers to students, from adults to children, and from the dominant culture that controls policy to subordinate subcultures that are affected by policy but have little official say regarding this process.

Translation to Explicit Assumptions and Tensions

The specific tensions between assumptions described in this chapter are affected by this underlying philosophical dichotomy, this nature–nurture argument (**4.-B.**).

Translation to Explicit Policy

This dilemma works its way up almost invisibly through the conceptual hierarchy of tensions listed in this chapter (through Tension 3 to Tension 2 and finally to Tension 1, as in Figure 11.1) until it emerges, well camouflaged and almost unrecognizable, into the realm of explicit tensions, explicit policies, and their consequences (**4.-C.**).

IMPACTS

The interrelationships among the four tensions become apparent when their impacts are considered. No single impact suggested here is exclusively related to one particular tension or to any other single factor, whether included here or not. Rather, it is the whole of the tangled web of assumptions that forms the intangible machinery of implicit intelligence policy that manifests these impacts and, in turn, feeds on them. Given this grand but subtle relationship between implicit assumptions and policy impacts, a few general impacts of intelligence policy are suggested in the following paragraphs.

Selected Immediate Impacts

• *The policy response to the tension between merit-based and fair representation approaches shapes the student body in a socially and academically hetero-*

geneous manner (**I.-1.**). Clearly, the composition of the student body is dictated by the mix of criteria applied to select students for admission. As Figure 11.3 shows, some high school students will not qualify for Tier-1-type admission, and among those who do qualify there may be broad variation as to academic merit. This results in the composition of an academically as well as socially heterogeneous student body.

• *Mixed admission standards admit students according to different criteria* (**I.-2.**). A student body admitted entirely on the basis of fair representation criteria would replicate the profile of the surrounding population, as depicted in Figure 11.5. Where fair representation is *modulated by academic criteria*, it creates from the representative sample of the population rendered by purely fair representation admission a new sample. This sample admits varying percentages of each subgroup, applying a differential merit-based modulator to admissions criteria for each subgroup (see Figure 11.6). While the university then opens itself to

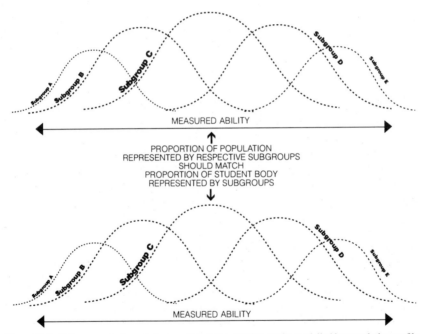

Figure 11.5. Fair representation admissions. Fair representation can be modelled by population profile. In this adaptation of Cattell's model, when these proportions are matched, and the student body (lower) set of curves generally mirrors the population (upper) set of curves, there is fair representation. Whether it be admissions, hiring, or any other distribution of opportunity, fair representation must meet this criterion. Refer to Figures 11.2 and 11.3 for further definition of the components of these figures.

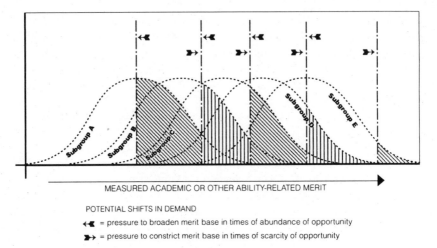

MEASURED ACADEMIC OR OTHER ABILITY-RELATED MERIT

POTENTIAL SHIFTS IN DEMAND

◄ = pressure to broaden merit base in times of abundance of opportunity

► = pressure to constrict merit base in times of scarcity of opportunity

Figure 11.6. Fair representation with merit-based modulation. When opportunities (in the form of admissions, jobs, or other gateways to social viability) are abundant, there is pressure to lower the lower limits of the standard merit base. Sub-bases form when the merit base is lowered for selected subpopulations only, for political or social reasons. Conversely, when opportunities are scarce, there is pressure to raise the lower limits of the merit base (and of any related sub-bases). Clearly, fair representation is more readily achieved in times of great abundance.

criticism, and even lawsuit, related to reverse discrimination and preferential admissions policy, it also applies some degree of academic merit selection to the fair representation process.

• *Fair representation admission places new demands on the university for supportive services* (**I.-3.**). The differences in preparation become apparent when students arrive in the classroom. It is there that admissions policy gains a face. Dinesh D'Souza claims, "You cannot hide the gap in preparation from students in the same classroom." [31] A U.C. Berkeley chemistry professor was quoted in the *San Francisco Chronicle* as saying, "The difference between the ability of students I teach is clear. . . . There are some students in my courses who shouldn't be there." [32] Whenever half of the student body is admitted at a lower standard of academic merit than the other half, a portion of the first half may require supportive services. In fact, the *Karabel Report* suggested exactly this point when it called for additional secondary review categories. [33]

Selected Midrange Impacts

• *The Academic Index Score (AIS) offers inadequate prediction of college academic performance for some students* (**I.-4.**). The soundness of the AIS as a predictor of academic performance has been examined in terms of the soundness of its two components, the high school grade point average (GPA) and the combined SAT and achievement test scores. The validity of tests as predictors of academic performance was explored in Part I and Part II of this book; the validity of the GPA as a predictor is also worthy of discussion. An examination of the records of undergraduate students entering U.C. Berkeley in 1983, a cohort composed of 3,770 freshman, revealed that high school GPA is not a clear-cut (positively correlated and linear) predictor of academic performance in college. [34] Instead, the relationship between high school GPA and college GPA varies, depending on the high school GPA. That is, at the upper end of the distribution of high school GPAs the relationship is strong and positive; students with high GPAs in high school show high GPAs in college. However, this strongly positive relationship "deteriorates" to no relationship (or to a "null relationship") when high school GPAs drop to about 3.0. [35] This means that admissions based on GPA, or partially on GPA, may not be based on adequate predictors of college performance for all applicants. Universities may be drawn to select applicants with the highest GPAs owing to the positive predictability of their high college GPAs. This same study also examined SAT scores as predictors and compared their validity as predictors to the validity of the GPA. The relationship between SAT scores and college GPAs was found to be more direct (more linear) than the relationship between high school GPAs and college GPAs. Interestingly, SAT scores were found to have a weaker relationship than high school GPAs under one set of conditions: where high school GPA did manifest a relationship to college GPA (i.e., for high school GPAs above 3.0), it was a stronger relationship than that between the SAT and the college GPA. [36] This finding was examined for variation by gender and race; however, instead of variation in the pattern, consistency was found. The power of this finding thus appears universal. [37]

• *There can be continuing shifts in selection ranges due to external political, economic, and population pressures* (**I.-5.**). The balance between merit-based and fair representation criteria is a sensitive one. Political pressure over time can lead to shifts favoring one or the other approach. Specifically, economic pressure, in times of scarcity, can reduce scholarship and funding options and raise tuition. Most critically, it can limit the ratio of admissions slots to number of applicants, thus responding to the increasing societal emphasis placed on high-quality higher education. The midrange effect of the tension between the two admissions policy approaches is that the university selection process reflects external pressures and shifts in response to them. Figure 11.7 depicts the various shifts in selection range that can occur with respect to different subgroups when selection criteria change.

• *Shifts in public trust and constituent support* (**I.-6.**). The *Karabel Report* explained that the public's trust in the fairness of the university's admissions procedures had been "eroded" by doubt regarding the appropriateness of the various selection criteria applied by the university. [38] The rise and fall of public

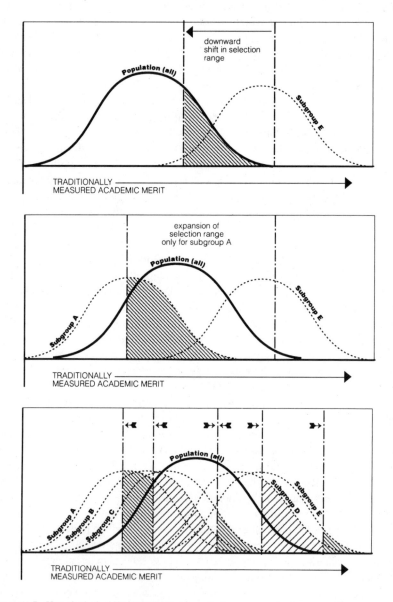

Figure 11.7. Hypothetical shifts in selection ranges in response to the economic pressures of abundance and scarcity. (*Above*) A downward shift in selection range. (*Center*) Expansion of selection range only for subgroup A. (*Below*) Multiple shifts among varying subgroups.

support for admissions criteria indicates the shifting level of trust held by the public. In that U.C. Berkeley is taxpayer and constituent supported, public trust is an important ingredient in continuing support.

Selected Potential Long-Term Impacts

• *Alteration of the character of the university can be difficult to reverse* **(I.-7.)**. Whether or not the changes brought about by shifting admissions standards are desirable, the results of these changes may be difficult to reverse. The university environment adapts to the characteristics of its student body, which is, in turn, molded by admissions policy. However, adaptations become institutionalized, officially mandated, and bureaucratically established, and cannot be readily reversed.

• *Potential alteration of the contribution of the university to society* **(I.-8.)**. As the pressure to fairly respond to the needs of all quarters of society mounts, academic excellence is no longer the sole goal of the university. Serving the public, broadening the distribution of opportunity, educating the future labor force, and other social goals emerge as priorities. Whether or not the shifting and mixing of goals is desirable, it alters the contribution of the university to society.

• *University admissions policy is continuously reflective of prevailing assumptions regarding the acquisition of knowledge and the demand for that knowledge* **(I.-9.)**. As political and economic pressures from outside the university gain power to dictate who gains admission into the university, the effects of implicit intelligence policy will be increasingly registered in admissions policy. The societal investment in admitting students who manifest a broader range of mental ability and academic achievement will increase as their ability is increasingly viewed as malleable. (This quintessential relationship has been captured in Figure 13.1.)

12

Recommendations and Conclusions
Toward a Coherent and Explicit Intelligence Policy

People are different from one another in ways that are both meaningful and measurable. But somehow, without sufficient deliberation, we have taken a great collective leap from the commonplace belief to the conviction that there are precise, measurable graduations of ability (and stability) that can be used to send children to the right classrooms, adults to the right job slots, and patients to the right psychological interventions.

Decision-makers need a sound, fair, and reasonably efficient mechanism to help them make difficult decisions about the allocation of opportunity among individuals and institutions. In many circumstances, standardized tests serve a useful role. Certainly, people have different abilities and skill levels. Another way to say this is that life is not fair. But that does not relieve us of the burden of being as fair as we can possibly be as we measure differences and assign meaning to them.

BERNARD R. GIFFORD [1]

As Gifford contends, decision makers need a mechanism to assist in making difficult decisions regarding the allocation of opportunity. It is suggested herein that a special form of impact analysis be used to extract, and make more explicit, the powerful tensions inherent in the implicit intelligence policy behind explicit college admissions and other policies. Although this mechanism will not necessarily resolve the many difficulties of opportunity allocation, it will force the specification, even illumination, of the biases that drive policy and its outcome. Greater control over the effects of these biases should result.

179

Assigning meaning to differences in ability is likely to persist as long as human beings differ from one another. The allocation of opportunity, especially educational opportunity, will, most likely, continue to present dilemmas of efficiency and fairness wherever mental ability is identified, educated, and utilized. Given the ongoing reality of a dilemma-ridden implicit intelligence policy, a concerted effort must be made to connect the elements and tensions of such policy to their explicit counterparts and explicit impacts. In this endeavor, admissions policy provides an especially interesting challenge. It is, by nature, relatively succinct and, by administrative standards, very explicit. Yet admissions policy is built on an array of bureaucratic, political, economic, and cultural expectations. As tangible, succinct, and explicit as it purports to be, it has an ambiguous underbelly filled with unspecified tensions regarding academic merit versus fair representation, intelligence versus education as a determinant of worldly success, aptitude versus achievement, and, at a deep level, a modern counterpart of the rationalist-versus-empiricist argument. These tensions percolate up from the realm of ancient philosophy into scientific research, sociopolitics, and explicit college admissions policy. To deny their power is to allow them to invisibly manipulate policy. This denial is dangerous.

BASIC QUESTIONS TO ASK OF ADMISSIONS POLICY

Policy makers and their constituents must therefore routinely question higher education admissions (and other) policies in order to make more explicit the elements of implicit intelligence policy. They must do the following:

A. GOALS
1. Seek to determine and describe what, if any, implicit assumptions regarding intelligence drive the general goals of higher education. Examine all missions, goals, and objectives statements.
2. Seek to determine and describe what, if any, implicit assumptions regarding intelligence drive the specific goals of higher education admissions policy. Use an impact analysis of implicit intelligence policy to assess this.
3. Seek to determine and describe what, if any, relationship admissions policy has to the explicit goals of the institution.

B. MEASUREMENT
1. Seek to determine and describe what, if any, implicit assumptions regarding intelligence are held by those who design the instruments and methods of evaluation of student admission applications. If met with a refusal to answer such inquiries, seek out settings, statements, and documents from which these assumptions can at least be inferred.

2. Seek to determine and describe what, if any, implicit assumptions regarding intelligence are held by those who design the instruments and methods of assessment of individual student performance following college admission. If met with a refusal, again seek out means of inferring these assumptions.

3. Seek to determine and describe what, if any, implicit assumptions regarding intelligence are held by those who design the instruments and methods of evaluation of institutional performance. Note where these differ and/or resemble the assumptions behind the assessment of individual student performance.

C. POLITICAL INFLUENCE

1. Seek to determine and describe what, if any, implicit assumptions regarding intelligence are held by those who support, propose, and mandate higher education admissions and other policies. Clearly specify these assumptions.

2. Seek to determine and describe what, if any, implicit assumptions regarding intelligence are held by those who fund higher education admissions and other policies. Once again, clearly specify these assumptions.

D. STUDENT VIEWS

1. Seek to determine and describe what, if any, implicit assumptions are held by the students regarding their own intelligence.

2. Seek to determine and describe what, if any, implicit assumptions are held by the students regarding their own ability to compete academically.

3. Seek to determine and describe what, if any, implicit assumptions are held by students and would-be students regarding their ability to raise their own academic performance.

E. INSTITUTIONAL EVALUATION

1. Seek to determine and describe what, if any, implicit assumptions regarding intelligence are held by those who are in a position to interpret and to utilize the findings of assessments in institutional evaluation.

2. Seek to determine and describe what, if any, implicit assumptions regarding intelligence drive the determination of type of student evaluation that is used in university assessment.

3. Seek to determine and describe what, if any, information institutional assessment findings feed to the admission-selection process.

THE POTENTIAL ROLE OF IMPACT ANALYSIS

In the case of implicit intelligence policy, impact analysis must be relatively hypothetical, theoretical, qualitative, and prospective. Steps of an impact analysis should include the following:

1. Begin implicit policy impact analysis by clarifying and stating specific explicit assumptions and tensions regarding mental ability and its utilization. Seek the sociopolitical, scientific, philosophical, and economic sources of these assumptions. Seek to determine how these assumptions drive policy design and its eventual outcome.
2. Make it one of the preliminary goals of policy development to achieve some type of consensus not on the nature of mental ability and intelligence but on the definition and wording of the explicit forms of the implicit assumptions and tensions regarding mental ability and intelligence. *This translation process is essential.*
3. Commit a portion of policy development to discovering the aforementioned assumptions and tensions. One of the preliminary goals of policy development must be the conversion of these assumptions and tensions into an explicit form and a clarification of them. Map policy and its potential impacts onto assumptions (as shown in Figures 11.1 and 13.1).
4. One of the goals of higher education policy makers must be to determine what, if any, assumptions and tensions regarding intelligence underlie educational goals and how these affect policy. These effects must be thoroughly clarified for students, educators, administrators, and the public.

SPECIFIC PROPOSALS FOR ADMISSIONS POLICIES THAT SPECIFY THEIR RELATIONSHIP TO INTELLIGENCE POLICY

The 50–50 criterion, set forth in the *Karabel Report* (see Chapter 5) and implemented at U.C. Berkeley beginning in the fall of 1991, split the difference equally between conflicting views regarding the goals of the university with respect to opportunities to develop abilities. Thus, 50% of all admissions are to be merit based, and 50% are to be aimed at fair representation. The policy solution to the "tension" [2] is to apportion opportunity evenly according to these two different modes of allocation. While at first glance this appears to be splitting the difference, the reality is that even the admission via the fair representation process is academically based. It must be inferred that maintaining an academic base even in the fair representation process means that some assumption regarding the necessity to uphold or match academic standards is still operative.

Other mechanisms of allocation can be designed to distribute opportunity perhaps even more fairly than the 50–50 approach (with its contiguous academic baselines). Some of these would require a greater degree of self-selection (prior to application) on the part of the students, placing more of the burden of their selection for admission on them, thereby extending and making explicit the boundaries in which self-selection is assumed to be viable. Alternative allocation mechanisms include the following:

1. Require that all students enter the university via the junior college route. Carry this requirement to the extreme by refusing to admit any student to the university before the junior year. Do not consider admission for students who still need to take preliminary "core" courses or basic requirements. Have the junior college perform *all* remediation of educational gaps, including *all* basics. Have the junior college *refuse* to graduate students who do not meet all requirements at a certain level of respectable competence. If junior college students are still interested in further education (self-selection) after choosing and committing to a major and completing the required course work, upon graduation they can apply to specific university departments as per the graduate school model.

2. Institute voluntary tracking. Establish explicit tracks for the bachelor of arts degree. Allow students to select the track for which they feel most fit. Grade students competitively and encourage voluntary "retracking" if they are not matched properly or are dissatisfied with their grade averages. At graduation, explicitly specify the track completed by awarding "B.A., track 1," "B.A., track 2," and so on. This method would allow future employers to understand what level of education job applicants' grade averages correspond to.

3. Combine these two procedures into a bundle. Make explicit to the public, to applicants, to graduate schools, and to employers the processes used for admissions, self-selection, grading, and tracking. A bachelor of arts degree on track 1 would be recognized as one awarded to students in the highest echelon.

Controlled self-selection is, of course, not devoid of institutional and individual assumptions regarding mental ability and intelligence. To remove self-selection almost entirely from the process, while also avoiding institutional selection, the following lottery method could be adopted.

4. Institute a lottery for selection. Whether or not they seek admission, all young people who are of a particular age and meet certain very basic criteria would be selected by means of a blind lottery. The criteria would be set by the state legislature with or without advice provided by university faculty and administrators and would include residence in the state or the nation, high school graduation, and a passing grade average. Obviously, fewer biases regarding ability differences would enter the admissions picture. Fairness would be established by allowing—even forcing or drafting—equal probability of opportunity for everyone.

Blind lottery selection, while perhaps most egalitarian, could prove a disincentive to high school students who might otherwise study hard to qualify for college admission. But perhaps blind admission would offer new incentive to disadvantaged youth who never expected to go to college.

If some or all of the above suggested approaches seem unreasonable, readers should inquire of themselves and their colleagues what assumptions regarding mental ability and intelligence are influencing their perceptions. This may be an opportunity to lift the shroud of denial. The drive for egalitarian reform has hit the tough reality of its implementation. But the struggle to redistribute opportunity in the form of college admissions and other functions is not over. In a sense, it has barely begun. Policies are uncontrollable when underlying forces have not been made explicit. Answers to critical questions such as the following must be sought: Are increasingly egalitarian measures problematic because of preconceived and rigid assumptions regarding ability? Or is there an undeniable reality to preset individual differences in mental ability? And are the interactions of preset individual differences with motivational and cultural factors so powerful that, whatever the preset conditions are, they are minimally potent by comparison to the interactions? How much of our reality is determined by our perceptions of it?

13

From Here to a Coherent and Explicit Intelligence Policy

> The ingenuity of the economists may be said to have postponed recognition of the fact that the most important factor is people—the distribution of intelligence in the people. For the rest of what economics deals with, the rule is allowed to hold that what is valuable and useful will be produced in proportion to the demand for it.
>
> RAYMOND B. CATTELL [1]

Whatever course of evolution college admissions and other selection policies take, they will serve as a meter of the evolution of all the implicit assumptions, tensions, and unwritten policies behind them. This meter must be read with ever-watchful eyes. All opportunities for the development of an explicitly articulated intelligence policy must be accepted as a challenge for the betterment of all social policy.

MAPPING INTELLIGENCE POLICY TO MAKE IT EXPLICIT

In the central instance of higher education admissions policy, it is critical that policy makers, administrators, students, and the public understand how education policy maps itself onto the network of implicit intelligence policy. A literal mapping is useful in accomplishing this goal. Figures 11.1 and 13.1 are maps that aim to unearth and make explicit what is otherwise implicit. Figure 11.1 tracks the flow of implicit assumptions into tensions that crystallize into explicit policies and their various outcomes. The tracking of elements in Figure 11.1 suggests that with diligent scrutiny the effects of implicit policy on specific components of explicit policy can be related to certain outcomes, actual and projected. In this way, strands of logic (or of what is assumed to be logical reasoning) can be pulled from the

185

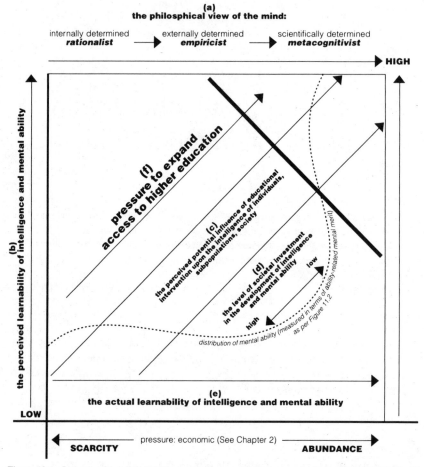

Figure 13.1. Impacts of implicit intelligence policy on admissions and other social policies. In this figure the distribution curve of mental ability and the fluctuation in demand (thick black line) for mental ability (as depicted in Cattell's model, diagrammed in Figures 2.1, 2.2, 2.3, and 2.4) are inverted and placed over the map of hypothetical relationships depicted in Figure 4.1. A culmination of the models set forth herein, this figure brings together the significant impacts of, and forces at work in, all implicit intelligence policies.

unspoken into the spoken, from the obscure into the more distinct realms of identifiable policy impact. Such an impact analysis must always be placed in the context of larger forces.

In a culmination of the theoretical review and synthesis on which this book has been constructed, Figure 13.1 charts the context for Figure 11.1. In Figure 13.1

the economically oriented Figure 2.4 (p. 20) and Figure 11.2 (p. 165) are imported into Figure 4.1 (p. 61). Figure 13.1 thus represents the *inextricable relationship* between policies that utilize ability, such as college admissions policy (as per Cattell's economic model), and the forces and tensions of implicit policy as delineated in this book. A "continuum f," which represents the pressure to increase or decrease emphasis on merit-based admissions, has been added to Figure 13.1. Unlike Cattell's original ability-shift model (Figure 2.4), this model recognizes multiple forces, with economic pressure being not the sole force but the force that allows the others to operate or constrains them in their operation. All of the pressures charted in Figure 13.1 are seen as contextually relevant.

Coherent intelligence policy can give birth to itself by becoming explicit. This mapping of selection policy onto the network of implicit assumptions (as in Figure 11.1), aided by a theoretical impact analysis (as in Figure 13.1), serves as a beginning. Policy makers must ultimately commit to making explicit the relationships between their policies and underlying assumptions regarding the malleability of intelligence. Seekers and providers [2] of educational opportunities must unearth the assumptions that drive related policies.

SPEAKING TRUTH TO POWER

The previous chapters have looked at intelligence from a broad variety of perspectives. If but one truth were to emerge from the concatenation of definitions, assumptions, theories, findings, and policies regarding intelligence and its utilization, this truth would be a simple one: There is, to date, no single prevailing and satisfactory definition of intelligence. Implicit intelligence policy has no solid immutable core. Rather, it is composed of an insubstantial but highly complex and powerful web of conflicting assumptions that crystallize into the four basic tensions around which college admissions and other social policies form.

In light of Cattell's models of the shifting demand for intelligence, a second truth can be detected: It is through the unstable lens of economic subjectivity that the value and usefulness of intelligence are perceived. The standards used in defining and satisfying demand for intelligence shift in response to shifts in the supply of opportunity. The standards during times of scarcity, when opportunity is limited, are restrictive and perceived as elitist. In times of abundance, when there is plenty of opportunity to go around, standards defining intelligence are generous and perceived as egalitarian. Even the political forces that define intelligence ebb and flow with economic tides.

Perhaps the ultimate truth to be ferreted out here is one that upon closer, more piercing reflection, rises out of the subjective muddle of implicit assumptions: The "concept of intelligence has outlived its usefulness in science." [3] To take this sad reflection one step further and create a broader and more ironic message, it may not be the *concept* of intelligence but intelligence itself that has outlived its usefulness, and not only in science but in social policy as well. Either way, we seem to be asking intelligence to fade out of our awareness.

Especially in selection policies, which distribute opportunity according to economically and politically influenced formulas, intelligence is a moving target. The definition of and even references to intelligence are perpetually dependent on its perceived value, usefulness, and political appropriateness. Intelligence becomes just a word, often a negative one that, having been associated with IQ and genetic determination of social status, is frequently replaced by less loaded terms such as *mental ability* and *human talent*.

College admissions and other selection policies, whether public or private, must respond to the scrutiny of the courts that judge them, the mandates of executive offices that monitor them, and the requirements of the legislative actions that dictate their characteristics. In this sense, most selection policies are, to a great degree, *public* policies. While private universities and private employers have more freedom to dictate their own selection policies than do their public counterparts, they are nevertheless required to function within the realm of publicly ordained controls on prejudice, bias, and other unfair selection practices. Such external or public controls are necessary in a societal environment in which organizations do not initiate self-control of their own accord.

Selection policies are mirrors of the times. In recent decades these policies have been increasingly based on factors that have little to do with the intelligence of the applicants, by any definition of intelligence. Other characteristics, including experience, gender, ethnicity, and more loosely defined talents, are increasingly important data in the selection process. It is this trend that must be closely monitored. As the distribution of opportunity takes increasing precedence over the identification and utilization of mental talent, the polity and its members, the citizens, must learn to spot the point at which balance is lost, the point at which implicit intelligence policy drives explicit policy too far in a particular direction, be it the restrictive or expansive extreme. A balance is essential. For example, the tension between fair representation and academic or intellectual merit (Tension 1) is useful if it protects both causes, if it protects admissions policy from one or the other extreme.

But exactly when is the balance between the extremes lost? How can a shift in the balance or a trend of shifting balances be detected? Such questions are not easily answered nor are they easily asked.

One reason for failure to question is the enormity of overarching trends, which are almost too enormous to see and large enough in scope to ward off true scrutiny. Another reason is the complexity of the question. The time and tools needed to examine social policies or the implicit factors molding them may be lacking. Instead, large political, economic, and philosophical forces are left to determine the course of these policies, as well as the opportunities they afford.

Is there a remedy that might prompt the questioning of these matters? A logical response is to create the opportunity for all citizens to have an adult educational experience that provides them with the time and analytical training to look for imbalances in policy. Here, a strong case for less stringent college admissions policies, and perhaps even universal public college admissions, can be made. An educated citizenry is a strong citizenry. A case for making policy analysis a required undergraduate course can also be made here.

Yet from quite the opposite perspective emerges another reason for the growing ignorance or denial regarding imbalances in selection policies. Questions regarding and monitoring imbalances may be too painful if the process forces a confrontation with the notion that intelligence itself has outlived its usefulness in a mechanistic, institutionalized, diversely and densely populated world. Is there a real desire to ask whether or not intellectual excellence is still held in high esteem? Will there be a discovery that many of the best and brightest minds are being lost in the shuffle or, worse, that a great many of these minds are systematically sacrificed in the name of economic and political values? Does society still value intellectual excellence? Did it ever? Is such excellence even recognizable?

DIMINISHING DEMAND FOR INTELLIGENCE DIMINISHES ITS SUPPLY

The most painful of truths may indeed be that intelligence has outlived its usefulness. As selection policies shift away from an emphasis on intelligence, first to mental ability, then to human talent, and on to other more socioeconomic characteristics of applicants, the demand for what was once considered intellectual excellence appears to wane.

From a general economic perspective, as quoted by Cattell at the beginning of this chapter, "what is valuable and useful will be produced in proportion to the demand for it." Cattell offered this observation as part of a larger statement that says that the ingenuity of economists has actually "postponed recognition of the fact that the most important factor is people—the distribution of intelligence in the people." And, yes, the actual distribution of intelligence within the population is important in terms of the preservation, education, and utilization of intelligence. But basic economic influences overpower what is important even in the special domain of intelligence. Economic and related political forces may be the unbeatable pressures that select out intelligence. Alas, it is unfortunate but undeniably possible that as selection policies demand less in the area of intelligence and intellectual excellence, the supply of such excellence will diminish. When other attributes are selected for, are emphasized by policy, those will be the ones presented, stimulated, and preserved. The human intellect may recede into hiding to survive, its supply and demand restricted to a small, hidden subculture.

FOR WHOM THE BELL TOLLS

Higher education admissions policy can overlook the most promising of minds, even a mind as great as that of Albert Einstein. In the case of Einstein, a brilliant mind was able to overcome the failure to be selected and to go on to share itself with the world. [4] However, it is essential to ask: How much of this precious, albeit elusive, resource—intelligence—is lost in the selection shuffle? The failure of a society to utilize its wealth of mental ability may be its death knell. Were this failure obvious at any one point in time, action could perhaps be taken to correct it. But if this failure were slowly and obscurely overtaking society, would it be detected?

Higher education now faces growing pressure to provide opportunity to a broader segment of society. And higher education is thus becoming overloaded with the responsibility for correcting social imbalances originating well outside its domain. Certainly, there is much that begs correction. As social critic Mortimer Adler wrote of what he perceived to be the "inadequacy of the schools":

> Not only are distressingly large numbers of high school graduates unable to read and write to that minimum degree which must be possessed by free minds participating in a democratic community, but the evidence further shows that after graduation they have neither appetite nor capacity for reading anything better than the local newspaper or mediocre fiction. Some of these high school graduates have terminated their schooling. For them there is little hope. School has given them neither the equipment nor the impulse to continue their education out of school. Their intelligence, of whatever degree, has been so untrained and so uncultivated, that they will be ready to follow the first demagogue who seeks to beguile them. [5]

If higher education can actually train and cultivate intelligence, it may be society's—the human species'—greatest investment. If this be the case, let us compel all citizens to go to college. This, of course, is a major investment of taxpayers' money. To protect and enhance any socially just system, there must be a judicious, ethical, and conscious weighing of societal investments in the development of mental ability (and in the distribution of knowledge) against the assumptions and tensions that drive those investments. As global economic and environmental pressures mount, this weighing of societal investments against the tensions that drive them may be the human species' only opportunity to ensure the survival of the very intelligences (plural intended) that are required to carry on the existence of human life on earth. The bell tolls for all of society when opportunity is denied or misallocated due to ignorance. The bell tolls for all of humanity when the keen and diverse intelligences it has evolved are neglected. After all, who is to say what forms of intelligence will best meet the dramatic challenges of life on a changing planet in a harsh cosmos?

APPENDIXES

A

Relevant Models of
Impact Analysis

A thing is safe if its risks are judged to be acceptable.
W. W. LOWRANCE [1]

GENERAL EXPLANATION

When conceptualizing an impact analysis methodology that can be applied to obscure, vague, implicit policy, existing precedents must be examined. However, most of these precedents deal with explicit policies and their impacts. Nevertheless, exploring these existing impact analyses can be quite instructive. Various approaches have been taken in the analysis of the impact of actions and nonactions dictated by public as well as private policies.

While policy impacts have long been the focus of political and legislative debates, a distinctly analytical perspective has emerged in the form of environmental impact analysis (EIA). There has been a great deal of in-depth planning of procedures for analyzing the impact of an environmental policy on an existing or potential environmental condition, especially when the problem being analyzed has called for the enactment of a policy to control or prevent it. A map of the EIA process is found in Figure A.1.

Systems theory and general systems thinking have become central to scientific, political, and cultural understandings of environmental ecology. The environment is now viewed as a system or network of relationships. Figure A.2 shows what is termed a "network approach to systems diagramming," an approach in which relationships between various components of an environment (in this case an upland ecosystem) are linked. Figure A.2 also includes statistically derived numbers that indicate the relative weights of these relationships.

Many interrelationships have been identified in environments, resulting in numerous methods being devised (including computer programs) for measuring

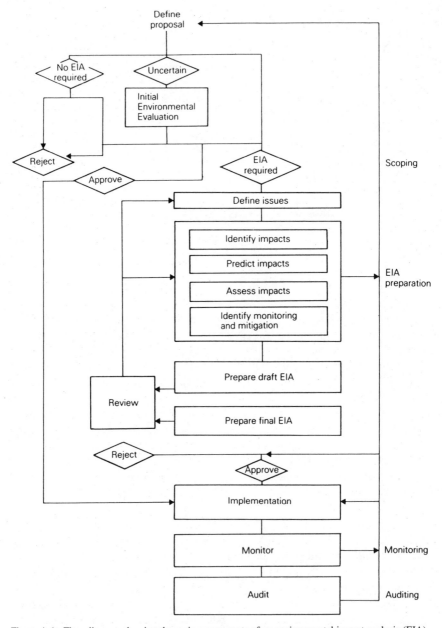

Figure A.1. Flow diagram showing the main components of an environmental impact analysis (EIA) system. [17]

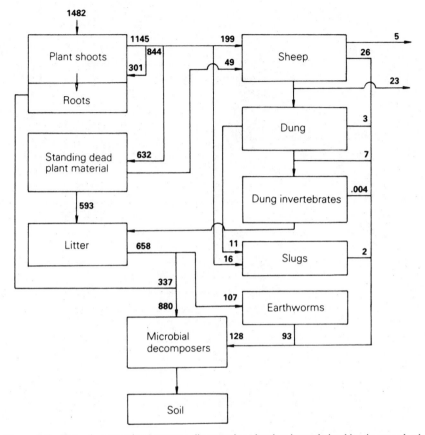

Figure A.2. Network approach to systems diagramming showing interrelationships in an upland ecosystem. [18]

the relationships among the multitude of components under study. Figure A.3, a section of what is called the "Leopold matrix," lists all actions associated with a proposed project or policy along its horizontal dimension, with the vertical dimension listing the impact of these actions on any and all areas or components. Such a chart or matrix makes it possible to trace the impact stemming from the implementation of an action or policy through to subsequent subactions or steps.

Social policy analysts have built on the systems thinking approach used in environmental impact analysis. Systems thinking was already in place when urban impact analysis (UIA) emerged. Figure A.4 models the levels of impact of policies and projects on a city or urban area. The theoretical breakdown of policy impacts

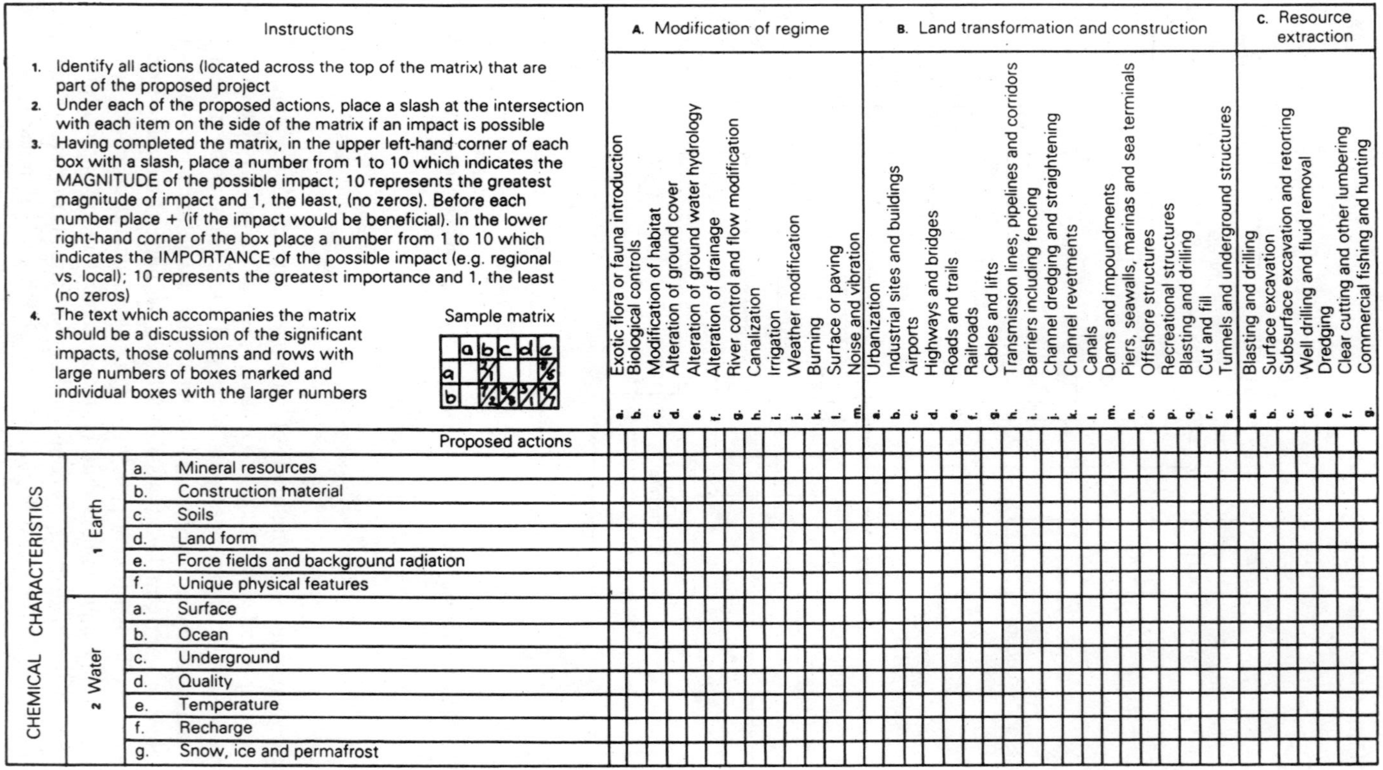

Instructions

1. Identify all actions (located across the top of the matrix) that are part of the proposed project
2. Under each of the proposed actions, place a slash at the intersection with each item on the side of the matrix if an impact is possible
3. Having completed the matrix, in the upper left-hand corner of each box with a slash, place a number from 1 to 10 which indicates the MAGNITUDE of the possible impact; 10 represents the greatest magnitude of impact and 1, the least, (no zeros). Before each number place a + (if the impact would be beneficial). In the lower right-hand corner of the box place a number from 1 to 10 which indicates the IMPORTANCE of the possible impact (e.g. regional vs. local); 10 represents the greatest importance and 1, the least (no zeros)
4. The text which accompanies the matrix should be a discussion of the significant impacts, those columns and rows with large numbers of boxes marked and individual boxes with the larger numbers

Sample matrix

	a	b	c	d	e
a		X			%
b	%%				

Proposed actions

A. Modification of regime
a. Exotic flora or fauna introduction
b. Biological controls
c. Modification of habitat
d. Alteration of ground cover
e. Alteration of ground water hydrology
f. Alteration of drainage
g. River control and flow modification
h. Canalization
i. Irrigation
j. Weather modification
k. Burning
l. Surface or paving
m. Noise and vibration

B. Land transformation and construction
a. Urbanization
b. Industrial sites and buildings
c. Airports
d. Highways and bridges
e. Roads and trails
f. Railroads
g. Cables and lifts
h. Transmission lines, pipelines and corridors
i. Barriers including fencing
j. Channel dredging and straightening
k. Channel revetments
l. Canals
m. Dams and impoundments
n. Piers, seawalls, marinas and sea terminals
o. Offshore structures
p. Recreational structures
b. Blasting and drilling
r. Cut and fill
s. Tunnels and underground structures

C. Resource extraction
a. Blasting and drilling
b. Surface excavation
c. Subsurface excavation and retorting
d. Well drilling and fluid removal
e. Dredging
f. Clear cutting and other lumbering
g. Commercial fishing and hunting

CHEMICAL CHARACTERISTICS

1 Earth
a. Mineral resources
b. Construction material
c. Soils
d. Land form
e. Force fields and background radiation
f. Unique physical features

2 Water
a. Surface
b. Ocean
c. Underground
d. Quality
e. Temperature
f. Recharge
g. Snow, ice and permafrost

Figure A.3. Leopold matrix. [19]

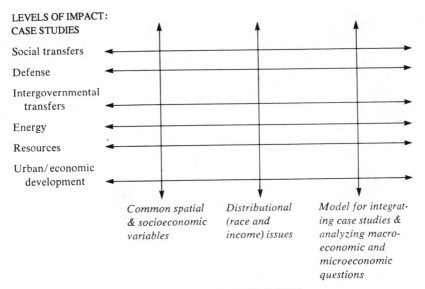

LEVELS OF IMPACT:
CASE STUDIES

Figure A.4. Expanding the scope of an urban impact analysis (UIA) across levels of impact. [20]

into levels of impact was, therefore, natural when societal, or social, impact analysis (SIA) emerged.

Whatever form of impact analysis is being conducted (EIA, UIA, SIA, or other, including the implicit policy impact analysis proposed in this book), the identification of multiple impacts is a necessary part of the analysis. Any impact arena is vulnerable to impact on multiple levels, as pictured in Figure A.5.

The vertical axis of the diagram in Figure A.6 depicts the respective levels of government from which policies originate. These policies take many forms, from general policies to specific projects, as shown on the horizontal axis.

When policies are analyzed in terms of their actual or potential impacts, the dimension of time is often overlooked. Figure A.7 diagrams the thinking behind an impact analysis in which environmental factors are projected and/or actually measured over time, with and without the implementation of a particular project or policy.

For readers seeking more information regarding the impact analyses deemed relevant by the author, the following section has been included.

THEORETICAL BACKGROUND TO IMPACT ANALYSIS

Given that there exists some degree of social rationality within a particular policy (see Chapter 9), an impact analysis can denote the impacts of that policy

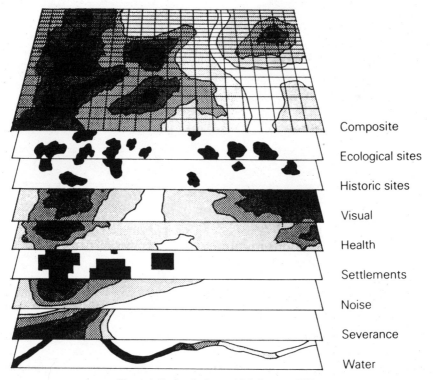

Composite

Ecological sites

Historic sites

Visual

Health

Settlements

Noise

Severance

Water

Figure A.5. Overlaying multiple impacts. [21]

on a web of intricate societal conditions and relationships. Typically, among all impacts there is a range from desirable to undesirable, and along this range, impacts disaggregate and are felt unevenly across socioeconomic subgroups and various levels of organization. This means that one man's meat may be another man's poison; impacts will compete and conflict and therefore must be weighed against each other. Noted in the following paragraphs are concepts, theories, and literature that can be useful in the application of impact analysis to intelligence policy.

In this era of ecological awareness, application of environmental impact analysis has been brought to the forefront. Transferring impact analysis from an environmental system to an educational system moves from a higher degree of physical tangibility to a lower one. Nevertheless, educational systems share basic characteristics of systems with environmental systems, including boundaries (however obscure they may be), elements, and time frames.

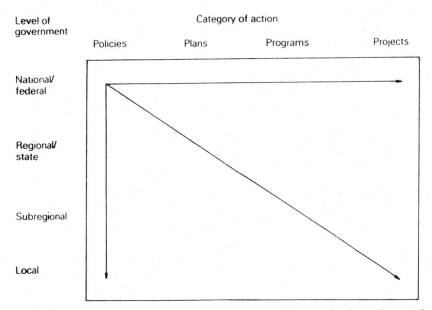

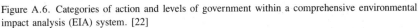

Figure A.6. Categories of action and levels of government within a comprehensive environmental impact analysis (EIA) system. [22]

Hazards and Risks

Some of the weighing of competing impacts can be anticipated and done prospectively. Anticipation of outcomes creates policies that are designed to drive desired outcomes. Similarly, anticipation of impacts should create policies with the greatest degree of positive or "good" social rationality. Once a set of potential societal impacts is projected, the overall "safety"—or what might be called the "cumulative reasonableness" of the policy or program under examination—can be estimated. As Lowrance wrote on the relationships between the hazards and risks of scientific developments to society, safety is determined in terms of acceptable risks. [2] It is but a simple conceptual shift to transfer such thinking to the societal impact of social (in this case, intelligence-related) policies. The notion of overall safety can be replaced with overall reasonableness, and various policy outcomes can be weighed in terms of the overall reasonableness of their societal impacts.

Prospective Multidisciplinary Impact Analysis

The value of a prospective impact analysis is derived when the implications of policies in the making and in the early phases of implementation are assessed

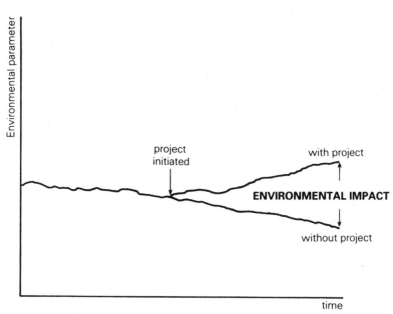

Figure A.7. An impact over time. [23]

and weighed and imbued with a social rationality from the outset. Prospective impact analysis has been applied in the area of environmental impact analysis (EIA), in the form of "adaptive environmental assessment and management" (AEAM). [3] AEAM is a specialization of simulation modeling based on the work at the Institute of Animal Resource Ecology in the late 1970s. [4] This method was developed in response to perceived weaknesses of standard "environmental impact statements" (EISs). [5] These weaknesses include (1) the increasing length and unwieldy nature of the EIS, which includes massive amounts of environmental data (a result of the "measure everything" syndrome that evolved out of the drive to avoid the criticism of lacking comprehensiveness); (2) the deficiency of EISs in the area of impact prediction; and (3) the breakdown between EIS personnel and those making decisions about the future of the project. [6]

The predictive and multidisciplinary modeling approach of AEAM influenced EIA. However, because most AEAM literature focuses specifically on resource management, the environmental impact field awaits applications and reports allowing for the development of a generic EIA method. [7] (See Figure A.1 for a general flow chart of an EIA system.) Nevertheless, the general prospective and multidisciplinary approach typical of AEAM can be valuable in many forms of impact analysis.

The Problem with Indexing

As just noted, EISs tend to be unwieldy documents owing to the drive to measure everything. This "indexing" tendency results in vast amounts of quantification. But the index approach to EIA was one of the first developed. EISs break into two basic groups: the checklist and the "complex quasi-mathematical form," in which "impacts are transformed into units on a common, national scale, weighted in terms of relative importance, and finally manipulated mathematically to form various indices of 'total' impact." [8] Whether the quantification typical in indexing actually improves the utility of an impact statement is unclear. Decision makers tend to feel that quantitative data facilitates and justifies decision making. This technocratic approach to decision making assumes that technologically trained people will conduct and read impact analyses. It also assumes that there is a general consensus regarding the choice of relevant outcome or impact variables. [9]

The fundamental arguments against index methods point to, in the main, the ultimate weakness of standard EISs. With indexing, the subjectivity involved is "hidden within spurious objectivity"; the subjective views incorporated are those of an elite group of experts and decision makers; the reports are "needlessly technocratic and complex"; and the findings are not readily interpreted by the general population. Moreover, despite its apparent systems approach, an index approach tends to compartmentalize and fragment the environment into almost arbitrary variables. [10] Therefore, it is important to seek out and apply other, more qualitative, impact analysis methods, including systems diagramming and matrix formatting, to intelligence policy impact analysis.

Systems Diagramming

The systems diagram, another method of impact analysis, has distinct advantages over index methods of impact analysis in that it acknowledges the complexity and the interdependence of the parameters of the system. When used in environmental impact analysis, data on energy flow are applied (see Figure A.2). However, quantified energy flow data do not necessarily characterize all ecological relationships. When socioeconomic impacts are to be studied, the energy flow concept cannot be practically applied [11]; however, other quantifications—such as cost increments, time/cost ratios, head counts (e.g., total female students admitted to a freshman class during a particular year), head/cost ratios, and heads admitted/heads graduated ratios—have been used to determine systemic outcomes.

The type of systems diagram in Figure A.2 is one of the several "network approaches" available. [12] This one uses interlinked networks to reveal multiple and often indirect impacts. The ramifications of a change can be followed through a chain of intermediaries.

Matrix Formatting

This book takes a contemporary and prospective multidisciplinary approach (as done in AEAM) to impact analysis, combining systems diagramming (a variation of which is in Figure A.2) and the matrix form of analysis first suggested in 1971, now known as the Leopold matrix (see Figure A.3). It is always a challenge to condense information on complex variables into manageable form. Leopold was the first to suggest a matrix form for environmental impact analysis (EIA). As shown in Figure A.3, Leopold's impacts result from the interaction of development activities and the environment, which creates a complex matrix. In full form it includes 8,800 cells: 88 environmental parameters on one axis and 100 developmental categories on the other. This matrix format is ideally suited for identification of multiple impacts, although its ability to identify indirect impacts is questioned. [13]

Multiple Levels and Regions of Policy Impact

Thus far, the discussion has referred primarily to environmental impact analysis. Much of the learning that has come out of urban impact analysis (UIA) is also relevant here. UIA grew out of the city-focused social programming of the 1960s and early 1970s. Early on, urban impact analysis found that a good UIA can cover a single local initiative, a broad-based initiative, and even the federal budget. Impact analysis can also reach across several different policy domains (as in Figure A.4), providing a useful clarification of several types of impact. These impact categories include direct and indirect impacts, qualitative as well as quantitative impacts, absolute and differential impacts, and analysis takes into account the relative size of programs and their relative impacts, and the spatial dimension (in which effects on one region, city, or neighborhood are compared with effects on others). [14] The latter categorization of impacts is one that reminds the impact analyst that policies are created and implemented at various levels of and for various regions within the political system and that the impacts branch out from each of these points (see Figure A.4). The author's adaptation of impact analysis in Chapter 11 seeks a way to avoid the pitfalls that studies by the Rand Corporation encountered.

Rand UIA studies illustrated how widely varied impacts of federal programs are between and within regions and in different types of urban areas. These studies brought out the limitations of some analytical formats (such as charting of effects) in their ability to assess the often conflicting effects of policies in specific areas, for example, tax incentives for new development in new areas versus those for rehabilitation of the inner city and the effect of minimum wage regulations on economic growth and employment in different areas. [15] As noted earlier, there is a need to combine systems diagramming with matrix formatting in order to remain cognizant of interacting effects and competing outcomes.

Modeling Societal Impact

There is also a distinct body of literature on societal impact assessment (SIA). "Knowledge systems accounting" is SIA, a field that seeks to establish the effects of science on society. [16] Defining indicators of social effects is, perhaps, more difficult than defining those of environment. Socioeconomic indicators (SIS) are useful. These are often applied in knowledge systems accounting, where the measures of interest are called "policy indicators." This approach avoids unproductive distinctions between social and economic indicators. This assessment typology includes any useful measure of human conditions and related variables.

The impact analysis model presented in Chapter 11 was developed by drawing on, but not being restricted to, societal impact literature for guidance. The valuable multilevel and multiregional perspectives, shown in Figures A.5 and A.6, were also applied in order to broaden the scope of the impact analysis. Recognition and differentiation of direct (or "primary") and indirect (or "secondary," "tertiary," and "higher-order") impacts is critical. Often overlooked, indirect impacts can be as profound as direct impacts. The relationship between events and the impacts of those events is difficult to identify when the impacts are several steps away from the original event. Both temporal and spatial distance from the original event must be considered in impact analysis (see Figure A.7). Failure to establish a time frame broad enough to project (in prospective analysis) and detect (in retrospective analysis) specific impacts results in a limited impact analysis. In environmental impact analysis, changes in a chain of environmental parameters may have impacts on biological systems not considered part of the original study. For example, construction of a dam on a river might directly affect the fish swimming upstream. It might also indirectly affect life in streambeds both a long distance down- and upstream from the dam. EIAs have demonstrated that an impact analysis can be expanded well beyond a particular time, region, program, or policy. The practicality and nature of an EIA differ at various levels of EIA analysis (see Figure A.6).

The policy-design-level to implementation-level sequence can be regarded as a theoretical hierarchy, one characterized by the increasing generality and uncertainty of implementation. Prediction of impacts must allow for the uncertainty inherent in implementation as well as for long-range outcomes that may manifest long after official (and explicit) implementation is concluded.

B

Adaptation of Impact Analysis to Intelligence Policy Analysis

Society will value and devalue skills as they satisfy individual and group needs, which may be dictated by cultural, as well as biological, propensities.

S. IRVINE AND J. SANDERS [1]

Public universities, because of their implicit commitment to serving a broad cross section of society, might have a broader range of curriculum offerings but somewhat lower average SAT scores than a large private counterpart.

EDWARD B. FISKE [2]

CONCEPTUAL FOUNDATION

The impact of an implicit policy is elusive by virtue of the very fact that it is implicit. Figure B.1 shows schematically the conceptual structure for the implicit policy impact analysis designed by the author. (The foundation of Chapter 11 rests primarily on this schematization, building on the concepts diagrammed in Figures B.2 and B.3.) First, the implicit assumptions must be identified. Second, these must be linked to components of implicit policy, which must also be identified. Third, the explicit assumptions driving specific components of explicit policy must be linked to implicit policy. Fourth, explicit policy must be clearly related to the explicit assumptions that drive it. Fifth, impacts of the explicit policy must be projected (if the impact analysis is a prospective one) or measured (if the impact analysis is retrospective or concurrent to policy implementation). The interrelationships between assumptions, actions, and their impacts can be seen in terms of a matrix of relationships. Therefore, Figure B.2 adapts the Leopold matrix analysis (Figure A.3) to an implicit policy impact analysis. Impacts are identified as short-, middle-, and long-term outcomes. These outcomes must include expected impacts as well as undesigned consequences. Figure B.3 shows this

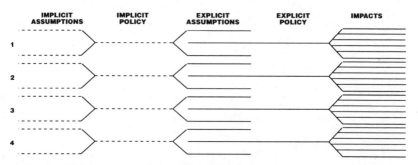

Figure B.1. Implicit intelligence policy is composed of tensions that impact to varying degrees policies of educational opportunity (such as higher education admissions policy) and their outcomes. In standard impact analysis methodology, explicit policy serves as the independent variable while impact serves as the dependent variable. To analyze the effects of implicit assumptions and implicit policy, a longer chain of dependent and independent variables is necessary, as seen here.

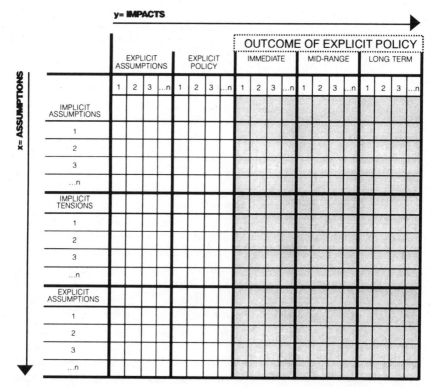

Figure B.2. Adaptation of matrix analysis to the analysis of the effects of implicit policy on explicit policy and on the general impact of affected explicit policy.

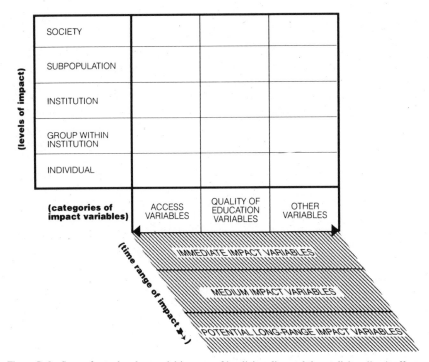

Figure B.3. Span of actual and potential impacts of implicit policy and the explicit policy it affects. Impacts of implicit policy extend through explicit policy to multiple levels of time and social organization.

scheme three-dimensionally, indicating the levels of impact against the categories of impact variables over a time range.

As noted in Appendix A, impact analysis has been conducted in several different domains of policy. In this appendix, various models of impact analysis have been selected and adapted in order to model a theoretical and primarily qualitative analysis of the effects of implicit intelligence policy on higher education admissions policy and the outcomes of that policy.

The network approach to impact analysis, demonstrated in Appendix A, promotes tracing of relationship chains, that is, chains of possible causality or, at least, of sequence. The diagramming of chains (as seen in Figure A.2) can be applied to the tracing of the assumptions and relationships that drive implicit policy into the components and outcomes of explicit policy. The author's network model of implicit–explicit policy relationships is shown in Figure B.1.

From this elucidation of implicit–explicit policy relationships, a matrix similar to the Leopold matrix (Figure A.3) has been designed by the author to clarify and differentiate specific impacts (see Figure B.2).

The span of impacts must also be taken into account. A simple matrix of impacts and outcome variables is modeled in Figure A.4. In Figure B.3, a schematization of actual and potential impacts is presented. As stated earlier, intelligence policy impact analysis must be relatively speculative, qualitative, and prospective because it is aimed at demonstrating the effects of unstated assumptions on explicit policies and their impacts.

C

Relevant Documents

C.1. Introduction to U.C. Berkeley [1]

BERKELEY

Berkeley, the oldest University campus, is a place of diversity and abundance—in academics, in extracurricular activities, and in the faculty and students.

The Cal campus is stately and beautiful, surrounded by wooded hills and the city of Berkeley (population 112,000). Strawberry Creek meanders through the grounds amid spacious lawns and groves of redwood and eucalyptus. The campus architecture is a blend of the old and the new, including rustic South Hall built in 1873, the classical Greek Theater, and the modern, new addition to the Life Sciences Building.

Berkeley has a long history as one of the most lively, culturally diverse, and politically adventurous communities in the country. The surrounding San Francisco Bay Area—much of it within easy reach by BART, the high speed transit system—is known for its natural beauty and outstanding cultural and entertainment offerings.

It would be difficult to find a more varied and interesting mix of students anywhere. Cal students are bright, motivated, and eager to meet the tough academic challenges they face here. More graduates of Berkeley go on to earn Ph.D. degrees than graduates of any other university in the country.

Academics

Berkeley's academic programs are recognized internationally for their excellence. You may choose from hundreds of courses in the sciences, humanities, arts, social sciences, and natural resources. If one of the more than 100 majors offered does not suit your interests, you may design one of your own. A number of special programs for freshmen and sophomores feature small classes and seminars.

Your professors at Cal will include some of the most distinguished novelists, poets, thinkers, and researchers in the world. There are 9 Nobel Laureates on the faculty, and more Guggenheim Fellows than at any other university in the country.

Berkeley has one of best university libraries in the nation. As an undergraduate, much of your study out of the classroom will take place in Moffitt Undergraduate Library. You also have access to the 23 specialized libraries on campus. There are distinguished museums of anthropology, paleontology, and science, and The University Art Museum includes one of the country's leading film exhibition centers, the Pacific Film Archive.

Campus Life

Cal students are serious about their studies, but life here doesn't revolve completely around academics. A kaleidoscope of activity goes on outside the classroom. Thousands of students pass through Sproul

Total Enrollment:	30,618
Undergraduate Enrollment:	21,853
Women:	10,190
Men:	11,663
Graduate Enrollment:	8,765
Undergraduates by Ethnicity:	
African American 6.0%, American Indian 1.1%, Asian/Pacific Islander 32.5%, Chicano/Latino 14.3%, White 35.7%, Other/Not Stated 10.5%	
Undergraduates Living on Campus:	25.0%
Colleges: Chemistry, Engineering, Environmental Design, Letters and Science, Natural Resources	
Schools: Business Administration, Education, Journalism, Law, Library and Information Studies, Optometry, Public Health, Public Policy, Social Welfare	

Plaza every day, making it a popular place for rallies, exhibits, and concerts. There are more than 500 different student organizations on campus, so you'll have no trouble finding other Cal students who share your interests. The Associated Students is very active, the Cal Band is a continuing source of campus pride, and fraternities and sororities are popular.

Sports are also important to Cal students. There is a beautiful recreational Sports Center, and a host of other fitness facilities. About half of Cal's students team up for friendly intramural competition, and the campus has a strong intercollegiate athletic program for men and women. The Big Game, the traditional football match-up between Cal and Stanford, is the focus of a weekend of special events each fall.

Visiting Berkeley

Tours of the campus are given Monday, Wednesday, and Friday at 10:00 a.m. and 1:00 p.m. starting at the Visitor's Center in University Hall. You may arrange a tour at a different time by calling (510) 642-5215.

◄

C.2. Admission to the University of California [2]

ADMISSION TO THE UNIVERSITY

UNIVERSITY
ADMISSIONS POLICY

The undergraduate admissions policy of the University of California is guided by the University's commitment to serve the people of California and the needs of the state, within the framework of the California Master Plan for Higher Education.

The entrance requirements established by the University follow guidelines set forth in the Master Plan, which requires that the top one-eighth of the state's high school graduates, as well as those transfer students who have successfully completed specified college work, be eligible for admission to the University of California. These requirements are designed to ensure that all eligible students are adequately prepared for University-level work.

Mindful of its mission as a public institution, the University of California has an historic commitment to provide a place within the University for all eligible applicants who are residents of California, and to achieve, on each campus, a student body that both meets the University's high academic standards and encompasses the cultural, racial, geographic, economic, and social diversity of California itself.

Each campus of the University makes every effort to provide a place for all California resident applicants who meet the minimum admissions requirements and who file an application during the appropriate filing period. If the number of applicants exceeds the spaces available for a particular campus or major—as is often the case—the campus uses criteria that exceed the minimum requirements to select students. Meeting the minimum requirements, therefore, is not enough to gain admission to many UC campuses and programs.

When there are more eligible applicants than spaces available, the campus uses academic criteria alone—grade point average, SAT or ACT results, achievement test scores—to select between 40 and 60 percent of

I didn't come in with a 4.0 GPA, so I was afraid I might really have some serious trouble academically. But, as I found out, it really depends on how you apply yourself. If you have a commitment to doing well in high school, that should follow you to college. You might be able to get good grades in high school without studying, but the same attitude won't get you through college. I always studied hard in high school, and I do the same here. It's really challenging, it's tough— but that's just another attraction to me.

those accepted. The campus uses a combination of academic and supplemental criteria to select the remaining admittees.

Selection criteria for applicants for fall 1994 are described by campus beginning on page 23. You will find them most useful as a guide—to help you to better understand the selection process, rather than to predict whether you will be accepted to the campus and program of your choice. Criteria vary from year to year and from campus to campus according to the number and qualifications of applicants to each campus and program. Because the level of competition for admission to certain campuses and programs is very high, you should consider applying to more than one campus and to programs that, while not your first choice, will allow you

to fulfill your educational goals. To give you some idea of the competition at each campus, the academic qualifications of recently enrolled freshmen at each campus are summarized in the Freshman Profile beginning on page 29. Again, you will find these figures most useful as a guide to the selection process, rather than to predict your chances for admission.

If you have questions about admissions policies, selection criteria, or the level of competition for admission to a particular campus or program, please contact the Admissions Office at the appropriate campus.

PREPARING FOR
UNIVERSITY WORK

If you are in high school and considering the University for your college education, this discussion will help you plan your high school program. It will provide you with guidelines on the basic subjects and skills you should master to increase your chance of academic success at the University.

As a prospective University freshman, you should make sure that you complete the high school courses required for admission described on page 19. You should give careful thought to adequately preparing yourself in reading, writing, mathematics, and in other areas related to your major. The more comprehensive and challenging your high school program is, the better prepared you will be for University work.

The University urges prospective students to take particular care in planning the senior year program. Your senior year should be used to prepare you for your first year at the University and should include honors and advanced courses as well as courses that will strengthen your overall preparation. A challenging senior year program, successfully completed, is a natural bridge between high school and University coursework in your intended major. A strong senior program will also strengthen your chances for admission to the campus and program of your choice.

▶

C.3. Admission as a Freshman [3]

ADMISSION AS A FRESHMAN

The University considers you a freshman applicant if you have graduated from high school and have not enrolled in a regular session at any college or university. If you attend a summer session immediately after graduating from high school, you are still a freshman applicant.

California Residents*

To be eligible for admission to the University, you must meet the Subject, Scholarship, and Examination Requirements described below and on page 20. There is also an explanation of how you may qualify for admission by examination alone.

Subject Requirement

To satisfy this requirement, you must complete the high school courses listed below with a grade point average defined by the Scholarship Requirement. This sequence of courses is also known as the "a-f" requirements.

You must take 15 units of high school courses to fulfill the Subject Requirement, and at least 7 of the 15 units must be taken in your last two years of high school. (A unit is equal to an academic year, or two semesters, of study.)

Applicants from California high schools: To be acceptable to the University, the courses must appear on a list certified by your high school principal as meeting the University's admissions requirements. Your counselor or principal will have a copy of this list.

* *Residency Status:* The requirements for bona-fide California residents also apply to dependents of University of California graduates and employees. The manner in which legal residence is defined for tuition purposes is different. If you have questions about your residency status, contact the Admissions or Registrar's Office at the campus you wish to attend.

a. **History/Social Science**—2 years required.
Two years of history/social science, including one year of U.S. history or one-half year of U.S. history and one-half year of civics or American government; and one year of world history, cultures, and geography.

Taking honors courses in high school was something that really prepared me for the workload in college. It wasn't as difficult for me to make the transition from high school to college.

b. **English**—4 years required.
Four years of college preparatory English that include frequent and regular writing, and reading of classic and modern literature. Not more than two semesters of 9th grade English can be used to meet this requirement.

c. **Mathematics**—3 years required, 4 recommended.
Three years of college preparatory mathematics that include the topics covered in elementary and advanced algebra and two and three dimensional geometry. Math courses taken in the 7th and 8th grades may be used to fulfill part of this requirement if your high school accepts them as equivalent to its own courses.

d. **Laboratory Science**—2 years required, 3 recommended.
Two years of laboratory science providing fundamental knowledge in at least two of these three areas: biology, chemistry, and physics. Laboratory courses in earth/space sciences are acceptable if they have as prerequisites or provide basic knowledge in biology, chemistry, or physics. Not more

than one year of 9th grade laboratory science can be used to meet this requirement.

e. **Language Other than English**—
2 years required, 3 recommended.
Two years of the same language other than English. Courses should emphasize speaking and understanding, and include instruction in grammar, vocabulary, reading, and composition.

f. **College Preparatory Electives**—
2 years required.
Two units (four semesters), in addition to those required in "a-e" above, chosen from the following areas: visual and performing arts, history, social science, English, advanced mathematics, laboratory science, and language other than English (a third year in the language used for the "e" requirement or two years of another language).

Scholarship Requirement

The Scholarship Requirement defines the grade point average (GPA) you must attain in the "a-f" subjects to be eligible for admission to the University.

If your "a-f" GPA is 3.3 or higher, you have met the minimum requirement for admission to the University. If your GPA is below 3.3 but above 2.81, you have met the minimum requirement if you achieve the necessary college entrance test score indicated in the Eligibility Index on the following page.

The University calculates your GPA in the "a-f" subjects by assigning point values to the grades you earn, totaling the points, and dividing the total by the number of "a-f" course units. Points are assigned as follows: A = 4 points, B = 3 points, C = 2 points, D = 1 point, and F = 0 points.

Only the grades you earn in "a-f" subjects in the 10th, 11th, and 12th grades are used to calculate your GPA. Courses you take in 9th grade can be used to meet the Subject Requirement if you earn a grade of C or better, but they will not be used to calculate your GPA.

▶

C.4. University of California Selection Criteria [4]

SELECTION CRITERIA

The University makes every effort to provide a place on one of its campuses for all California resident applicants who meet the minimum admission requirements (see pages 19–21) and file an application during the appropriate filing period.

In recent years, the number of applicants for some campuses and some majors has far exceeded the number of spaces available. When a campus cannot accept all eligible applicants, it uses standards that are more demanding than the minimum requirements to select students. These standards, which the University calls selection criteria, identify those students who have demonstrated the capacity for high academic achievement and who have a variety of other qualities that can contribute to the strength and diversity of the campus community.

The selection criteria for freshman and advanced standing (transfer) applicants for fall 1994 are described by campus in this section. In the box to the right are general guidelines the campuses use to develop the selection procedures. The campuses use similar indicators of academic and personal qualifications to evaluate applicants. The specific evaluation process and weight of factors differ from campus to campus depending upon enrollment targets and the number and qualifications of applicants. Some campuses use a formula or academic index to identify the types of students they wish to admit. At all campuses, faculty members are involved in establishing the selection criteria and often participate in the selection process.

The selection criteria described below are only for applicants for the fall 1994 term. The criteria may differ for the winter and spring terms because enrollment targets and applicant qualifications change. Applicants for winter or spring should contact the appropriate campus Admissions Offices for more information.

ADMISSION GUIDELINES

To be eligible for admission, applicants must meet the University's undergraduate admission requirements. The following guidelines provide the framework within which the campuses establish procedures for selecting applicants when the number of eligible applicants exceeds the places available.

Each campus, in consultation with the Office of the President, develops enrollment targets that specify the number of new freshman and advanced standing students expected to enroll. Campuses that receive more applications than the number required to meet their enrollment target admit students using the criteria described below.

FRESHMAN APPLICANTS

At least 40 percent and no more than 60 percent of freshmen admitted by each campus are selected on the basis of the academic criteria described below. The remaining freshmen, with the exception of those admitted through special action, are selected using some or all of the academic criteria and supplemental criteria.

Academic Criteria

• Academic grade point average (GPA) calculated for all academic courses completed in the "a–f" subject areas specified by the University's minimum admission requirements, including additional points for completing honors courses. The maximum value allowed for the GPA is 4.00.

• Test scores on the following standardized tests: Scholastic Aptitude Test (SAT) or American College Test (ACT) and the College Board Achievement Tests (Ach).

• The number and content of courses completed in academic subjects beyond the minimum specified by the University's eligibility requirements.

• The number of University-approved accelerated, advanced placement, and honors courses completed or in progress.

Supplemental Criteria

• Special talents, interests, or experiences—beyond those indicated by the academic criteria—that demonstrate unusual promise of leadership, achievement, and service in a particular field such as civic life or the arts.

• Special circumstances that have adversely affected the applicant's life experiences. These circumstances may include, for example, disabilities, personal difficulties, low family income, refugee status, or veteran status.

• Ethnic identity, gender, and location of residence. These factors are considered to provide cultural, racial, geographic, and socio-economic diversity in the student population.

ADVANCED STANDING APPLICANTS

The campuses use the academic criteria described below as the primary means of evaluating advanced standing applicants. The same supplemental criteria described above for freshman applicants are used when relevant to assess the applicant's overall promise of success at the campus or potential to contribute to the strength and diversity of the student population.

The highest priority for advanced standing admission is given to junior level transfers from California community colleges.

Academic Criteria

• Completion of a specified pattern or number of courses that meet general education or breadth requirements.

• Completion of a specified pattern or number of courses that provide continuity with upper division courses in the major.

• GPA in all transferable courses.

• Participation in academically selective honors courses or programs.

Supplemental Criteria

The same supplemental criteria described above for freshmen are used.

▶

C.5. Description of Selection Process at U.C. Berkeley [5]

BERKELEY

A more detailed description of the selection process at Berkeley is included in the Berkeley *General Catalog.*

FRESHMAN APPLICANTS

All Colleges

Academic Criteria

Used to Select Approximately 50% of Admits to the College of Letters and Science, College of Natural Resources, College of Environmental Design, and College of Engineering; and 60% of Admits to the College of Chemistry

Berkeley ranks all freshman applicants, by college, based on academic performance. An academic index is used, comprised of the high school GPA (capped at 4.00), the SAT or ACT score, and Ach scores. Additional academic criteria that may be used include college preparatory courses completed beyond the minimum required and honors or advanced placement courses completed.

Supplemental Criteria

Used to Select Approximately 50% of Admits to the College of Letters and Science, College of Natural Resources, College of Environmental Design, and College of Engineering; and 40% of Admits to the College of Chemistry

The academic criteria are used with supplemental criteria that take into account specific applicant circumstances, such as California residency and socioeconomic background. Additional factors considered are other academic accomplishments, extracurricular activities, and personal experiences that indicate a potential to contribute to the vitality of the campus learning environment.

ADVANCED STANDING APPLICANTS

All Colleges

Lower Division

There are very few openings for applicants who wish to transfer to Berkeley at the advanced standing freshman or sophomore level. Most applicants considered are members of underrepresented ethnic groups, have demonstrated hardship, or are recruited athletes.

Upper Division

Academic Criteria

All programs turn away qualified applicants because of space limitations. In recent terms, less than 40 percent of transfer applicants were admitted. Upper division transfer applicants to the most competitive programs are expected to have completed the lower division prerequisites for the major and satisfied the college or school breadth requirements or Intersegmental General Education Transfer Curriculum (IGETC). Applicants are selected primarily on the basis of strength of academic preparation and GPA.

Supplemental Criteria

Supplemental criteria considered may include these factors: membership in groups historically underrepresented, attendance at California community colleges, California residency, reentry status, presence of a disability, qualification for the Educational Opportunity Program, or recruitment as an athlete. Students' essays may be carefully considered in the review of applications to nearly all programs.

GLOSSARY

Below are definitions of the terms and abbreviations used in the discussion of selection criteria:

UC Eligible: This means that the applicant has met the University of California's minimum admission requirements.

SAT: Scholastic Aptitude Test, a college entrance examination given by the College Board.

ACT: American College Test, a college entrance examination given by the American College Testing Program.

Ach: Achievement Test, given by the College Board. The University requires freshman applicants to take three Ach—English Composition, Mathematics (Level 1 or 2), and a third test chosen from English literature, foreign language, science, or social science. Reference to third Ach means the test the applicant has the option to choose.

DAVIS

FRESHMAN APPLICANTS

All Colleges

Academic Criteria

Used to Select 60% of Admits

Davis selects freshman applicants who have demonstrated the greatest effort to fully prepare academically as measured by the following criteria:

1. Calculated GPA on all academic courses completed in the "a–f" subject areas, with additional grade points given for honors courses (maximum value is 4.00);

2. College entrance test scores—SAT or ACT and three required Ach;

3. The number and content of college preparatory courses completed in academic subjects beyond UC minimums;

4. The number of University-approved honors or advanced placement courses completed or in progress.

Supplemental Criteria

Used to Select 40% of Admits

Applicants are evaluated using the academic criteria described above in conjunction with the following supplemental criteria:

1. Personal accomplishments, talents, experiences, or interests that will contribute to the educational environment of the campus;

2. Special circumstances which may have affected the applicant's life, including personal hardship, disabilities, economic disadvantage, and membership in groups historically underrepresented at the University.

ADVANCED STANDING APPLICANTS

All Colleges

Academic Criteria

Admission of advanced standing applicants is based upon GPA in academic coursework, course preparation for intended major if major is impacted, level at entry, and type of school of origin. The highest priority for admission is given to California community college transfer applicants with 56 semester or 84 quarter units. Priority is next given to junior level transfers from other UC campuses and other four-year institutions in and out of state. Finally, if space is available, lower division transfers from

▶

C.6. University of California Eligibility Index [6]

Honors Courses

The University assigns extra points for up to four units of certified honors level and advanced placement courses taken in the last three years of high school: A = 5 points, B = 4 points, C = 3 points. No more than two units of certified honors level courses taken in the 10th grade may be given extra points. A grade of D in an honors or advanced placement course does not earn extra points.

The courses must be in the following "a-f" subjects: history, English, advanced mathematics, laboratory science, and foreign language, and they must be certified at your high school as offered at the honors level. In these fields, as well as in the fields of computer science, social science, and the visual and performing arts, courses that are designed to prepare students for an Advanced Placement Examination of the College Board or a Higher Level Examination of the International Baccalaureate and college courses that are transferable to the University are acceptable honors level courses.

D and F Grades

D and F grades in the "a-f" courses must be repeated or validated. Consult with your counselor to determine how these grades can be improved and how the University will use them in evaluating your scholarship record.

Grades for repeated courses in which you initially earned a grade of C or better will not be used.

Examination Requirement

You must submit the following test scores:

☐ One aptitude test, either the Scholastic Aptitude Test (SAT) or the American College Test (ACT). The verbal and mathematics scores on the SAT must be from the same sitting. The ACT composite score must be submitted.

☐ Three College Board Achievement Tests (Ach), including English Composition, Mathematics Level 1 or Level 2, and *one* test in one of the following areas: English literature, foreign language, science, or social studies.

ELIGIBILITY INDEX

"a-f" GPA	ACT[1] Composite	SAT[2] Total	"a-f" GPA	ACT[1] Composite	SAT[2] Total
2.82	36	1590	3.06	25	1030
2.83	36	1570	3.07	24	1010
2.84	35	1540	3.08	23	980
2.85	35	1520	3.09	23	960
2.86	35	1500	3.10	22	940
2.87	34	1470	3.11	22	910
2.88	34	1450	3.12	21	890
2.89	33	1430	3.13	21	870
2.90	33	1400	3.14	20	840
2.91	33	1380	3.15	20	820
2.92	32	1360	3.16	19	800
2.93	31	1330	3.17	19	770
2.94	31	1310	3.18	18	750
2.95	31	1290	3.19	18	730
2.96	30	1260	3.20	17	700
2.97	30	1240	3.21	17	680
2.98	29	1220	3.22	16	660
2.99	28	1190	3.23	16	630
3.00	28	1170	3.24	15	610
3.01	27	1150	3.25	15	590
3.02	27	1120	3.26	14	560
3.03	26	1100	3.27	14	540
3.04	26	1080	3.28	13	520
3.05	25	1050	3.29	12	490

1. ACT is scored in intervals of 1 point, from a minimum of 1 to a maximum of 36.
2. SAT is scored in intervals of 10 points, from a minimum of 400 to a maximum of 1600.

Admission by Examination Alone

If you do not meet the Subject and Scholarship Requirements, you may be able to qualify for admission to the University by examination.

To satisfy the minimum requirements for qualifying by examination alone, you must achieve a total score of 1300 or higher on the SAT, or a composite score of 31 or higher on the ACT. In addition, you must earn a total score of 1650 or higher on the three College Board Achievement Tests, with a minimum score of 500 on each test.

You cannot qualify for admission by examination alone if you have completed 12 or more units of transferable coursework at another college or university following high school graduation, or if you have taken transferable college courses in any subject covered by the College Board Achievement Tests.

Nonresidents

The minimum freshman admission requirements for nonresidents of California are the same as those for residents except for the following:

☐ **Scholarship Requirement:**
Your grade point average in the "a-f" subjects must be 3.4 or higher, regardless of your college entrance examination score. The Eligibility Index is used only for California residents.

☐ **Admission by Examination Alone:**
You must score at least 1300 on the SAT or 31 on the ACT. Your total score on the three College Board Achievement Tests must be at least 1730, with a minimum score of 500 on any single test.

If the number of applicants exceeds the spaces available for a particular campus or major— as is often the case—the campus uses criteria that exceed the minimum requirements to select students. (See the discussion of Selection Criteria beginning on page 23 for more information.) Meeting the minimum requirements, therefore, is not enough to gain admission to many UC campuses and programs.

◀

C.7. University of California Freshman Profile for Two Campuses: Berkeley and Davis [7]

FRESHMAN PROFILE

The Freshman Profile summarizes by UC campus the qualifications of applicants and admitted freshmen for fall 1992. The Profile is most useful as a guide to the selection process, rather than to predict your chances for admission to the University. Separate figures are included for non-engineering and engineering programs.

Grade point average (GPA) intervals are listed vertically and Scholastic Aptitude Test (SAT) composite score (mathematics plus verbal) intervals are listed horizontally. Each block in the chart represents a pool of applicants with GPA and SAT scores within the specific intervals indicated.

In each block, the first figure is the total number of applicants and the second figure is the number of applicants regularly admitted. The figure in bold type on the second line is the percentage of students who were regularly admitted.

GPA is defined as a student's GPA in the "a–f" requirements as calculated by a UC admissions evaluator or, if the evaluated GPA was not available, the student's GPA as self-reported on the application for admission.

The campus overall total includes freshman applicants whose GPA and/or SAT composite score were out of range or unavailable. Data as of September 1992.

ALL PROGRAMS EXCEPT ENGINEERING

GPA	SAT COMPOSITE					
	490–790	800–990	1000–1190	1200–1390	1400–1600	OVERALL
BERKELEY						
2.82–2.99			131/21 **16%**	39/0 **0%**	3/0 **0%**	173/21 **12%**
3.00–3.29	179/11 **6%**	500/79 **16%**	729/127 **17%**	304/50 **16%**	26/7 **27%**	1738/274 **16%**
3.30–3.59	173/24 **14%**	608/165 **27%**	1133/247 **22%**	569/136 **24%**	44/21 **48%**	2527/593 **23%**
3.60–3.89	116/15 **13%**	573/160 **28%**	1489/408 **27%**	1081/449 **42%**	125/111 **89%**	3384/1143 **34%**
3.90–3.99	11/3 **27%**	97/23 **24%**	332/104 **31%**	325/219 **67%**	47/45 **96%**	812/394 **49%**
4.00	39/12 **31%**	345/115 **33%**	1908/769 **40%**	3363/2770 **82%**	997/980 **98%**	6652/4646 **70%**
OVERALL	518/65 **13%**	2123/542 **26%**	5722/1676 **29%**	5681/3624 **64%**	1242/1164 **94%**	17063/7326 **43%**
DAVIS						
2.82–2.99			180/39 **22%**	36/14 **39%**	1/1 **100%**	217/54 **25%**
3.00–3.29	259/76 **29%**	745/244 **33%**	876/272 **31%**	245/159 **65%**	11/11 **100%**	2136/762 **36%**
3.30–3.59	231/138 **60%**	838/307 **37%**	1312/589 **45%**	467/397 **85%**	17/17 **100%**	2865/1448 **51%**
3.60–3.89	140/80 **57%**	730/348 **48%**	1485/1102 **74%**	631/614 **97%**	45/43 **96%**	3031/2187 **72%**
3.90–3.99	20/13 **65%**	94/61 **65%**	265/246 **93%**	177/177 **100%**	11/11 **100%**	567/508 **90%**
4.00	45/26 **58%**	347/267 **77%**	1399/1330 **95%**	1453/1440 **99%**	243/240 **99%**	3487/3303 **95%**
OVERALL	695/333 **48%**	2754/1227 **45%**	5517/3578 **65%**	3009/2801 **93%**	328/323 **98%**	13903/8631 **62%**

ENGINEERING PROGRAMS

GPA	SAT COMPOSITE					
	490–790	800–990	1000–1190	1200–1390	1400–1600	OVERALL
BERKELEY						
2.82–2.99			17/2 **12%**	5/0 **0%**	0/0 **0%**	22/2 **9%**
3.00–3.29	25/0 **0%**	42/0 **0%**	78/2 **3%**	42/7 **17%**	0/0 **0%**	187/9 **5%**
3.30–3.59	13/0 **0%**	75/0 **0%**	153/10 **7%**	110/14 **13%**	12/2 **17%**	363/26 **7%**
3.60–3.89	19/0 **0%**	94/5 **5%**	231/22 **10%**	232/75 **32%**	41/20 **49%**	617/122 **20%**
3.90–3.99	2/0 **0%**	22/0 **0%**	68/11 **16%**	81/30 **37%**	10/8 **80%**	183/49 **27%**
4.00	8/0 **0%**	60/4 **7%**	393/87 **22%**	870/523 **60%**	387/353 **91%**	1718/967 **56%**
OVERALL	67/0 **0%**	293/9 **3%**	940/134 **14%**	1340/649 **48%**	450/383 **85%**	3409/1204 **35%**
DAVIS						
2.82–2.99			14/4 **29%**	5/3 **60%**	0/0 **0%**	19/7 **37%**
3.00–3.29	10/0 **0%**	55/4 **7%**	110/30 **27%**	40/28 **70%**	1/1 **100%**	216/63 **29%**
3.30–3.59	10/1 **10%**	77/17 **22%**	199/91 **46%**	95/85 **89%**	6/6 **100%**	387/200 **52%**
3.60–3.89	5/0 **0%**	86/45 **52%**	235/163 **69%**	171/168 **98%**	15/14 **93%**	512/390 **76%**
3.90–3.99	1/0 **0%**	13/6 **46%**	65/57 **88%**	48/48 **100%**	6/6 **100%**	133/117 **88%**
4.00	4/1 **25%**	53/43 **81%**	310/292 **94%**	424/422 **100%**	79/77 **97%**	870/835 **96%**
OVERALL	30/2 **7%**	284/115 **40%**	933/637 **68%**	783/754 **96%**	107/104 **97%**	2279/1636 **72%**

LEGEND: applicants/regular admits
percent regularly admitted

C.8. Fall Freshman Yield by Admissions Tier: 1986–1988 [8]

	1986 yield	1987 yield	1988 yield	Average yield
Tier 1	38.1%	34.5%	40.0%	37.6%
Tier 2	58.1%	51.0%	49.1%	52.6%
Tier 3	44.0%	47.5%	47.5%	46.6%
Special action	60.3%	69.0%	62.6%	64.0%
Total	44.8%	44.5%	45.7%	45.0%

SOURCE: Office of Student Research, U.C. Berkeley.

C.9. Freshman Registrants 1988–1989 (Year-Round): All Colleges at Berkeley [9]

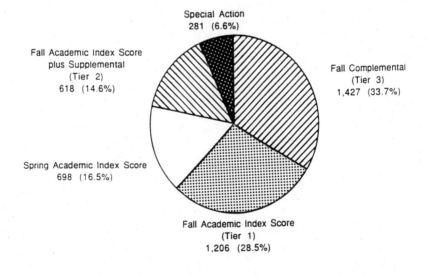

Special Action
281 (6.6%)

Fall Academic Index Score
plus Supplemental
(Tier 2)
618 (14.6%)

Fall Complemental
(Tier 3)
1,427 (33.7%)

Spring Academic Index Score
698 (16.5%)

Fall Academic Index Score
(Tier 1)
1,206 (28.5%)

Source: Office of Student Research, UC Berkeley

C.10. Fall Freshman Tier Admits by Complemental Group: 1986–1988 [10]

Group	1986		1987		1988		Average number	Average percentage
	Admits	% of total	Admits	% of total	Admits	% of total		
Athletes	257	12.4	302	10.5	300	10.0	286	10.8
Disabled	51	2.5	39	1.4	29	1.0	40	1.5
Special talent	0	0.00	0	0.0	12	0.4	4	0.2
Administative review	65	3.1	28	1.0	55	1.8	49	2.0
High school w/o stand. GPA[a]	48	2.3	41	1.4	58	1.9	49	1.9
Rural high school	0	0.00	83	2.9	185	6.3	89	3.4
High tester	106	5.1	189	6.5	313	10.4	203	7.6
Affirmative action	1330	63.9	1900	65.7	1799	59.8	1676	63.0
Filipino	224	10.8	309	10.7	256	8.5	263	9.9
Total	2081	100.0	2891	100.0	3007	100.0	2660	100.0

[a]Without standard grade-point average.
SOURCE: Office of Student Research, U.C. Berkeley.

C.11. Student-Estimated Annual Parental Income: Fall 1987 Entering Freshmen [11]

			Percentage in each income category			
Income category	White	Asian[a]	American Indian	Black	Chicano	All freshmen
Under $30,000	11	24	24	34	40	22
$30,000–49,999	18	25	35	24	31	24
$50,000–74,999	31	27	18	29	19	28
$75,000 and above	40	25	24	13	10	27
Median income (Number in sample)	$67,000 (503)	$51,000 (306)	$47,000 (17)	$39,000 (161)	$34,000 (208)	$53,500 (1360)

[a]Asian includes Filipino.
SOURCE: CIRP/ACE Annual Freshman Survey—U.C. Berkeley Freshmen.

C.12. University of California Fees, Expenses, and Aid [12]

MONEY MATTERS

FEES AND EXPENSES

The University's educational and registration fees are the same at all campuses. Other fees and living expenses vary from campus to campus. The box on this page gives estimates of typical costs for the 1993-94 academic year (three quarters or two semesters). Actual costs for the 1994-95 academic year are likely to be higher. Students who are not residents of California must pay an additional $7,699 tuition fee each year. All University fees are subject to change without notice.

FINANCIAL AID AND SCHOLARSHIPS

The University wants every student it accepts to be able to attend regardless of his or her economic background, so it has a strong financial aid program, including scholarships, grants, loans, and work-study. In 1991-92, 55,577 UC undergraduates received $302 million in financial aid and scholarships. The average award was $5,436.

To determine your financial need, the Financial Aid Office compares your resources to your probable educational and living expenses. The resources the University considers include:

☐ **Your own contribution:** You may be expected to contribute to your own educational expenses, depending upon the information you provide on the financial aid application. This money might come from your savings or a part-time job.

☐ **Your parents' contribution:** If you are financially dependent on your parents, the amount of their expected contribution is based upon the information you submit on the financial aid application about their income, assets, and household size.

☐ **Other resources:** These include scholarships and grants you receive from other sources.

If the University determines that your resources are not sufficient to meet your educational and living expenses, you will be eligible for financial aid. You will be offered a financial aid package that may include a combination of funds from the available aid programs—scholarships, grants, loans, and work-study. You must maintain satisfactory progress in your coursework to continue to be eligible for aid.

The basic types of financial aid are described below. Because many financial aid programs are funded by the federal and state governments, they are subject to change from year to year.

TYPICAL COSTS, 1993-94	
Costs for an Undergraduate California Resident Living in a University Residence Hall	
Average Required Fees	$ 3,898 - 4,380
Books and Supplies	600 - 827
Room and Board	5,355 - 6,313
Miscellaneous Expenses	957 - 1,582
TOTAL	$11,820-13,320
AVERAGE	$12,550

Scholarships

The University has a strong scholarship program for students with outstanding academic records and potential. Need-based scholarships are limited to students who are eligible for financial aid. Honorary scholarships are awarded without regard to need. Honorary scholarships range from $300 to several thousand dollars, while need-based scholarships cover a portion or all of a student's financial need. Scholarships do not have to be repaid.

Scholarship programs available at all campuses include Regents and Alumni Scholarships. Most campuses award a variety of other scholarships and many are National Merit Scholarship Program sponsors. In addition, the University offers a wide range of scholarships endowed by private individuals that are limited to students who meet specific requirements.

Grants

Grants are awarded on the basis of financial need and do not have to be repaid. The grants available include the Pell Grant, Supplemental Educational Opportunity Grant (SEOG), Cal Grant A and Cal Grant B, and the University of California Grant.

Nearly all financial aid applicants must apply for a Pell Grant. California residents must also apply for a Cal Grant. Cal Grant A is the only grant program awarded on the basis of academic achievement. You may receive Cal Grant A or Cal Grant B, but not both. Every eligible financial aid applicant is considered for the SEOG and University of California Grant.

Loans

Loans from a variety of sources are awarded to students on the basis of financial need or creditworthiness. Most loans have below-market interest rates and must be repaid over a period of several years, beginning six to nine months after you stop attending school or cease to be at least a half-time student.

The major loan programs are the Perkins Loan, Stafford Loan, Supplemental Loans for Students (SLS), and Parent Loans for Undergraduate Students (PLUS). Perkins and Stafford subsidized loans are available only to students who qualify for financial aid. You do not have to qualify for financial aid to obtain the unsubsidized Stafford, SLS, and PLUS loans. The University will assist you in applying for the Stafford, SLS and PLUS loans, which are awarded by banks, savings and loans, and other private lenders.

Work-Study Program

Various work-study programs, funded by the University, employers, and the federal government, offer part-time jobs to students eligible to work in the U.S.

How to Apply

More information about how to apply for financial aid and scholarships is included in the *Undergraduate Application Packet*.

◀

Notes

Chapter 1

1. Donne, J. (1626), 17. Devotions upon Emergent Occasions. London: Simpkin, Marshall, Hamilton, Kent & Co., Ltd. (This work can also be found in 1926 edition of Abbey Classics, Vol. 20.)
2. Gould, S. J. (1981). The Mismeasure of Man. New York: Norton and Davis, B. D. (1986), Neo-Lysenkoism, IQ, and the press. In Storm over Biology. New York: Prometheus Books, pp. 114–131 (reprinted from The Public Interest, Fall 1983, pp. 41–59).
3. Sternberg, R. J. (1988). The Triarchic Mind: A New Theory of Human Intelligence. New York: Viking, p. 9.
4. Sternberg, R. (1986). A framework for understanding conceptions of intelligence. In Sternberg, R. and Detterman, D. (Eds.), What Is Intelligence? Norwood, NJ: Ablex.
5. Kamin, L. (1974). Introduction. The Science and Politics of I.Q. Potomac, MD: Erlbaum, pp. 1–4. See also Shanker, A. (1990). The social and educational dilemmas of test use. In The Uses of Standardized Tests in American Education (Proceedings of the 1989 ETS Institute and Conference). Princeton, NJ: Educational Testing Service.
6. Kearns, D. and Doyle, D. (1991). Winning the Brain Race. San Francisco: ICS Press, pp. xi, 3, 140.
7. Ibid, pp. xi–xii.
8. Gardner, D. (1991). Gardner's letter of resignation, November 13, 1991 (speech addressed to Meredith Khachigian, chairman of the board of regents). Cal Report, Winter 1992, p. 4.
9. Quoted in U.C. President Gardner to step down October 1. Cal Report, Winter 1992, p. 4.
10. Humphreys, L. (1980). Race and intelligence re-examined. The Humanist, July/August, p. 55.

Chapter 2

1. Peters, R. J. (1988). Working smarter: The business of practical intelligence. Phi Kappa Phi Journal, Spring, p. 13.

2. Jensen, A. R. (1986). g: Artifact or reality? *Journal of Vocational Behavior*, 29:3, p. 317.
3. Ibid.
4. Ibid.
5. See, for example, Gould, S. (1981). *The Mismeasure of Man*. New York: Norton.
6. Cattell, R. B. (1987). Intelligence and society. In Stelmach, G. E. and Vroon, P. A. (Eds.), *Advances in Psychology* (Vol. 35). New York: N.H.C., pp. 580–591.
7. Lipset, S. M. and Riesman, D. (1975). *Education and Politics at Harvard*. New York: McGraw-Hill, p. 306.
8. Ibid., p. 318.
9. Ibid., p. 331.
10. Ibid., p. 332.
11. The Tennessee and Alabama Female Institute (1853). 1853-1854 Catalogue of the Mary Sharp College of Tennessee. Quoted in Taylor, J. M. (1914, reprinted in 1972). *Before Vassar Opened: A Contribution to the History of the Higher Education of Women in America*. Freeport, NY: pp. 4–6, 9–12, 27, 235; Gilchrist, B. B. *The Life of Mary Lyon*, pp. 207–208, cited in Taylor, op. cit., p. 7; Oberlin College (1834). *Catalogue of 1834*, quoted in Taylor, op. cit., p. 6; Solberg, W. U. (1968). *The University of Illinois, 1867–1894*. Urbana: University of Illinois Press, pp. 160–161; *University of Illinois, 1871–1872 Catalogue*, p. 52; and Lawton, M. (1992). Schools' glass ceiling imperils girls: Study cites barriers erected in school that prohibit the advancement of girls. *Education Week*, February 12, pp. 1, 17.
12. Adams, W. (1971). *The Test*. New York: Macmillan, pp. 183–184.
13. Gardner, D. P. (1991). Gardner's letter of resignation, November 13, 1991 (speech addressed to Meredith Khachigian, chairman of the board of regents). *Cal Report*, Winter 1992, p. 4.
14. Solberg, op. cit., pp. 5–6.
15. Adams, op. cit., p. 184.
16. Adams, op. cit., p. 185.
17. Based on telephone conversation with Edith Zinn, director of Hawthorn College Application Services, Berkeley, CA, September 30, 1991.
18. Plan to reform college budget: Assemblyman Hayden proposes linking fees to income. *San Francisco Chronicle*, January 22, 1992, p. A12.
19. Ibid.
20. Ibid.
21. Lauder, H. (1991). Education, democracy and the economy. *British Journal of Sociology of Education*, 12:4, p. 418.
22. Ibid., p. 425.
23. Ibid., p. 427.
24. Ibid., p. 428.
25. Cattell (1987), op. cit., p. 585.
26. Ibid., p. 588.
27. Ibid., p. 589.
28. Ibid., p. 591.

Chapter 3

1. William Hiss, dean of Admissions and Financial Aid at Bates College in Lewiston, ME, quoted in Pitsch, M. (1991). Study affirms Bates College officials' hunch in dropping requirement for admissions test. *Education Week*, November 27, p. 6.

2. Beyer, L. E. (1986). Schooling for moral and democratic communities. *Issues in Education*, 4:1, Summer 1986, p. 1.

3. Jacobi, M., Astin, A., and Ayala, F., Jr. (1987, Fall). A philosophy of assessment. In *College Student Outcomes Assessment: A Talent Development Perspective* (Ashe–Eric Higher Education Report No. 7). Washington, DC: Association for the Study of Higher Education, p. 15.

4. College Outcomes Evaluation Program Advisory Committee (1987, October). *Report to the New Jersey Board of Higher Education*. Trenton, NJ: Office of College Outcomes, Dept. of Higher Education, p. 6; and California State University System (1989). Outcomes assessment in the California State University: Cooperation without coercion. Specific list of missions. *The Mission of the California State University*. Material on Assessment in the CSU System, 1985–1989. Handed out during a panel presentation at the AAHE National Conference, Chicago, April 1989.

5. Jensen, A. R. (1989). *Psychometric "g" and Manifest Achievement*. Monograph. U.C. Berkeley: School of Education.

6. Jensen, A. R. (1989). The relationship between learning and intelligence. *Learning and Individual Differences*, 1:1, p. 37.

7. Ibid., p. 7.

8. Browne, A. (now Browne-Miller, A.) and Wildavsky, A. (1984). Implementation as mutual adaptation. In Pressman, J. L. and Wildavsky, A. (Eds.), *Implementation*. Berkeley: University of California Press, pp. 206–231.

9. Ibid.

10. Ibid.

11. Sternberg, R. J. (1988). *The Triarchic Mind: A New Theory of Human Intelligence*. New York: Viking, p. 46.

12. Baron, J. (1986). Capacities, dispositions, and rational thinking. In Sternberg, R. and Detterman, D. (Eds.), *What Is Intelligence?* Norwood, NJ: Ablex, p. 29.

13. Gottfredson, L. S. (1988). *Ability Differences in a Democracy: Challenge to Educational Policy*. Paper presented to College of Education Colloquium Mini-Series 1988–1989. College of Education, University of Delaware, p. 2.

14. Scarr, S. (1989). Protecting general intelligence. In Linn, R. L. (Ed.). *Intelligence: Measurement, Theory and Public Policy*. Chicago: University of Illinois Press, p. 76.

15. Linn, op. cit., p. 1.

16. Lerner, B. (1989). Intelligence and law. In ibid., p. 173.

17. Table (1986). A framework for understanding conceptions of intelligence. In Sternberg, R. and Detterman, D. (Eds.), *What Is Intelligence?* Norwood, NJ: Ablex, pp. 4–5.

18. Linn, op. cit., p. 2; and Eysenck, H. J. (1973). *The Measurement of Intelligence*. Lancaster, UK: MTP Medical and Technical Pub. Co. Ltd.

19. Spearman, C. (1904). General intelligence, objectively determined and measured.

American Journal of Psychology, 15, pp. 201–293; and Spearman, C. (1927). *The Abilities of Man and Their Measurement*. New York: Macmillan.

20. A concept argued by Ulrich Neisser of Emory University; see Neisser, U. (1976). General academic and artificial intelligence. In Resnick, L. (Ed.), *The Nature of Intelligence*. Hillsdale, NJ: Erlbaum.

21. Ibid.

22. Ibid.

23. Sternberg, op. cit., p. 211.

24. Ibid.

25. Ibid.

26. Neisser, op. cit.

27. Jensen, A. R. (1987). Intelligence as a fact of nature. *Zeitschrift Fur Padagogische Psychologie*, Heft 3, p. 157.

28. Ibid.

29. Davis, B. D. (1986). Neo-Lysenkoism, IQ and the press. In *Storm over Biology*. Buffalo, NY: Prometheus Books, p. 114.

30. Hartle, T. W. (1986). The growing interest in measuring the educational achievement of college students. In Adelman, C. (Ed.), *Assessment in American Higher Education: Issues and Contexts*. Washington, DC: OERI, pp. 201–211.

31. Marchese, T. J. (1987). Third down, ten years to go. *American Association of Higher Education Bulletin*, 40:4, December, pp. 3–8.

32. Hartle (1986), op. cit., p. 4.

33. Millman, J. (1988). Designing a college assessment. In Adelman, op. cit., pp. 9–31.

34. Ibid.

35. Halpern, D. F. (1987, Fall). Student outcomes assessment: Introduction and overview. In *Student Outcomes Assessment: What Institutions Stand to Gain* (New Directions for Higher Education series, No. 59). San Francisco: Jossey-Bass, p. 6.

36. Hartle (1986), op. cit., p. 2.

37. Marchese, op. cit.

38. McClain, C. J. and Kruger, D. W. (1985, September). Using outcomes assessment: A case study in institutional change. In Edwell, P. T. (Ed.), *Assessing Education Outcomes* (New Directions for Institutional Research Series; No. 47). San Francisco: Jossey-Bass, pp. 38–39.

39. Hartle, op. cit; and El-Khawas, E. (1987). Campus trends. *Higher Education Panel Reports, No. 75*, August, pp. vi–19.

40. Sternberg, op. cit., p. 9.

41. College Outcomes Evaluation Program Advisory Committee, op. cit., p. 6.

42. Hartle (1986), op. cit., p. 1.

43. Ibid.

44. Ibid.

45. Ibid.

46. Ibid.

47. Ibid., pp. 7–8.

48. Edwell, P. T. (1987, May). Assessment, accountability and improvement: Managing the contradiction. Paper prepared for the American Association for Higher Education.

Washington, DC: National Center for Higher Education Management Systems, pp. 1–22.

49. Ibid., p. 7.

50. California State University System, op. cit.

51. Baird, L. L. (1988). Value-added: Using student gains as yardsticks of learning. In Adelman, C. (Ed.), *Performance and Judgment: Essays on Principles and Practices in the Assessment of College Student Learning*. Washington, DC: Office of Educational Research and Improvement, p. 206.

52. Ibid; see also Astin, A. W. (1982). Why not try some new ways of measuring quality? *Educational Record*, 63, pp. 10–15.

53. Value-added assessment (VA) can be initiated without developing an entirely new set of procedures; an institution can build on what it has in place. Institutional identity is enhanced using VA. A common institution-wide mission is engendered by VA, and a clear vision on the part of all players is formed. A general understanding that improving education is a continuous process is encouraged. See Astin, A. W. (1987). Assessment, value-added, and education excellence. In Halpern, op. cit., pp. 89–107; see also Krueger, D. W. and Heisserer, M. L. (1987). Assessment and involvement: Investments to enhance learning. In Halpern, op. cit., pp. 45–56.

54. Jacobi et al. (1987), op. cit., p. 15.

55. Ibid., p. 19.

56. Baird (1988a), op. cit., p. 206.

57. Hanson, G. R. (1988). Critical issues in the assessment of value-added education. In Banta, T. W. (Ed.) *Implementing Outcomes Assessment: Promise and Perils* (New Directions for Institutional Research, No. 59). San Francisco: Jossey-Bass, pp. 53–67.

58. Manning, W. H. (1987). *AACJC Journal*, February/March, p. 52; and Warren, J. (1984). The blind alley of value-added. *AAHE Bulletin*, 37, pp. 10–13.

59. Manning (ibid., p. 52) asserts that value-added testing "implies that education is merely additive, piling more of the same ability or knowledge on top of where you started," but higher-order learning is not additive. It is "a dynamic reorganization of component skills and abilities in new and more complex ways," which is impossible to fully measure. See Power, J. (1987, March). Value-added testing: Is it coming your way? *NEA Today*, p. 3. See also Hanson, op. cit., pp. 58–59.

60. Pascarella, E. T. (1987). Are value-added analyses valuable? *Assessing the Outcomes of Higher Education: Proceedings of the 1986 Invitational Conference*. Princeton, NJ: Educational Testing Service, pp. 71–92.

61. Baird, L. L. (1988b). Diverse and subtle arts: Assessing the generic academic outcomes of higher education. In Adelman (1988), op. cit., p. 50.

62. Ibid.

63. Ibid.

64. Ibid., p. 39.

65. Ibid., pp. 39–62.

66. Ibid.

67. See, for example, Barkowski, J. G. and Milstead, M. (1984). *Components of Children's Metamemory: Implications for Strategy Generalization*. Munich, Germany: Institute for Psychological Research.

68. See Baird (1988b), op. cit., pp. 40–41, 50–51.
69. Dunbar, S. B. (1988). Issues in evaluating measures of basic language skills for higher education. In Adelman (1988), op. cit., p. 86.
70. Baird (1988a), op. cit., p. 211.
71. Centra, J. A. (1988). Assessing general education. In Adelman (1988), op. cit., p. 107.
72. Baird (1988a), op. cit., pp. 213–214.
73. Jacobi et al. (1987). Outcome taxonomies. In Jacobi et al., op. cit. (1987), p. 18.
74. Baird (1988a), op. cit., p. 207.
75. Dunbar (1988), op. cit., p. 89.
76. Baird (1988b), op. cit., p. 51.
77. Dunbar (1988), op. cit., p. 80.
78. Baird (1988a), op. cit., p. 208.
79. Ibid., pp. 210–211.
80. Baird (1988b), op. cit., p. 43.
81. Baird (1988a), op. cit., p. 207.
82. Ibid.
83. Ibid., p. 205.
84. Parker, C. A. and Schmidt, J. A. (Eds.) (1982). Effects of college experience. *Encyclopedia of Educational Research* (5th ed.). New York: The Free Press, p. 535.
85. Baird (1988b), op. cit., pp. 40–41, 50–51.
86. Millman, J. (1988). Designing a college assessment. In Adelman (1988), op. cit., p. 25.
87. Jacobi et al. (1987), op. cit., p. 15.

Chapter 4

1. Ortiz de Montellano, professor of anthropology, made this statement in a speech before the American Association for the Advancement of Science; it is quoted in West, P. (1992). Scientists debate claims of Afrocentric teachings. *Education Week*, February 19, p. 10.

Chapter 5

1. Committee on Admissions and Enrollment (1989). *Freshmen Admissions and Beyond (The Karabel Report)*. Berkeley, CA: Berkeley Division, Academic Senate, University of California, p. 55.
2. Gottfredson, L. (1986). Societal consequences of the g factor in employment. *Journal of Vocational Behavior*, 29:3, December, p. 403.
3. Ibid., pp. 403–404.
4. Ibid., p. 404. See also Herrnstein, R. and Murray, C. (1994). *The Bell Curve*. New York: The Free Press.
5. Ibid., p. 405; and Manning, W. and Jackson, R. (1984). College entrance examinations: Objective selection or gatekeeping for the economically privileged. In Reynold,

C. and Brown, R. (Eds.), *Perspectives on Bias in Mental Testing*. New York: Plenum Press, pp. 189–220.

6. Gottfredson (1986), op. cit., p. 404.
7. Rohranbacher, D. (Rep.) (1989). Evidence of Asian American Discrimination in College and University Admissions: Fact Sheet, June.
8. D'Souza, D. (1992). *Illiberal Education: The Politics of Sex and Race on Campus*. New York: Random House, p. 3.
9. Ibid., p. 27.
10. Ibid., p. 28.
11. Ibid., p. 28.
12. Ibid., p. 31.
13. California State Department of Education (1960). *A Master Plan for Higher Education in California, 1960–1975*. Sacramento: Liaison Committee of the State Board of Education and the Regents of the University of California, pp. 72–73.
14. Ibid.
15. Commission for the Review of the Master Plan for Higher Education (1987). *The Master Plan Renewed: Unity, Equity, Quality and Efficiency in California Post Secondary Education*. Sacramento: California State Government.
16. Committee on Admissions and Enrollment (1989), op. cit., pp. 1–2.
17. Ibid., p. 1.
18. Ibid., p. 4.
19. Ibid., pp. 4, 35.
20. Ibid., p. 7.
21. Ibid., p. 11.
22. Ibid., pp. 22, 36.
23. University of California at Berkeley, Office of Student Research (1983). *Ethnic Distribution of New Freshman at U.C. Berkeley, Fall Terms 1979–1983*. Berkeley, CA: Office of Student Research.
24. Committee on Admissions and Enrollment (1989), op. cit.
25. Joint Committee for Review of the Master Plan for Higher Education (1988). *California Faces, California's Future*. Sacramento: California State Government, p. 19.
26. Committee on Admissions and Enrollment (1989), op. cit., pp. 22–23; see also Office of the Chancellor: Budget and Planning (1988). *Freshman Admissions at Berkeley, February 1988*. Berkeley: University of California at Berkeley, pp. 3–4.
27. Office of the Chancellor: Budget and Planning (1988), op. cit., pp. 3–4.
28. Ibid.
29. Committee on Admissions and Enrollment (1989), op. cit., p. 22.
30. Ibid.
31. Ibid.
32. Ibid., p. 23.
33. Ibid.
34. Ibid., p. 25.
35. Ibid.
36. Ibid., pp. 25–26.

37. Ibid., p. 43.
38. Ibid., p. 46.
39. Ibid., p. 46.
40. Ibid.
41. Ibid.
42. Ibid., p. 51.
43. Ibid., p. 52.
44. Ibid., pp. 29, 35.
45. Ibid., p. 29.
46. Ibid., pp. 29, 35.
47. Ibid.
48. Ibid., pp. 29–34.
49. D'Souza, op. cit., p. 28–31.
50. Committee on Admissions and Enrollment (1989), op. cit.
51. Gifford, B. (1989). The allocation of opportunities and the politics of testing: A policy-analytic perspective. In Gifford, B. (Ed.), *Test Policy and the Politics of Opportunity Allocation.* Boston, MA: Kluwer Academic Publishers, pp. 3–32.
52. Committee on Admissions and Enrollment (1989), op. cit. p. 56.

Chapter 6

1. Academic Senate, Berkeley (1989). *Freshman Admissions at Berkeley: A Policy for the 1990s and Beyond (The Karabel Report*, a report by the Committee on Admissions and Enrollment, Berkeley Division, with Professor Jerome Karabel as chair, Berkeley, CA: U.C. Berkeley, p. 15.
2. Ibid.
3. Ibid., pp. 15–16.
4. Goodlad, J. (1984). *A Place Called School: Prospects for the Future.* New York: McGraw-Hill, pp. 148–149.
5. Ogbu, J. U. (1978). *Minority Education and Caste: The American System in Cross-Cultural Perspective.* New York: Academic Press, pp. 355–370.
6. Sternberg, R. J. (1987). Second game: A school's eye view of intelligence. In Langer, J. A. (Ed.), *Language, Literacy and Culture: Issues of Society and Schooling.* Norwood, NJ: Ablex, p. 280.
7. Jensen, A. (1972). Assessment of racial desegregation in the Berkeley schools. In Adelson, D. (Ed.), *Man as the Measure: The Crossroads* (Community Psychology Series, American Psychological Association, Division 27). New York: Behavioral Publications.
8. Jacobs, P. (1980). *The Economics of Health and Medical Care.* Baltimore, MD: University Park Press, pp. 90–91.
9. Ogbu (1978), op. cit., p. 358.
10. Goodlad (1984), op. cit., p. 130.
11. Lightfoot, S. L. (1978). *Worlds Apart: Relationships between Families and Schools.* New York: Basic Books, p. 4.

12. Labov, W. (1982). Competing value systems in the inner-city schools. In Gilmore, P. and Glathorn, A. A. (Eds.), *Children in and out of School*. Washington, DC: Center for Applied Linguistics, p. 149.
13. Heath, S. B. (1983). *Ways with Words*. New York: Cambridge University Press. See also Sternberg, R. J. (1987), op. cit.
14. Sternberg, R. J. (1987), op. cit., pp. 38–40.
15. Lightfoot (1978), op. cit., p. 176.
16. Ibid.
17. Estes, C. L. (1981). The social construction of reality: A framework for inquiry. In *The Aging Enterprise*. San Francisco, CA: Jossey-Bass, p. 2.
18. Stromquist, N. P. (1989). Determinants of educational participation and achievement of women in the third world: A review of the evidence and a theoretical critique. *Review of Educational Research*, 59:2, pp. 143–183.
19. Ibid., pp. 143–144.
20. Ibid., p. 152.
21. Ghosh, R. (1986). Women's education in the land of Goddess Saraswati. *Canadian and International Education*, 15:1, pp. 25–44.
22. Stromquist (1989), op. cit., p. 153.
23. Seetharamu, A. S. and Ushadevi, M. D. (1985). *Education in Rural Areas*. New Delhi, India: Ashish Publishing House.
24. Ogbu, J. U. (1987). Opportunity structure, cultural boundaries, and literacy. In Langer, J. A. (Ed.), *Language, Literacy and Culture: Issues of Society and Schooling*. Norwood, NJ: Ablex, p. 165.
25. Schiefelbein, E. and Farrell, J. (1980). Women, schooling, and work in Chile: Evidence from a longitudinal study. *Comparative Education Review*, 24:2, pp. 160–179; based on categorization by Levin, H. (1976). Educational opportunity and social inequality in Western Europe. *Social Problems*, 24, pp. 148–172.
26. Sternberg (1987), op. cit., p. 47.
27. Sternberg (1987), op. cit., p. 47.
28. Brown, A., Bransford, J., Ferrara, R., and Campione, R. (1983). Learning, remembering and understanding. In Mussen, P. H. (Ed.), *Handbook of Child Psychology* (Vol. 3). New York: Wiley, pp. 106–129.
29. Ibid., p. 122.
30. Ibid. and Vygotsky, L. S. (1978). *Mind in Society: The Development of the Higher Psychological Processes*. Cambridge, MA: Harvard University Press.
31. This concurs with Immanuel Kant's argument that the content of knowledge comes a posteriori from sensory perception but that its form is determined by a priori categories in the mind. Kant, I. (1960). Selections from the critique of pure reason (abridged). In *The European Philosophers from Descartes to Nietzsche*. New York: The Modern Library.
32. Newton, E. (1950). *The Meaning of Beauty*. New York: McGraw-Hill, p. 10.
33. Nelson, G. (1973). *How to See* (U.S. DHEW Publication No. 73-10063; SSA). Washington, DC: U.S. Government Printing Office, p. 15.
34. Boas, F. (1939). *The Primitive Mind of Man*. New York: The Free Press, p. 199.
35. Wiener, N. (1948). The great ravelled knot. *Scientific American*, 179:5, p. 17.

36. Bloom, A. (1987). *The Closing of the American Mind*. New York: Simon & Schuster, p. 26.

37. Lightfoot, op. cit., pp. 191–192.

38. Ibid., pp. 193–194.

39. Labov, op. cit., pp. 168–169.

40. Ibid., p. 169.

41. Ibid., p. 169.

42. Rebell, M. A. (1989). Testing, public policy and the courts. In Gifford, B. R. (Ed.), *Test Policy and the Politics of the Workplace and the Law*. A publication sponsored by the National Commission on Testing and Public Policy. Boston, MA: Kluwer Academic Publishers, p. 151.

43. Simon, H. (1980). Problem solving and education. In Turner, D. and Reif, F. (Eds.), *Problem Solving and Education: Issues in Teaching and Research*. Hillsdale, NJ: Erlbaum, p. 81.

44. Ibid.

45. Lave, J., Murtaugh, M., and de la Rocha, O. (1984). The dialectic of arithmetic in grocery shopping. In Rogoff, B. and Lave, J. (Eds.), *Everyday Cognition: Its Development in Social Context*. Cambridge, MA: Harvard University Press, pp. 67–94.

46. Brown, A. L. (1982). Learning and development: The problems of compatibility, access and induction. *Human Development*, 25:1, p. 95. See also Brown, A. L. (1979). The development of memory: Knowing, knowing about knowing, and knowing how to know. In R. Reese (Ed.), *Advances in Child Development and Behavior* (Vol. 10). New York: Academic Press; and Brown, A. L. (1979). The zone of proximal development: Implication for intelligence testing in the year 2000. *Intelligence*, 3, pp. 255–277.

47. Brown (1982), op. cit., pp. 90–115.

48. Ibid., p. 103.

49. Ibid., p. 108.

50. Ibid.

51. Ibid.

52. Ibid.

53. Ibid.

54. Campione, J. C. and Brown, A. L. (1978). Towards a theory of intelligence: Contributions from research with retarded children. *Intelligence*, 2, pp. 279–304.

55. Wong, B. (1989). Musing about cognitive strategy training. *Intelligence*, 13, pp. 1–4.

56. Brown et al., op. cit., pp. 106–108.

57. Ibid., pp. 106–120.

58. Barkowski, J. and Milstead, M. (1984). *Components of Children's Metamemory: Implications for Strategy Generalization*. Munich, Germany: Max Planck Institute for Psychological Research, p. 14.

59. Ibid.

60. Ibid., p. 16.

61. Bowles, S. and Nelson, V. I. (1974). The inheritance of I.Q. and the intergenerational reproduction of economic inequality. *The Review of Economics and Statistics*. 56:39.

62. Herrnstein, R. J. (1973). *I.Q. in the Meritocracy*. Boston: Little, Brown, p. 5.

63. Wilson, R. S. (1983). The Louisville twin study: Developmental synchronies in behavior. *Child Development*, 54, pp. 298–316.
64. Piaget, J. (1978). *The Psychology of Intelligence Testing*. Totowa, NJ: Littlefield Adams.
65. Ibid.
66. Vygotsky, L. S. (1978). *Mind in Society: The Development of Higher Psychological Processes*. Cambridge: Harvard University Press.
67. Chapman, P. (1988). *Schools as Sorters*. New York: New York University Press, p. 19.
68. Ibid.; and Spearman, C. (1923). *The Nature of "Intelligence."* London, UK: Macmillan.
69. Thurstone, L. (1938). Primary mental abilities. *Psychometric Monographs* (No. 1). Chicago: University of Chicago Press.
70. Cattell, R. B. (1987). Fluid and crystallized intelligence. In *Intelligence: Its Structure, Growth and Action*. New York: NHC, p. 97.
71. Ibid.
72. Plonim, R., DeFries, J., McLearn, G. (1990). *Behavioral Genetics: A Primer*. New York: Freeman; see p. 340, for example.
73. Eells et al. (1951). *Children and Cultural Differences*. Chicago: University of Chicago Press, p. 58.
74. Jensen, A. (1980). *Bias in Mental Testing*. New York: The Free Press, pp. 368–369.
75. Gardner, H. (1983). *Frames of Mind: The Theory of Multiple Intelligences*. New York: Basic Books.
76. Gifford, B. R. (1989). Introduction. In Gifford, B. R. (Ed.), *Testing Policy and Test Performance: Education, Language and Culture*. Boston: Kluwer Academic Publishers, p. ix.
77. Herrnstein (1971), op. cit., p. 198.
78. Ibid., pp. 189, 198.

Chapter 7

1. Quoted in Gould, S. (1981). *The Mismeasure of Man*. New York: Norton, p. 21.
2. Chapman, P. D. (1988). *Schools as Sorters*. New York: New York University Press, p. 17.
3. Ibid., p. 1.
4. Ibid.
5. Ibid.
6. Ibid.
7. Ibid.
8. Ibid., pp. 6, 1–106.
9. Ibid., pp. 1–106.
10. Gifford, B. R. (1989). The allocation of opportunities and the politics of testing: A policy-analytic perspective. In Gifford, B. R. (Ed.), *Test Policy and the Politics of Opportunity Allocation: The Workplace and the Law*. Boston: Kluwer Academic Publishers, National Commission on Testing and Public Policy, pp. 3–32.

11. Ibid., p. 4.
12. Ibid., p. 13.
13. Ibid., p. 3.
14. Ibid., p. 13.
15. Ibid., p. 15.
16. Ibid., pp. 15–16.
17. Ibid., p. 18.
18. Patterson, P. O. (1989). Employment testing and Title VII of the Civil Rights Act of 1964. In ibid., p. 83.
19. Ibid.
20. Jensen, A. (1980). *Bias in Mental Testing*. New York: The Free Press, pp. 2, 370–373.
21. Rebell, M. A. (1989). Testing, public policy, and the courts. In Gifford (1989), op. cit., p. 151.
22. Chapman (1988), op. cit.
23. Anastasi, A. (1981). Coaching, test sophistication, and developed abilities. *American Psychologist*, 36:10, pp. 1086–1093.
24. Anastasi, A. (1982). *Psychological Testing*. New York: Macmillan, p. 393.
25. Anastasi, A. (1981), op. cit.
26. Hargadon, F. (1981). Tests and college admissions. *American Psychologist*, 36:10, pp. 1112–1119.
27. Jencks, C. (1989). If not tests, then what? In Gifford, B. (Ed.), *Test Policy and Test Performance: Education, Language and Culture*. Boston: Kluwer Academic Publishers, p. 118.
28. Hanford, G. (1989). Advice to the Commission. In Gifford, op. cit., p. 124.
29. Ibid.
30. Ibid.
31. Jencks (1989), op. cit., p. 119.
32. Gardner, H. (1983). *Frames of Mind: The Theory of Multiple Intelligences*. New York: Basic Books, p. 368.
33. Ibid.
34. Ibid., p. 5.
35. Sternberg, R. (1986). A framework for understanding conceptions of intelligence. In Sternberg, R. and Detterman, D. (Eds.), *What Is Intelligence?* Norwood, NJ: Ablex, pp. 4–5.
36. Adapted from Sternberg, op. cit.
37. Plonim, R., De Fries, J. C., and McClearn, G. E. (1990). *Behavioral Genetics: A Primer*. New York: Freeman. See also Jensen, A. R. (1991). Spearman's g and the problem of educational equality. *Oxford Review of Education*, 17:2.
38. See Plonim et al. (1990), op. cit.
39. Spearman, C. (1923). *The Nature of "Intelligence" and the Principles of Cognition*. London, UK: Macmillan.
40. Ibid., p. 90.
41. Cattell, R. (1987). Intelligence: Its structure, growth and action. In Stelmach, G. and Vroon, P. (Eds.), *Advances in Psychology*. New York: NHC, 35, p. 225.

42. Ibid., p. 97.
43. Noted in Jensen, A. (1969). How much can we boost I.Q. and scholastic achievement? *Harvard Educational Review*, 39, pp. 1–123.
44. Ibid.
45. See, for example, Gleitman, H. (1986). *Psychology* (2nd ed.). New York: Norton, Chapter 17; Humphreys, L. G. (1980). Race and intelligence re-examined. *The Humanist*, 40:4, pp. 52–55; Jensen, A. (1980). *Bias in Mental Testing*. New York: The Free Press; Jensen, A. (1981). *Straight Talk about Mental Tests*. New York: The Free Press; Neisser, U. (1986). New answers to an old question. In Neisser, U. (Ed.), *The School Achievement of Minority Children: New Perspective*. Hillsdale, NJ: Erlbaum, pp. 1–17; Papalia, D. E. and Olds, S. W. (1988). *Psychology* (2nd ed.). San Francisco: McGraw-Hill, Ch. 7; and Plomin, R., DeFries, J. C., McClearn, G. E. (1990). *Behavioral Genetics: A Primer* (2nd ed.). New York: Freeman.
46. Plomin et al. (1990), op. cit., pp. 367, 401.
47. Jensen, A. (1991). Spearman's g and the problem of educational quality. *Oxford Review of Education*, 17:2, p. 9. Regarding the reference to any setting or any age, see also Jensen, A. (1986). g: Artifact or reality? *Journal of Vocational Behavior*, 29:3, p. 316.
48. Bouchard, T. J., Jr. and McGue, M. (1981). Familial studies of intelligence: A review. *Science*, 212, pp. 1055–1059; Scarr, S. and Carter-Salzman, L. (1982). Genetics and intelligence. In Sternberg, R. J. (Ed.), *Handbook of Human Intelligence*. Cambridge, UK: Cambridge University Press; Erlenmeyer-Kimling, L. and Jarvick, L. F. (1963). Genetics and intelligence: A review. *Science*, 142, pp. 1477–1479; Loehlin, J. C. and Nicols, R. C. (1976). *Heredity, Environment and Personality*. Austin, TX: University of Texas Press; Nicols, R. C. (1965). The National Merit Twin Study. In Vandenberg, S. (Ed.), *Methods and Goals in Human Behavior Genetics*. Orlando, FL: Academic Press; and Husen, T. (1960). Abilities of twins. *Scandinavian Journal of Psychology*, 1, pp. 125–135.
49. Benirschke, K. and Harper, V. (1977). The acardiac anomaly. *Teratology*, 15, pp. 311–316.
50. See, for example, Wallace et al. (1982). Neonatal precursors of cognitive development in low-birth-weight children. *Seminars in Perinatology*, 6, pp. 327–333; and Record, R., McKeown, T., and Edwards, J. (1969). The relation of measured intelligence to birthweight and duration of gestation. *Annals of Human Genetics*, 33, pp. 70–79.
51. Ibid.
52. Bouchard and McGue (1981), op. cit. Note also that a comprehensive international analysis of the literature on the correspondence between measured intelligence and familial relationships (which included 111 studies) reported the average findings among studies surveyed. Strong biological relationships prevailed with average correlations of IQ being .42 between parent and child living together, .50 between child and "midparent" I.Q., .47 between nontwin siblings reared together, .72 for mid-parent-midoffspring, and .31 for half siblings reared together. These correlations are considered quite high by statisticians.
53. See Storfer, H. (1990). *Intelligence and Giftedness: The Contributions of Heredity*

and Early Environment. San Francisco: Jossey-Bass, pp. 68–69, for a summary of findings of the Texas Adoption Study, the Colorado Adoption Study, the Transracial Adoption Study, the "First" Minnesota Study, and the Stanford Adoption Study. Note also that the average correlations between adopted children and adoptive parents are +.16 for one adoptive parent and +.19 for midadoptive parents IQ. (Midadoptive parent IQ is the average IQ of the two parents who adopt a child.) These studies also indicate that IQs of adoptive mothers correlate more highly with those of adopted children than do IQs of adoptive fathers and that there are greater correlations on verbal measures than on nonverbal measures.

54. Kamin, L. J. (1974). I.Q. in the uterus. In Kamin, L. J. (Ed.), *The Science and Politics of I.Q.* Potomac, MD: Erlbaum, pp. 161–174.

55. Zajonc, R. B. and Markus, G. B. (1975). Birth order and mental development. *Psychological Review,* 82, pp. 74–88.

56. Vining, D. R. (1982). On the possibility of the re-emergence of adysgenic trends with respect to intelligence in American fertility differentials. *Intelligence,* 6, pp. 241–264.

57. Scarr, S. (1989). Protecting general intelligence: Constructs and consequences for interventions. In Linn, R. L. (Ed.), *Intelligence: Measurement, Theory and Public Policy.* Urbana, IL: University of Illinois Press.

58. Wachs, T. D. and Gruen, G. (1982). *Early Experience and Human Development.* New York: Plenum Press.

59. Toynbee, A. (1964). Is America neglecting her creative talents? In Taylor, C. W. (Ed.), *Widening Horizons and Creativity.* New York: Wiley, 1964.

60. Karnes, M.B., Shwedel, A. M., and Kemp, P. B. (1985). Preschool: Programming for the young gifted child. *Roeper Review,* 7:4, pp. 204–211.

61. See Wilson, R. S. (1986). Continuity and change in cognitive ability profile. *Behavior Genetics,* 16:1, p. 46.

62. From an interview with B. de Vries, past president of the Association for Gifted Children, May 10, 1991.

63. Wallace, B. (1987). An exploration of some definitions of giftedness. *Gifted Education International,* 4:3, pp. 136–138.

64. Chang, L. L. (1985). Who are the mathematically gifted? *Roeper Review,* 7:2, November, p. 76.

65. Galton, F. (1869). *Hereditary Genius: An Inquiry into Its Laws and Consequences.* London, UK: Collins.

66. Terman, L. (1915). The mental hygiene of exceptional children. *Journal of Educational Psychology,* 6, November, pp. 529–537.

67. Piechowski, M. M. (1979). Developmental potential. In Colangelo, N. and Zaffran, R. T. (Eds.), *New Voices in Counseling the Gifted.* Dubuque, IA: Kendall/Hunt, pp. 25–27.

68. Bachtold, L. M. (1980). Psychoticism and creativity. *Journal of Creative Behavior,* 14, pp. 242–248; and Geortzel, M. G., Geortzel, V., and Geortzel, T. G. (1978). *Three Hundred Eminent Personalities.* San Francisco: Jossey-Bass.

69. Renzulli, J. S. (1978). What makes giftedness? Reexamining a definition. *Phi Delta Kappan,* 60, pp. 180–184, 261.

70. Sternberg, R. J. (1981). A componential theory of intellectual giftedness. *Gifted Child Quarterly*, 25, pp. 86–93.

71. Wilms, D. (1986). Patron's opening address. In Cropley, A. J., Urban, K. K., Wagner, H., and Wieczerkowski, W. (Eds.), *Giftedness: A Continuing Worldwide Challenge*. New York: Trillium Press, p. 17.

72. Cropley et al. (1986), op. cit., p. 13.

73. Ibid., p. 11. See also Shaughnessy, H. (1986). Cognitive structures of the gifted. In Cropley et al. (1986), op. cit., pp. 65–69; Sternberg (1988), op. cit.; and Gardner, H. (1983). *Frames of Mind: The Theory of Multiple Intelligences*. New York: Basic Books.

74. Sternberg, R. J. (1984). Mechanisms of cognitive development: A componential approach. In Sternberg, R. J. (Ed.), *Mechanisms of Cognitive Development*. New York: Freeman. See also Davidson, J. and Sternberg, R. (1984). The role of insight in intellectual giftedness. *Gifted Child Quarterly*, 28:2, pp. 58–64.

75. Kranz, B. (1986). Curriculum by design. In Cropley (1986), op. cit., pp. 378–384.

76. Parlett, M. R. (1973). The syllabus-bound student. *Human Development*, 16, pp. 1–2.

77. Kranz (1986), op. cit., p. 379.

78. Fliegler, L. A. (1961). *Curriculum Planning for the Gifted*. Englewood Cliffs, NJ: Prentice-Hall, p. 16.

79. Ibid.

80. Renzulli, J. S. (1978). What makes giftedness? Re-examining a definition. *Phi Delta Kappan*, November, p. 261.

81. Browne-Miller, A. (1991). Evaluating gifted programs. The state of the art. *Gifted Child International*, Winter.

82. Ibid.

83. Healy, C. (1986). Creating a gifted ghetto from the principle of 'no policy.' In Maker, J. C. (Ed.), *Critical Issues in Gifted Education*. Rockville, MD: Aspen Publishing.

84. Gallagher, J. J. (1986). The conservation of intellectual resources. In Cropley et al. (1986), op. cit., p. 21.

85. Flynn, J. (1983). Now the great augmentation of American I.Q. *Nature*, 301, p. 655; see also Humphreys, L. (1971). Theory of Intelligence. In Canco, R. (Ed.), *Intelligence: Genetic and Environmental Influences*. New York: Grune & Stratton, pp. 31–55.

86. Storfer (1990), op. cit., p. 421.

87. Storfer (1990), op. cit., pp. 421–422.

88. Ibid.

89. Ibid.

90. For example, see Ogbu, J. U. (1978). *Minority Education and Caste: The American System in Cross-Cultural Perspective*. New York: Academic Press.

91. Ogbu, J. U. (1982). Cultural discontinuities and schooling. *Anthropology and Education Quarterly*, 13:4, pp. 290–306 at p. 298.

92. Ogbu, J. U. (1978), op. cit.; and Ogbu, J. U. (1985). Research currents: Cultural–ecological influences in minority school learning. *Language Art*, 62:8, pp. 860–869.

93. Ogbu, J. U. (1987). Teaching in secondary schools: A contextual perspective. *Educational Psychologist*, 22:2, p. 27.

94. Ogbu, J. U. (1986). The consequences of the American caste system. In Neisser, U. (Ed.), *The School Achievement of Minority Children: New Perspectives*. Hillsdale, NJ: Erlbaum, pp. 19–56.

95. Lewontin, R. C., Rose, E., and Kamin, L. J. (1984). *Not in Our Genes*. New York: Pantheon, p. 116.

96. Ibid., p. 125.

97. Ibid., p. 127.

98. Ibid., p. 116.

99. diSessa, A. (1979). On learnable representations of knowledge: A meaning for the computational metaphor. In *Cognitive Process Instruction*. Philadelphia: Franklin Institute Press, p. 239.

100. Ibid.

101. See Ranney, M. (1988, November). *Contradictions and Reorganizations among Naive Conceptions of Ballistics*. Paper presented at the meeting of the Psychometric Society, Chicago.

102. Clement, J. (1983). A conceptual model discussed by Galileo and used intuitively by physics students. In Genther, D. and Stevens, A. (Eds.), *Mental Models*. Hillsdale, NJ: Erlbaum, p. 338.

103. Gardner, H. (1985). *The Mind's New Science: A History of the Cognitive Revolution*. New York: Basic Books, p. 383.

104. Cattell, R. (1987). *Intelligence: Its Structure, Growth and Action*. New York: NHC, p. 94.

105. Gardner (1985), op. cit., p. 383.

106. Ibid.

107. Ibid., p. 86.

108. Ibid., p. 863.

109. Spiro, R. (1980). Constructive processes in prose comprehension and recall. In Spiro, R. J., et al. (Eds.), *Theoretical Issues in Reading Comprehension*. Hillsdale, NJ: Erlbaum, pp. 245–278.

110. diSessa, A. (1979). On learnable representations of knowledge: A meaning for the computational metaphor. In *Cognitive Process Instruction*. Philadelphia: Franklin Institute Press, p. 240.

111. Ibid.

112. McCloskey, M. (1983). Naive theories of motion. In Genther, D. and Stevens, A. (Eds.), *Mental Models*. Hillsdale, NJ: Erlbaum, pp. 318–322.

113. Clement, J. (1983). A conceptual model discussed by Galileo and used intuitively by physics students. In Genther, D. and Stevens, A. (Eds.), *Mental Models*. Hillsdale, NJ: Erlbaum, p. 338.

114. McCloskey (1983), op. cit., pp. 318–319.

115. Clement (1983), op. cit., pp. 335–336.

116. Ibid., p. 337.

117. McCloskey (1983), op. cit., p. 321.

118. di Sessa (1979), op. cit.

119. Ibid.

120. Clement (1983), op. cit., p. 337.

121. Ranney, M. (1988, November). *Contradictions and Reorganizations among Naive*

Conceptions of Ballistics. Paper presented at the meeting of the Psychonomic Society, Chicago, p. 2.

122. Ranney, M. and Thagard, P. (1988). Explanatory coherence and belief revision in naive physics. In *Proceedings of the Tenth Annual Conference of the Cognitive Science Society.* Hillsdale, NJ: Erlbaum, pp. 426–432; see also p.2.
123. diSessa (1979), op. cit.
124. Ibid., p. 241.
125. Ibid., p. 243.
126. McCloskey (1983), op. cit., p. 320; diSessa (1979), op. cit.; Ranney (1988), op. cit.

Chapter 8

1. From *The Republic* by Plato. In Jowett, B. (1967). *The Works of Plato.* Montauk, NY: Tudor, p. 297.
2. Gardner, H. (1987). *The Mind's New Science.* New York: Basic Books, p. 49.
3. Gould, S. (1981). *The Mismeasure of Man.* New York: Norton, p. 19.
4. Dewey, J. (1939). The schools and the social welfare: Education and social change. In Ratner, J. (Ed.), *Intelligence in the Modern World: John Dewey's Philosophy.* New York: Random House, p. 692.
5. *The Republic* by Plato (Desmond Lee, Trans., 1979, rev. ed.) New York: Penguin Books, pp. 260–347.
6. Magill on Aquinas's *Summa Theologica.* In Magill, F. (Ed.) (1990), *Masterpieces of World Philosophy.* New York: Harper-Collins.
7. Angeles, P. (1981). *Dictionary of Philosophy.* New York: Barnes & Noble, pp. 62–63, 134–135, 268–269.
8. Magill (1990), op. cit., p. 192.
9. Ibid., pp. 191–194.
10. Ibid., pp. 224–228.
11. Ibid.
12. Ibid.
13. Descartes, R. Preface to the reader. In Donald A. Cress (Trans.), *Meditations on First Philosophy in Which the Existence of God and the Distinction of the Soul from the Body Are Demonstrated.* Indianapolis, IN: Hackett Publishing Co., p. 6.
14. Descartes, R. Meditation One: Concerning those things that can be called into doubt, op. cit., p. 12.
15. Descartes, R. Meditation Three: Concerning God, that He exists, op. cit., p. 12.
16. Magill on Spinoza's *Ethics,* op. cit., p. 250.
17. Magill, op. cit., pp. 250, 253.
18. De Spinoza, B. Ethics. In Hutchins, R. M. (Ed.) (1984). *Great Books of the Western World* (Vol. 31). London, UK: William Benton Publishing Co., p. 460.
19. Ibid., pp. 358–359.
20. Anastasi, A. (1988). *Psychological Testing.* New York: Macmillan, p. 381. See also Spearman, C. (1923). *The Nature of "Intelligence" and the Principles of Cognition.* London, UK: Macmillan.

21. Jensen, A., Cohn, J., and Cohn, C. (1989). Speed of information processing in academically gifted youths and their siblings. *Individual Differences*, 10:1, pp. 29–33.

22. Hume, D. An enquiry concerning human understanding. In (1977) *Classics of Western Philosophy*. Indianapolis, IN: Hackett Publishing Co., p. 645.

23. Darwin, C. The origin of species. In Alder, M. (Ed.) (1952). *Great Books of the Western World* (Vol. 49). Chicago: William Benton Publishing Co. See the chapter on "Natural Selection; or the Survival of the Fittest."

24. Locke, J. "An essay concerning human understanding" in *Book II: Of Ideas*. In Hutchins, R. M. (Ed.) *Great Books of the Western World* (Vol. 35). (1984). Chicago: William Benton Publishing Co., p. 121.

25. Ibid., p. 294.

26. Ibid., pp. 216–217.

27. Ibid., pp. 334–342.

28. Ibid.

29. Ibid., pp. 93–102.

30. Hume, D. An essay concerning human understanding. In Hutchins (1984), op. cit., pp. 457, 470, 484.

31. Ibid., p. 484.

32. Ibid.

33. Ibid.

34. Hume, D. Enquiry concerning human understanding. In (1977). *Classics of Western Philosophy*. Indianapolis, IN: Hackett Publishing Co.

35. Ibid., p. 643.

36. Bateson, G. (1972). *Steps to an Ecology of Mind*. New York: Ballantine Books, p. 504.

37. Rifkin, J. (1991). *Biosphere Politics: A New Consciousness for a New Century*. New York: Crown.

38. Bateson (1972), op. cit.

39. Rifkin (1991), op. cit., pp. 206–263.

Chapter 9

1. Cattell, R. B. (1987). Intelligence and society. In *Intelligence: Its Structure, Growth and Action*. In Stelmach, G. E. and Vroon, P. A. (Eds.), *Advances in Psychology* (Vol. 35). New York: N.H.C., p. 560.

2. Cattell, ibid., entire chapter.

3. Jensen, A. (1980). *Bias in Mental Testing*. New York: The Free Press, pp. 128, 201, 220.

4. National Commission on Testing and Public Policy (1990). *From Gatekeeper to Gateway: Transforming Testing in America*. Chestnut Hill, MA: National Commission on Testing and Public Policy, pp. 8–9.

5. Ibid., p. 17.

6. Ibid., pp. 5, 30.

7. Ibid., p. 7.

8. Ibid.

9. Ibid., p. 8.

10. Ibid.
11. Ibid., pp. x–xi, 40–42, 43.
12. Ibid., p. 38.
13. Ibid., p. 9.
14. Ibid., p. 8.

Chapter 10

1.   Committee on Admissions and Enrollment (1989). *Freshman Admissions at Berkeley (The Karabel Report)*. Berkeley: Berkeley Division, Academic Senate of the University of California, p. 35.
2.   Wildavsky, A. (1979). *Speaking Truth to Power*. Boston: Little, Brown, p. 18.
3.   Ibid., p. 19; see also pp. 205–211.
4.   Ibid., p. 3.
5.   Ibid., p. 5.
6.   Nathan, R. (1988). *The Uses and Misuses of Social Science in Government*. New York: Basic Books.
7.   Churchman, C. W. (1979). *The Systems Approach*. New York: Delta, p. viii.
8.   Bartlett, R. V. (1986). Ecological rationality: Reason and environmental policy. *Environmental Ethics*, 8, Fall, pp. 221–240, esp. p. 229.
9.   Ibid., p. 230.
10. Ehrenfeld, D. (1981). *The Arrogance of Humanism*. New York: Oxford University Press.
11. Bartlett, op. cit., p. 231.
12. Leopold, A. (1966). *A Sand County Almanac: With Essays on Conservation from Round River*. New York: Ballantine Books, p. 262.
13. Diesing, P. (1964). *Reason in Society: Five Types of Decisions and Their Social Conditions*. Urbana, IL: University of Chicago Press, pp. 88, 231–232.

Chapter 11

1.   Gardner, H. (1988). Beyond the IQ: Education and human development. *Phi Kappa Phi Journal*, Spring, p. 5.
2.   Odum, G. (1989). *Mothers, Leadership and Success*. Federalsburg, MD: Polyibus Press, p. 272.
3.   Watters, E. (1992). The new politics of race. *San Francisco Chronicle Focus*, Sunday, April, p. 58.
4.   U.S. News and World Report (1993). *America's Best Colleges: 1994 College Guide*. Washington, DC: U.S. News and World Report, Inc., p. 85.
5.   Ibid.
6.   Ibid. These data are reported throughout this volume.
7.   State of California, (1993). *Statistical Abstracts*, 1993 ed. Sacramento: State of California, p. 19.

8. U.S. News and World Report (1993), op. cit. These data are reported throughout this volume.
9. Ibid., p. 85.
10. Ibid.
11. Ibid. These data are reported throughout this volume.
12. Quoted in Watters, E. (1992). The new politics of race. *San Francisco Chronicle Focus*, Sunday, April, p. 58.
13. Ibid.
14. Parker, C. and Schmidt, J. (1982). Effects of college experience. In Mitzel, H. (Ed.), *Encyclopedia of Educational Research* (Vol. 2). New York: The Free Press, pp. 535–543, esp. p. 541.
15. Committee on Admissions and Enrollment (1989). *Freshman Admissions at Berkeley: A Policy for the 1990s and Beyond (The Karabel Report)*. Berkeley: Berkeley Division, Academic Senate, University of California, p. 33.
16. Watters (1992), op. cit.
17. Watters (1992), op. cit., p. 68.
18. Catanzaro, J. (1987). Counterpoint. *AAJCJ Journal*, February/March, p. 53; Advisory Committee to the College Outcomes Evaluation Program (1987, October). *Report to the New Jersey Board of Higher Education*. Trenton, NJ: Office of College Outcomes, Department of Higher Education, p. 13; Hartle, T. (1986). The growing interest in measuring the educational achievement of college students. In Adelman, C. (Ed.), *Assessment in American Higher Education: Issues and Contexts*. Washington, DC: OERI, pp. 1–11., esp. p. 6.
19. Watters (1992), op. cit.
20. Ibid., p. 55.
21. Ibid.
22. Committee on Admissions and Enrollment (1989), op. cit., p. 2.
23. Ibid., p. 46.
24. Gottfredson, L., and Crouse, J. (1986). Validity versus utility of mental tests: Example of the SAT. *Journal of Vocational Behavior*, 29:3, December, p. 365.
25. Jensen, A. (1986). g: Artifact or reality? *Journal of Vocational Behavior*, 29:3, December, p. 317.
26. Ibid.
27. Hunter, J. (1986). Cognitive ability, cognitive aptitudes, job knowledge and job performance. *Journal of Vocational Behavior*, 29:3, December, p. 360.
28. Gottfredson and Crouse (1986), op. cit., pp. 365–366.
29. Ibid., p. 366.
30. Committee on Admissions and Enrollment (1989), op. cit., pp. 45–52; see also Yale Daily News (1991). *The Insiders Guide to Colleges*. New York: St. Martin's Press, pp. 15–55.
31. Quoted in Watters (1990), op. cit., p. 68; see also d'Souza (1991). *Illiberal Education*. New York: Random House.
32. Watters (1990), op. cit., p. 70.
33. Committee on Admissions and Enrollment (1989), op. cit., p. 33.
34. Wilson, M., Moore, S., Gumpel, T., and Gifford, B. (1990). *Consequences of*

Nonlinearity for Validity and Selection (Monograph). Berkeley: School of Education and Office of Student Research, University of California, pp. 15–17.
35. Ibid.
36. Ibid.
37. Ibid.
38. Committee on Admissions and Enrollment (1989), op. cit., p. 38.

Chapter 12

1. Gifford, B. R. (1992). The learning society: On Ellis Island. *Education Week*, February 12, p. 17.
2. Committee on Admissions and Enrollment (1989). *Freshman Admissions at Berkeley: A Policy for the 1990s and Beyond (The Karabel Report)*. Berkeley, CA: Berkeley Division, Academic Senate, University of California.

Chapter 13

1. Cattell, R. B. (1987). Intelligence: Its structure, growth and action. In Stelmach, G. and Vroon, P. (Eds.), *Advances in Psychology* (Vol. 35). New York: NHC, p. 587.
2. As defined in Gifford, B. (1989). The allocation of opportunities and the politics of testing: A policy analytic perspective. In Gifford, B. (Ed.), *Test Policy and the Politics of Opportunity Allocation: The Workplace and the Law*. Norwell, MA: Kluwer Academic Publishers, pp. 3–32.
3. Horn, J. (1989). Models of Intelligence. In Linn, R. (Ed.), *Intelligence: Measurement, Theory and Public Policy*. Urbana, IL: University of Chicago Press, p. 30.
4. Clark, R. (1971). *Einstein: The Life and Times*. New York: Avon Books, p. 71.
5. Adler, M. (1988). *Reforming Education: The Opening of the American Mind*. New York: Collier Books, Macmillan, p. 46.

Appendix A

1. Lowrance, W. W. (1976). *Of Acceptable Risk: Science and the Determination of Safety*. Los Altos, CA: Kaufmann.
2. Ibid.
3. Wathern, P. (Ed.) (1988). Introduction. In *Environmental Impact Assessment: Theory and Practice*. Boston: Unwin Hyman, p. 15.
4. Bisset, R. Developments in EIA methods. In Wathern (Ed.) (1988), op. cit., p. 57.
5. Holling, C. S. (Ed.) (1978). *Adaptive Environmental Assessment and Management*. Chichester, UK: Wiley.
6. Bisset (1988), op. cit., p. 57.
7. Ibid., p. 58.
8. Ibid., p. 48.

9.   Ibid., p. 60.
10. Ibid., pp. 53, 60.
11. Ibid., pp. 56–57.
12. Wathern, op. cit., p. 13.
13. Ibid., pp. 12–13.
14. Glickman, N. J. (Ed.) (1980). *The Urban Impacts of Federal Policies*. Baltimore, MD: Johns Hopkins University Press, pp. 7, 8, 24, 29.
15. Glickman (1980), op. cit., pp. 36–37.
16. Bartlett, R. V. (Ed.) (1989). *Policy through Impact Assessment*. New York: Greenwood Press, p. 92.
17. Wathern (1988), op. cit., p. 18.
18. Ibid., p. 13.
19. Ibid., p. 12.
20. Glickman (1980), op. cit., pp. 24, 29.
21. Wathern (1988), op. cit., p. 15.
22. Wood, C. (1988). EIA in policy making. In Wathern (1988), op. cit., p. 99.
23. Wathern (1988), op. cit., p. 8.

Appendix B

1.   Irvine, S. H. and Sanders, J. T. (1972). Logic, language and method in construct identification across cultures. In Cronbach, L. J. and Drenth, P. J. (Eds.), *Mental Tests and Cultural Adaptation*. The Hague, Netherlands: Mouton, pp. 427–446.
2.   Fiske, E. (1990). *The Fiske Guide to Colleges*. New York: Random House, p. xxii.

Appendix C

1.   University of California (1994). *Introducing the University of California (1994–1995)*. Oakland, CA: Office of the President, p. 8.
2.   Ibid., p. 17.
3.   Ibid., p. 19.
4.   Ibid., p. 23.
5.   Ibid., p. 24.
6.   Ibid., p. 20.
7.   Ibid., p. 29.
8.   Committee on Admissions and Enrollment (1989). *Freshman Admissions at Berkeley: A Policy for the 1990s and Beyond (The Karabel Report)*. Berkeley: Berkeley Division, Academic Senate, University of California, p. 37.
9.   Ibid., p. 27.
10. Ibid., p. 48.
11. Committee on Admissions and Enrollment (1989), op. cit., p. 44.
12. University of California (1994), op. cit., p. 32.

Index

Ability
  academic outcome and, 33
  general learned, 46
  learnability of, 54–55
  learned vs. innate, 169
  school in channeling of, 87
  societal investment in, 52
  socioeconomic status effects on, 169
Ability-shift theory, 16–18, 164, 187
  in selection testing, 143–145
Ability tests, 49
Academic aptitude vs. achievement. *See*
  Aptitude vs. achievement
Academic criteria, 73–74
Academic Index Score (AIS), 74, 75, 76,
  174–175
  importance of, 73
Academic intelligence, 35
Academic merit vs. fair representation, 8,
  59, 82, 84, 126, 160, 188
  impacts of, 172–174
  substance of tension, 163–164
  translation to explicit assumptions/tensions,
  164
  translation to explicit policy, 164–165
  at U.C. Berkeley, 65–80. *See also*
  University of California at Berkeley
Academic outcome, 28–29, 33
  as admissions outcome, 26
  muddle of, 46–47
Achievement tests
  aptitude tests vs., 108
  measurement ambiguities in, 48–49
ACT-COMP, 49
Adaptive environmental assessment and
  management (AEAM), 200, 202
Adaptive value, 97
Adler, Mortimer, 190

Admissions outcome, 26
Admissions policies, 6–10, 188
  balance in, 76–77
  basic questions to ask of, 180–181
  blind, 74, 183
  demand and, 18–19
  educational foundation in, 77
  explicit intelligence policy and, 182–184
  guidelines for, 212
  implicit intelligence policy and, 153–177
    implicit undergrid formed by, 161–163
    matching in, 158–159, 167, 168
    tension caused by, 159–160
  implicit undergrid connecting to
    assessment, 29–32
  mapping against philosophical backdrop,
    59–64
  open, 109
  as opportunity allocation, 79–80
  self-monitoring in, 77
  specific proposals for, 182–184
  at U.C. Berkeley. *See* University of
    California at Berkeley
Adoption studies, 113
Affirmative action, 68, 158, 159, 160
African-Americans, 143, 156
  drop-out rate of, 81
  graduation rate of, 158
  IQ of, 112
  opportunity access and, 67–68
  percentage enrolled in U.C. Berkeley, 72,
    154
  percentage meeting U.C. system eligibility
    requirements, 81
  testing of, 107, 117
American College Testing Program (ACT),
  108
American Indians, 143, 154

245

American Psychological Association, 106
Anastasi, Anne, 108
Aptitude tests, 108
Aptitude vs. achievement, 8, 59, 105–124,
    160, 168–170
  cognitive science on, 118–124
  substance of tension, 169
  testing and, 106–109
  translation to explicit assumptions/tensions,
    169–170
  translation to explicit policy, 170
Aquinas, Thomas, 128
Aristotle, 127–128
Asian-Americans, 68, 74, 143, 156
  GPA of, 159
  graduation rate of, 158
  percentage enrolled in U.C. Berkeley, 154
  percentage meeting U.C. system eligibility
    requirements, 81
  reverse discrimination and, 160
Assembly Higher Education Committee, 23
Assessment, 25–55. See also Tests
  hidden intelligence policy in, 39
  implicit assumptions in, 50–51, 52
  implicit undergrid connecting to
    admissions, 29–32
  increasing public interest in, 40
  measurement ambiguities in, 48–49
  muddle created by, 46–47
  reliance on results of, 51
  role of, 38–39
  threatened homogenization of outcome
    and, 51
  value-added. See Value-added assessment
Autonomous social minorities, 117

Baird, Leonard, 47
Bateson, Gregory, 135
Belief systems
  conflict in, 88–90
  conflict regarding intelligence in, 90–92
  power of, 92–99
Bill for More General Diffusion of
    Knowledge, 21
Binet, Alfred, 1, 2, 102
Biological basis of intelligence, 119–120
Biological determinism, 136
Birth weight, 112–113
Blacks. See African-Americans
Blind admission policies, 74, 183

Bloom, Allan, 93
Boas, Franz, 92
Bowles, Samuel, 100
Brain, 119–120
Brain injury, 2
Broad representativeness principle, 72–73
Brown, Ann, 96, 97, 98
Butcher, John, 4

California State University system, 23, 41–42
Carnegie Commission on Higher Education,
    20
Cartesian philosophy, 129
Caste social minorities, 117
Cattell, Raymond B., 1, 10, 16–18, 60, 102,
    107, 109, 110, 119, 137, 141, 143–145,
    164, 185, 187, 189
Caucasians. See Whites
Causality
  as habitual association, 133
  undermining of, 131
Ceiling effect, 48
Checklists, 201
Christian Scholastics, 128
Churchman, C. West, 150
Cicero, 128
Civil rights movement, 87–88
Classicist views, 21–22
Closing of the American Mind, The (Bloom),
    93
Cognitive ability
  metacognition compared with, 98
  systematic transfer of, 94–95
Cognitive science, 118–124
Cognitive tests, 49
College admissions tests, 108–109. See also
    specific tests
College Entrance Board Achievement Tests
    (CEEB), 73
Commission on Testing and Public Policy,
    106
Competition, in college admissions, 156–158,
    163–164
Complemental admissions categories, 75, 79,
    83
  freshman yield by, 219
Complex quasi-mathematical environmental
    impact statements, 201
Control knowledge, 123
Core intelligence. See g

Criterial tasks, 97
Crouse, James, 167
Crystallized intelligence (g_c), 2, 102, 111, 119
Cultural bias, 103, 107, 140
Cultural confines, 93–94
Cultural discontinuity, 117
Cultural diversity. See Diversity
Cultural invention, intelligence as, 32
Culture-fair tests, 3

Darwin, Charles, 131
Darwinism, 100
Davis, Bernard, 36
Demand, 10, 141, 144–145. See also Supply
        and demand
    diminishing, 189
    occupational level and, 16–19
Democracy, education and, 22–24, 29
Descartes, René, 121, 128–129, 131, 135
Developmental psychology, 100–101
Dewey, John, 126, 131
Dianoetic functions, 128
Differential efficacy, 115
Direct impacts, 203
diSessa, Andrea, 62, 121, 123
Diversity, 65–66, 71–72, 77
Dominant cultures, 92, 172
    confines of, 93
    dichotomization of intelligence and, 102
    inequalities in, 103–104
    school as servant of, 86
    school failure and, 87–88
    social minorities in, 117
    testing and, 107
Dominated cultures
    confines of, 93
    dichotomization of intelligence and, 102
    heuristics and, 96
    school–home conflicts in, 94
Donne, John, 5
Drop-out rates, 81, 89, 109
D'Souza, Dinesh, 68, 174

Ecological empiricism, 135–136
Ecological rationality, 151
Education. See also School
    assumptions regarding influence of, 53–54
    concern over quality of, 41
    democracy and, 22–24, 29
    empiricism on, 132, 133

Education (cont.)
    intelligence vs. See Intelligence vs.
        education
Educational Opportunity Program (EOP),
        U.C. Berkeley, 71, 72
Educational Testing Service (ETS), 46
Egalitarianism, meritocracy vs., 109
Einstein, Albert, 190
Eiseley, Loren, 136
Emotional mode of giftedness, 114
Empiricism, 120, 125–127, 131–136. See also
        Rationalism vs. empiricism
    causality as habitual association in, 133
    causality undermined by, 131
    ecological, 135–136
    on environmental factors, 134–136
    on evolving intelligence, 136
    on knowledge acquisition, 132–133
    on metacognition, 91
    premises of, 126, 171
    sensory reduction of complexity in, 134
    tabula rasa concept in, 132
    unit-of-analysis problem and, 134
Energy flow data, 201
Environmental ecology, 151, 193
Environmental factors, 34. See also Nature–
        nurture controversy
    arguments supporting influence of, 101–
        102
    empiricism on, 134–136
    implicit intelligence policy and, 139
    IQ and, 116–118
Environmental impact analysis (EIA), 193–
        195, 197, 198, 200, 203
    index approach to, 201
    matrix formatting in, 202
Environmental impact statements (EIS), 200,
        201
Equality, complexity of, 85
Estes, Carol, 88–89
Ethnic groups. See Race/ethnicity
Evolution, 131
Excellence, 41
Explicit intelligence policy, 179–184, 185–
        190
    impact analysis and, 181–182, 185–187,
        205–208
    mapping in, 185–187
    truth behind, 187–189
Externality, 85–86

Factor analysis, 1, 34, 102
50–50 criterion, 71, 79, 165, 168, 182
Filipinos, 76
Financial aid, 221
First-degree relative studies, 113
First World Conference on Gifted and
    Talented Children, 115
Flexible targets, 76, 78
Fluid intelligence (g_f), 2, 102, 110–111, 119
Ford Foundation, 103
40–60 criterion, 71, 79, 165
Free-market competition, 23–24

g, 1–2, 16, 35, 50, 60, 141
    components of, 34
    failure to label in tests, 170
    giftedness and, 114
    in intelligence tests, 49, 102
    IQ as, 110–112
    job performance and, 167
    knowledge-within-process as, 124
    race and, 67, 140
    reasons for shifts in, 164
    selection testing and, 141–145
    unclear value of, 140
g_c. See Crystallized intelligence
g_f. See Fluid intelligence
Galton, Sir Francis, 114
Gardner, David, 7, 21
Gardner, Howard, 103, 109–110, 118–119,
    120, 140, 153
Gender. See Women
General factor. See g
General learned abilities, 46
Genetic factors, 36. See also Nature–nurture
        controversy
    in crystallized intelligence, 2
    environmental factor interaction with, 116–
        117
    in fluid intelligence, 2
    studies of, 112–113
GI Bill of Rights, 19
Gifford, Bernard R., 79, 103, 106–107, 179
Giftedness, 113–116
Glaucon, 125
God, rationalism on, 128–130, 131
Goodlad, John, 84, 86
Gould, Stephen Jay, 105
Grade point average (GPA), 73, 159, 175
Graduate Record Examination (GRE), 44, 46

Graduation rates, 158
Greece, ancient, 127, 128

Habitual association, causality as, 133
Hakstian, A. R., 2
Harvard Educational Review, 112
Harvard University, 19, 103
Hayashi, Patrick, 161
Hayden, Tom, 23
Headfitting, 96
Heath, S. B., 87–88
Hebb, Donald, 2
Heritability. See Genetic factors
Herrnstein, Richard, xiii, 67, 100, 104
Heuristics, 95–96
Heyman, Ira Michael, 68
Higher-order impacts, 203
High School Personality Scale, 3
Hispanics, 68, 156
    drop-out rate of, 81
    graduation rate of, 158
    percentage enrolled in U.C. Berkeley, 72,
        154
    percentage meeting U.C. system eligibility
        requirements, 81
    testing of, 107
Hiss, William, 25
Homogenization
    assessment as cause of, 51
    of intellectual standards, 82–83
Human capital theory, 49
Hume, David, 131, 133, 134
Humphreys, Lloyd, 10
Hunter, John, 167

Illiberal Education (D'Souza), 68
Imaginative mode of giftedness, 114
Immigrant social minorities, 117
Impact analysis, 193–203
    environmental. See Environmental impact
        analysis
    explicit intelligence policy and, 181–182,
        185–187, 205–208
    hazards and risks in, 199
    implicit intelligence policy and, 149–152,
        181–182, 205–208
    index approach to, 201
    matrix formatting in, 202, 203
    multiple levels and regions in, 202–203
    prospective, 150, 199–200

Impact analysis (*cont.*)
  societal, 197, 203
  steps of, 181–182
  systems diagramming in, 193, 201–202, 203
  urban, 195–197, 202–203
Implicit intelligence policy, 8–9, 10, 15, 137–145
  admissions policy and, 153–177. *See also* Admissions policy
  definitional face in, 140
  economic face in, 141
  environmental face in, 139
  explicit intelligence policy and, 185
  impact analysis and, 149–152, 181–182, 205–208
  insubstantiality of, 187
  seeking truth in, 138–139
  selection testing and, 141–143
Implicit undergrid
  admissions/assessment connected by, 29–32
  implicit intelligence policy and, 161–163
Index approach to impact analysis, 201
India, 89
Indirect impacts, 203
Inequalities, society constructed around, 103–104
Institute of Animal Resource Ecology, 200
Institutional evaluation, 181
Intellectual development stages, 100–101
Intellectual mode of giftedness, 114
Intellectual standards, homogenization of, 82–83
Intelligence, 109–113
  academic, 35
  adaptive value and, 97
  ancient notions of, 127–129
  assessment relationship to, 29–32
  assumptions about, 5–6, 32–33
  belief systems conflict regarding, 90–92
  biological basis of, 119–120
  brain in, 119–120
  as context dependent, 96, 98
  crystallized, 2, 102, 111, 119
  as cultural invention, 32
  definitions of, 32–33
  dichotomization of, 102
  as dynamic quality, 47–48, 169
  environmental factors in. *See* Environmental factors

Intelligence (*cont.*)
  evolving, 136
  fluid, 2, 102, 110–111, 119
  folk assumptions about, 33–34
  genetic factors in. *See* Genetic factors
  hidden policy on, 39
  implicit assumptions about, 36–38, 50–51
  learnability of, 30–31, 54–55, 60–62, 63, 104
    empiricism on, 125–127, 131–136
    rationalism on, 125–131
  as learning out, 98
  loci of, 34, 110
  macroenvironmental impacts on, 117–118
  misconceptions not signs of low, 121–122
  multiple, 109–110, 140, 169
  opportunities to restructure, 98–99
  perception of, 91
  practical, 35
  scientific assumptions about, 34–36
  single, 109, 140, 169
  social imagery of, 90, 91
  societal investment in, 52, 62–64
  sociological aspects of, 116–118
  species, 136
  supply and demand in. *See* Supply and demand
  systematic transfer of, 94–95
  technological opportunities for redefinition of, 118
  as transferable metaknowledge, 95
  two-factor theory of, 110
  usefulness of outlived, 187–189
  as valued metastrategy, 98–99
Intelligence-demanding educational requirements, 16
"Intelligence Objectively Determined and Measured" (Spearman), 1
Intelligence quotient (IQ), 109, 110–112
  cultural discontinuity and, 117
  environmental influence on, 116–118
  race and, 67–68, 140
  selection tests and, 143–145
  twin studies of, 112–113
  unclear value of, 140
Intelligence tests, 35, 102–103
  cognitive test overlap with, 49
  conflict regarding, 106–107
  cultural bias in, 103, 140
  early policy in, 106

Intelligence tests (*cont.*)
   measurement ambiguities in, 49
   race and, 140
Intelligence vs. education, 8, 59, 81–104,
      160. *See also* Sociopolitical
     perspective
   substance of tension, 166–167
   translation to explicit assumptions/tensions,
     167–168
   translation to explicit policy, 168
Internalization of social stimulation, 91–92
Intuitive knowledge, 130

Jefferson, Thomas, 21
Jencks, Christopher, 108
Jensen, Arthur, 16, 30–31, 35–36, 85, 112,
     167
Job performance, 167
Junior colleges, 183

Kamin, Leon, 117–118
Karabel Report, 70, 71, 72, 81, 158, 174,
     175, 182
   on 50–50 criterion, 79
   parity and, 78
   ten policy principles of, 77
   tier system amendments and, 75–77
   tier system prior to, 74–75
Knowledge
   ancient notions of, 127–129
   control, 123
   empiricism on acquisition of, 132–133
   intuitive, 130
   learning dependent on prior, 96–97
   material, 123
   receptivity to, 92–93
   structure of, 123–124
Knowledge-of-procedure, 123–124
Knowledge systems accounting, 203
Knowledge-within-process, 123–124

Labov, William, 87, 94
Language skills tests, 49
Learner-in-context, 96
Learning
   intelligence and. *See* Intelligence,
     learnability of
   prior knowledge dependence of, 96–97
   from specific to general, 97–98
Learning out, 98

Leopold matrix, 195, 202, 205, 208
Lightfoot, Sarah Lawrence, 87, 88, 93–94
Loci of intelligence, 34
Locke, John, 132–133
Lotteries, selection, 183
Lowrance, W. W., 193, 199

Macroenviromental impacts, 117–118
*1960 Master Plan for Higher Education
     Policy in California*, 69–70, 71
Matching, 158–159, 167, 168
Material knowledge, 123
Matrix formatting, 202, 203
McCloskey, Michael, 121
Measurement, 180–181
   ambiguities of, 48–49
Mental ability. *See* Ability
Mental retardation, 95, 107
Mental schemata, 120, 122–123
Meritocracy, 19–20
   egalitarianism vs., 109
Metacognition, 96, 98–99, 119, 120
   cognition compared with, 98
   enhancing, 99
   internalization of, 91–92
Metacognitive training, 118
Metaknowledge, 95, 97
Mind, essential traits of, 86–87
Minority groups. *See* Race/ethnicity
Montellano, Bernard Ortiz De, 59
Moral reasoning, 133
Multiple intelligences, 109–110, 140, 169
Murray, Charles, xiii, 67

Nathan, Richard, 150
National Commission on Testing and Public
     Policy, 103, 142–143
National Intelligence Tests, 106
Nature–nurture controversy, 105, 109, 169–
     170. *See also* Environmental factors;
     Genetic factors
   developmental psychology on, 100–101
   implicit intelligence policy and, 139
   intelligence testing and, 103
   multiple intelligences in, 110
   pendulum swings in, 99–100
   rationalism vs. empiricism on, 134, 172
Neisser, Ulrich, 35
Nelson, George, 100
Neoliberal political economy, 23

Network approach to systems diagramming, 193, 201–202
New Jersey College Outcomes Evaluation Program, 40
Newton, Edward, 92
Norris, Kenneth S., xii

Occupational level, 16–19
Odum, Guy R., 153
Oerectic functions, 128
Ogbu, John, 84, 86, 117
Open admissions policies, 109
Opportunity access, 66–69
Opportunity allocation, 15, 79–80, 107

Pacific Islanders, 143
Parental income, 220
Parity, 78
Peters, Roger J., 15
Physics, 121–122
Piaget, Jean, 101
Piechowski, M. M., 114
Place Called School, A (Goodlad), 84
Plato, 125, 127–128
Policies of exclusion, 68–69
Policies of inclusion, 68–69
Policy indicators, 203
Political influence, 181
Populist views, 21–22
Practical intelligence, 35
Primary cultural discontinuity, 117
Primary impacts, 203
Project Zero, 103
Prospective impact analysis, 150, 199–200
Prosperity, 40
Psychomotor mode of giftedness, 114

Quantitative ability, 46
Quota systems, 76, 77, 78

"Race and Intelligence Reexamined" (Humphreys), 10
Race/ethnicity. See also specific racial, ethnic groups
    cultural discontinuity and, 117
    IQ and, 67–68, 140
    in U.C. Berkeley student body, 154–158
    U.C. system eligibility requirements and, 81
Radcliffe College, 19
Rand Corporation, 202–203

Ranney, Michael, 122
Rational causality. See Causality
Rationalism, 120, 125–131. See also Rationalism vs. empiricism
    analytical reduction of composite ideas in, 130
    ancient notions of knowledge and intelligence in, 127–129
    God in, 128–130, 131
    on metacognition, 91
    premises of, 126, 171
Rationalism vs. empiricism, 8, 59, 60, 102, 160, 170–172. See also Empiricism; Rationalism
    on knowledge structure, 123
    substance of tension, 172
    translation to explicit assumptions/tensions, 172
    translation to explicit policy, 172
Reality, social construction of, 88–89
Renzulli, Joseph, 114
Republic, The (Plato), 127
Reverse discrimination, 160, 174
Riesman, David, 20
Rome, ancient, 128

s, 110
Scarr, Sandra Wood, 33
Schemata. See Mental schemata
Scholastic Aptitude Test (SAT), 76, 108–109, 158, 175
    academic outcome and, 46
    AIS and, 73
    measurement ambiguities in, 49
    race and, 67
    scores of U.C. Berkeley students on, 156, 159
School. See also Education
    as agent of social stasis, 83–88
    Dewey on, 126, 131
    dominant culture served by, 86
    rethinking failure of, 87–88
    social order perpetuated by, 84–85
School–home conflicts, 94
School Motivation Analysis Test, 3
Secondary cultural discontinuity, 117
Secondary impacts, 203
Secondary review categories, 75–76, 165
Selection tests
    ability-shift model and, 143–145
    implicit intelligence policy and, 141–143

Self-selection, 22, 182, 183
Sensual mode of giftedness, 114
Simon, Theodore, 1, 2
Single intelligence, 109, 140, 169
Sliding fee scale, 23
Social construction of reality, 88–89
Social imagery, 89–90, 91, 92
Social minorities, 117
Social order
  questioning of, 85–86
  school perpetuation of, 84–85
Social perception system, 89
Social rationality, 151, 152
Social stasis, school as agent of, 83–88
Social stimulation, internalization of, 91–92
Societal impact analysis (SIA), 197, 203
Socioeconomic factors, 169, 170
Socioeconomic indicators (SIS), 203
Sociological aspects of intelligence, 116–118
Sociopolitical perspective, 81–104
  belief systems conflicts and, 88–90
  belief systems conflicts regarding
      intelligence and, 90–92
  belief systems power and, 92–99
  homogenization of intellectual standards
      in, 82–83
  school as agent of social stasis in, 83–88
Socrates, 125–126
Sowell, Thomas, 158
Spearman, Charles, 1, 2, 34, 35, 50, 67,
      102, 110–112
Special Action admissions, 72, 79
  criteria for, 75
  Karabel Report on, 76
  matching and, 158–159
Species intelligence, 136
Specific factor (s), 110
Spinoza, Benedict Baruch de, 129–130
Stanford-Binet intelligence test, 106, 114, 141
Sternberg, Robert, 34, 84–85, 91, 110, 114–
      115
Storm over Biology (Davis), 36
Student fees, 22–23, 221
Student outcome assessments, 38
Students
  as nonpassive agents, 49–50
  views of, 181
Supplementary criteria, 74
Supply and demand, 15–24, 107. *See also*
      Demand

Supply and demand (*cont.*)
  diminishing, 189
  meritocracy and, 19–20
  populist vs. classicist views in, 21–22
Supportive services, 158, 174
Systems diagramming, 193, 201–202, 203
Systems theory, 193
Systems thinking approach, 193, 195

Tabula rasa, 132
Talent development assessments, 38
Temperamental scales, 3–4
Terman, Lewis, 106, 114
Tertiary impacts, 203
Testocratization, 103, 107
Tests, 106–109. *See also* Assessment; specific
      tests
  danger in reliance on results, 51
  opportunity allocation and, 79–80, 107
Thinking, as a process, 120
Thurstone, Louis, 1, 102, 110
Tier 1, 74, 160, 165, 173
Tier 2, 74, 75, 83, 158–159, 165
Tier 3, 75, 76, 78
Tier system
  freshman admits by complemental group,
      219
  freshman yield by, 218
  post-*Karabel Report* amendments to, 75–
      77
  pre-*Karabel Report*, 74–75
Total protection policy, 78
Toynbee, Arnold, 113
Tracking, 183
Twin studies, 112–113
Two-factor theory of intelligence, 110

Unitary intelligence. *See* Single intelligence
Unit-of-analysis problem, 134
University admissions policies. *See*
      Admissions policies
University of California at Berkeley, 7, 8,
      65–80, 81, 84, 153–177, 182
  academic admission criteria in, 73–74
  academic standards vs. fair representation
      in, 70
  AIS and. *See* Academic Index Score
  balanced admissions policy in, 76–77
  blind admissions policy in, 74
  broad representativeness principle in, 72–73

University of California at Berkeley (*cont.*)
  competition for admission to, 156–158,
    163–164
  diversity in, 65–66, 71–72, 77
  educational foundation in admissions
    policy, 77
  ethnic mix in, 154–158
  founding of, 154
  freshman profile for, 217
  freshman registrants in, 218
  introduction to, 211
  matching in, 158–159, 167, 168
  mission statement of, 69
  opportunity access in, 66–69
  raising academic standards in, 70
  selection process in, 215
  self-monitoring admissions policy in, 77
  shifts in public trust and constituent
    support for, 175–177
  shifts in selection ranges of, 175
  tier system in. *See* Tier system
  undercurrent of tension in, 159–160
University of California Davis, 217
University of California system
  admission as a freshman, 213
  admission to, 212
  eligibility index for, 216
  financial aid in, 221
  freshman profile for, 217
  racial/ethnic factors in eligibility for, 81
  selection criteria for, 214
  student fees in, 22–23, 221
University of Hawaii at Manoa, 154

Urban impact analysis (UIA), 195–197, 202–
    203

Value-added assessment, 38, 49–50, 51, 97
  as euphemism, 43–46
Verbal ability, 46
Vernacular culture, 94
Vining, Daniel, 3
Voluntary tracking, 183
Vygotsky, Lev, 91–92, 101

Wechsler Adult Intelligence Scale, 2, 141
Whites, 67–68, 74, 156
  drop-out rate of, 81
  GPA of, 159
  graduation rate of, 158
  IQ of, 112
  percentage enrolled in U.C. Berkeley, 154
  percentage meeting U.C. system eligibility
    requirements, 81
  reverse discrimination and, 160
  testing of, 107
Wiener, Norbert, 93
Wildavsky, Aaron, 150, 151
Women, 76
  classicist views of, 21
  drop-out rates of, 89
  meritocracy and, 19
  social imagery and, 89–90
  testing of, 107
Women's liberation, 90
World War I, 106

About the Author

Angela Browne-Miller holds two master's degrees and two doctorates from the University of California, Berkeley, where she has lectured in three departments. Dr. Browne-Miller is the author of numerous books on policy analysis as well as on educational, social, and psychological issues, including *Learning to Learn* (Insight Books) and *The Day Care Dilemma* (Insight Books). Her articles have been published nationally and internationally in the professional and the lay presses, and she has presented her work at national professional conferences and institutes as well as on national television and radio. She has served as a policy analyst for the White House Conference on Families and the U.S. Office of Juvenile Justice Task Force on Drug Abuse and as a National Institute of Mental Health Postdoctoral Fellow.